Ideology and Theory in Indian Sociology

Ideology and Theory in Indian Sociology

Yogendra Singh

RAWAT PUBLICATIONS
Jaipur • New Delhi • Bangalore • Guwahati • Kolkata

ISBN 978-81-7033-831-4 (HB)

Reprinted, 2024

Published by
Prem Rawat for **Rawat Publications**
Satyam Apts., Sector 3, Jawahar Nagar, Jaipur - 302 004 (India)
Phone: 0141 265 1748 / 7006 E-mail : info@rawatbooks.com
Website: rawatbooks.com

New Delhi Office
4858/24, Ansari Road, Daryaganj, New Delhi 110 002
Phone: 011-23263290

Also at *Bangalore, Guwahati* and *Kolkata*

Typeset by Rawat Computers, Jaipur
Printed at Nice Printing Press, New Delhi

Contents

Preface

Sociology, like most social sciences, is embedded in ideology. The essays contained in *Ideology and Theory in Indian Sociology* deal with theoretical underpinnings of the Indian sociology in the context of its ideological perspective. These essays, with the exception of a few, have been written most recently. In publishing them together in this volume our intention is to put across to the readers the ideological challenges which have overwhelmed sociology in India in the past and also continue to assume a great deal of relevance today. As we face up to the challenges of post-modernization and globalization, the need for sociologists to respond to the consequences of the changes that these processes may trigger in our society becomes urgent. It has both theoretical and ideological significance for our substantive studies of social structures, cultural systems and social processes. It is hoped that this volume would offer a perspective to the sociological studies of these problems.

In the preparation of this book the inspiration has come from diverse sources, such as several special lectures and participation in seminars and symposia. Without naming each of these sources individually I wish to acknowledge my grateful thanks to all of them. I also wish to thank the Rawat Publications for their keen interest in publishing this volume and also for their editorial assistance.

Yogendra Singh
Centre for the Study of Social Systems
Jawaharlal Nehru University
New Delhi

Introduction

The essays contained in *Ideology and Theory in Indian Sociology* can be read individually and each one of them is thematically complete within its theoretical boundary. Yet, taken in totality, these essays also demonstrate a convergence of concerns. The convergence is grounded in the discourse of ideology and its theoretical and explanatory boundaries. Most essays, with the exception of "The Concept of Man in Sociology" which deals with the theme in universalistic terms and attempts to link the changes in the concept of man with the changing theoretical orientations in the western sociology, are specifically addressed to the changing substantive and theoretical concerns of the Indian sociology. Ideological issues and their interface with the variety of ways in theorizing, sometimes explicit but often implicit or 'metaphorical' in nature, constitute the central discourse in most essays in this volume.

The changing relationship between ideology and theory is basic to the evolutionary course in sociology whether Indian or western. In the West, where sociology emerged as an independent discipline within the academic domain of the social sciences, the centrality of the significance of ideology is clearly visible. Its grounding in the Enlightenment ideology is self-evident which in general terms inaugurated the growth of a value orientation which celebrated 'reason'. It constituted the foundation of the 'progress ideology'. This ideology faced major challenges as the western societies increasingly encountered 'social anomie', impoverishment and exploitation of the working classes and exploitation of the women and children by the rapacious industrial capitalism. Marx made it the major theme of his sociology and his revolutionary praxis. Indeed, it is he who demonstrated the significance of ideology in social science and sociology. He demonstrated its role not only as reflected in the class or power interests of the capitalist and ruling classes inherent in the sociological formulations and analyses, but also went deeper in his treatment and unravelled how ideology was implicit in the conceptual and paradigmatic structure of the sociological language itself. This language mirrored the social reality not as much as it tended to hide the most crucial aspects bearing significance for the understanding of its true nature. His notion of the 'fetishism of commodities' fully illustrates this phenomenon.

Karl Marx has consistently demonstrated as to how social structures and relationships which outwardly maintain a semblance of institutionalization are indeed embedded into false consciousness. Whether it is ownership of estate by the feudal lord, or the investment of labour power in the production of commodity or the notion of rationality in the capitalist mode of production, all these social phenomena conceal the true nature of their social significance. Lord remains in the illusion of 'owning' the land, but as bound he is within the iron frame of traditional conventions, it is land which owns the lord, says Marx in his *The Economic and the Philosophical Manuscripts of 1884*. Capitalism, which celebrates its rationality and ability to move forward with perpetual innovations and accumulation of profits has built-in forces of history in its processes of growth that would inevitably invite the nemesis of its dissolution. The notion of commodity is itself merely a 'fetish' which is nothing but congealed form of labour power. Hence, according to Marx, the entire discourse of sociology and social sciences is embedded in ideology.

Similarly, Emile Durkheim refers to the centrality of ideology in his treatment of the relationship between social reality and social representations. Even though his early formulations, such as his theory of the division of labour in society, reflect positivistic orientation, in his later writings, he turns to unravel the fundamental nature of the categories and concepts used by sociologists and philosophers. In his *The Elementary Forms of Religious Life*, Durkheim refutes Kantian epistemology based as it is on idealistic and aprioristic assumptions about the nature of the basic social categories or concepts. He illustrates through his observations of religious rites and rituals as to how these basic social categories, such as the notions of 'time', 'space', 'number', etc., are grounded in social and cultural processes and their structural manifestations.

We may also notice the focus on ideology in Max Weber's notion of 'rationalization' which plays a basic role in the processes of integration, continuity and change in societies. In Weber's sociology, rationalization has double significance. First, it constitutes the boundary condition, as it were, of the application of principles of rationality in the process of institutionalization of social systems. The various forms of authority, viz., the 'traditional', the 'charismatic' and the 'legal', derive their legitimation based on their own course of the processes of rationalization and institutionalization. By the same measure, the forms of authority vary in the degree to which the principles of 'rationality' play a role in their legitimation. The institutions of bureaucracy and capitalism, according to Weber, conform nearest to the ideal type of rational authority. Weber's notions of 'charisma' and 'prophecy' constitute yet another dimension of how ideational and ideological innovations take place in society setting into motion new principles of rationalization which ultimately get 'routinized' and pass on to the corpus of 'tradition'. All these forms of authority, the principles of their rationalization and the process of their institutionalization belong to the domain of ideology.

The debate on ideology in the sociological discourse of the western sociology assumed importance during the entire period from 1889 to 1930. It was on account of two basic reasons: First, due to the limitations of positivistic theory in failing to explain the negative social and cultural consequences of the early 19th and 20th century industrial and capitalist social orders. The extent of poverty, social and cultural anomie and social conflict, which followed in the wake of capitalist-industrial growth in Europe, could not be explained by the 'rationality paradigm' on which the positivistic sociology was founded. Secondly, in the writings of sociologists of this period, of which Marx was a precursor, we find an attempt to offer theoretical and methodological alternatives. Generally, however, in most contributions of this period, we observe an attempt towards integrating the contending theoretical and meta-theoretical paradigms of sociology in order to arrive at a more satisfactory explanation of the contemporary social realities. For instance, Durkheim's theoretical explanation of division of labour tends to be positivistic, since he offers its explanation in terms of the increasing 'material' density (population) of the society which affects its 'moral' density reflected in the social and cultural institutions. The division of labour is, according to him, a consequence of this process. But, in his explanation of the phenomenon of religion, his focus shifts to studying the forms of 'representations' and 'rituals' which are basic to the emergence of the religious order (the realm of the sacred) and distinguish it from the economic or utilitarian social orders (the realm of the profane). The distinction between the sacred and the profane not merely offers a theoretical explanation of the religious phenomenon. It also provides a possibility of an integrative theoretical approach between positivism and phenomenology to analyze social realities. Weber similarly defines sociology as being a science capable of offering explanation of social processes and events and simultaneously he locates the foundation of this causal explanation in the 'ideal types' which are methodologically a mental construction and yet are not entirely heuristic in nature. The 'ideal types' are intuitively derived from the study of a period of history of the society or social phenomena under investigation and reflect its 'historical individual' or its most prominent features of social significance.

The sociologists of the 1889-1930 period were facing the challenges not only of anomie, social conflicts, deviance and urban decay, etc., induced historically by the early phase of industrialization, but they also had to take into cognizance the realities of the First World War and the violent revolutionary movement in Russia and the inaugural of the Marxist ideology of class struggle and inter-class conflict and violence. Sigmund Freud added to the disenchantment from the rational paradigm of the industrial society. He gave a new orientation to the theoretical and methodological perspective on human action and its relationship with the principles of social organization in which the significance of the irrational gained prominence. He formulated a theory of culture and society in which both these phenomena were seen to be in a state of perpetual threat of internal instability because, according to him, the basic impulses which guided human being to act and form social organization and institutions were trapped into the archetypical and dialectical tension between the libidinal (creative or sexual) and the destructive or violent orientations in human beings. This dialectic, according to Freud, was an inherent species attribute of human personality rooted in pre-history. The rational bases of the contemporary industrial society and its culture, therefore, were founded upon a fragile foundation as its strength was more apparent than real. Freud, therefore, envisaged that the cultural values and institutions, which are taken as the basis for stability in the social systems, are merely the surface reality arising out of the repression of the irrational and self-destructive impulses among men. Therefore, the equilibrium or stability or even progress that human societies demonstrated are fragile in nature and society may from time to time suffer from instability through eruption of violence.

The contributions both of Marx and Freud had deeper ideological significance and impacted with great force on the sociological theories which followed during and after the Second World War. The historical experience of the rise of Fascism and Nazism in Europe and the genocide of the Jews shocked the European conscience. Sociology assumed a new centrality in this period of intellectual introspection and self-criticism. The emergence of the 'critical school' in sociology symbolizes this development. Led largely by the German sociologists, of whom many had migrated to UK and USA, this school sponsored studies in which explorations of the nature and etiology of 'ideology' and its social and cultural foundations formed the central concern. Theodore Adorno, Max Horkheimer, Jurgen Habermas, H. Marcuse, Eric Fromm, Karl Mannheim, Paul Lazarsfeld and several other sociologists and social scientists have contributed to the study of ideology in both theoretical and methodological terms. The nature of ideology, its social and psychological foundations, its relationship with the personality system and the value system of society, its power structure, etc., constitute the major foci in these studies. These studies have also been innovative in integrating several theoretical paradigms into a meaningful synthesis. The major ones among these are Marxism, Freudianism, phenomenology, sociological voluntarism and history. The studies have also integrated the technique of discourse analysis with empirical researches using several tools of observation and measurement of social and psychological attributes and ideology.

Together with the emergence of the 'critical school' in sociology during the Second World War impetus towards 'structural-functional' studies based on empirical observations of social systems gained momentum. Systemic studies of rural-urban communities, factories and industrial systems, educational and political institutions, etc., came into vogue which continued to dominate the substantive and theoretical field of sociology from 1950's to 1970's. The structural-functional approach as a theory and methodology has been widely associated with and criticized for being the ideology of conservative-ism, status-quo-ism and the preservation of the vested interests which perpetuate the structures of domination in the society. This ideological spell was broken following the eruption during the 1970's of widespread youth unrest with its roots in their cultural and emotional disenchantment from the ideology of capitalism and consumerism that the industrial society perpetuated. This discontent from the structural-functional sociology which had its origin first in the European subcontinent soon engulfed the mainstream American sociology. The sociology of Talcott Parsons in the USA became an iconic symbol of the ideology of conservative-ism and forms the main theme for criticism in several writings of 1960's onwards. C. Wright Mills and E. Gouldner have made the Parsonian sociology as the centre piece of their critique of the functional sociology. The Parsonian sociology has also invited criticism from some of his own students, particularly from M. Zelditch Jr. and B. Cohen of the Stanford School of Sociology. Their criticism is based on the failure of Parsons general theory of action to offer a 'nomological' explanation of social action, and the structures of relationships or the processes that it engenders for change.

But the distinctive significance of the ideological criticism of the structural-functional theory rests on the revival of the philosophical debates in sociology on the questions related to theory and methodology. It is reflected in the growth of the neo-Marxist, phenomenological and critical approaches to the study of society and its institutions. There is now a marked shift in the debate on ideology. The centrality of economic and political domination in which most critiques of ideology were subsumed now seems to reflect the explorations of the cultural domination and its class character. This is pre-eminently present in the writings of Pierre Bourdieu, and his contemporary followers. The focus in several sociological studies had already shifted from the study of social structures to the study of social movements. Alain Touraine, among several European and American sociologists, has contributed richly to its theory by going beyond the study of ideological and structural dynamics in social movements to their phenomenology and praxis. This, according to him, adds new meaning to the study of sociological phenomena viewed as they are in the process of their 'self-production' and formation rather than their static existence. Unlike the concept of social action as formulated in Parsonian sociology where social action is perceived to be a 'system-integrative', the notion of social action in Touraine's analysis of social movements and social structures is constitutive of multi-directionality, it triggers the processes of open-ended self-creativity and is endowed with self-transformative qualities which are not merely system-integrative but also give rise to social practices and cultural or normative consequences totally unintended in the original agenda of action.

These developments in sociological theories and methodology have added new meaning to the notion of ideology itself. Ideology is no longer viewed as having a coherent discourse in command of itself. The rise of the post-modern and post-structuralist sociological paradigms, which are deeply influenced by the philosophical discourse on 'post-modernity' led by M. Foucault, J. Derrida and Jacques Lacan and their followers, has impacted on sociological meta-theory and the notion of ideology. Unlike the formulations of the concepts of social system and ideology in the neo-Marxist and 'new social movement' theories (e.g., Alain

Touraine) which challenged the concepts of the 'actor' and the 'social system' without denying their existence (ontologically) and faulted the older notions of social system only for not taking into account several of its collateral features, the post-modernist meta-theory rejects the very possibility of social system because it denies the ability in the 'subject' or the 'actor' to act rationally on the basis of voluntary choices. Its notion of social 'order' is ideologically submerged in the fluid and irrational structures either of 'power' without responsibility or in the 'discourse' or 'text' without meaning. The philosophical implosion which characterizes post-modernity puts notions both of ideology and sociology in jeopardy. It is symptomatic of a crisis in contemporary epistemological theories in philosophy which impacts negatively on sociology and its discourse on human society and civilization.

The civilizational and social structural settings in which sociology emerged as a discipline have, however, not lost their relevance about defining its scope and method. The emergence of the post-modern society, of which probably the surfacing of the philosophy of post-modernity is a result, even though its roots go back in the past to the Niezschean philosophy, only poses new challenges to sociological discourse and methodology. This viewpoint is well reflected in the writings of Earnest Gellner, Pierre Bourdieu, and a large number of contemporary western sociologists. According to Bourdieu, the post-modern philosophy is largely mired in the fallacy of 'scholasticism' and 'epistemocentrism' in which the emphasis on the 'text' or the 'language' is overemphasized to the exclusion of the reality of the life-world. He writes:

> "The vanity of attributing immense and immediate effects to philosophy, and to utterances of intellectuals, seems to me to be example par excellence of what Schopenhauer called 'pedantic comedy', by which he means the ridicule one incurs when performing an action that is not included in one's concept, like a stage horse that defecates on stage. Now if there is one thing that our 'modern' or 'post-modern' philosophers have in common, beyond the conflict that divide them, it is this excessive confidence in the power of language. It is the typical illusion of the *lector*, who can regard an academic commentary as a political act or critique of

text as a feat of resistance, and experience revolutions in the order of words as radical revolution in the order of things" (Bourdieu: 2000: 2).

Talking about his own intellectual journey from philosophy to ethnology and sociology, Bourdieu reflects:

> "The distance I have progressively taken from philosophy no doubt owes a lot to what are called the chance events of existence, in particular a forced stay in Algeria, which one could say, without looking further, was at the origin of my 'vocation' as an ethnologist and then as a sociologist. But I would not have been responsive to the call to understand and testify which I then felt if I had not been aware for a long time of a dissatisfaction with the philosophical game, even in its severest and most rigorous form, which still held my interest. And, rather than to have, myself, to indulge in confidences, I shall simply quote a passage from the correspondence of Ludwig Wittgenstein, with Jacques Bouveresse, a wonderful interpreter, brought to my attention, and which expresses rather well a good part of my feelings about philosophy: 'what is the use of studying philosophy if all that it does for you is to enable you to talk with some plausibility about some abstruse questions of logic, etc., and if it does not improve your thinking about the important questions of everyday life, if it does not make you more conscientious than many...journalists in the use of the *dangerous* phrases such people use for their own ends" (ibid.:42).

The Context of Indian Sociology

This volume opens with a discussion of the implications of the debate on post-modernity to sociological theory. We focus upon the significance that the methods of observation and critical analysis of the realities of everyday life have had right from the inception of sociology as an independent discipline. We argue that the merit of the sociological discourse does not depend merely on the sophistication of its deductive-logical or axiomatic conceptual categories and propositions. Of course, these are essential for initiating any observational or empirical study of social phenomena. But sociology distinguishes itself in the manner in which these logico-deductive concepts and propositions are put to test by matching them with the realities of the contemporary society or social facts under observation. Any theoretical generalization would remain problematic until the axiomatic propositions of sociology are empirically verified by observation of social realities which exist within a temporal or historical boundary. Theory attempts to outcross the temporal or historical boundaries, or in other words, it offers explanatory or general propositions. But, the validity of such propositions rests upon their affirmation by verifiable observation of social realities by methods that can be operationalized.

When we extend this logic on the construction of theory to the Indian sociology, we find that most theoretical approaches tend to be grounded in 'conceptual schema' rather than formal theory. As we have discussed in Chapter 5, "Functional Metaphor in Indian Sociology", most Indian sociological studies use a set of conceptual schemes to observe, analyze and compare the social structures, processes and changes in the society. The theoretical orientations in these studies are more metaphoric than formal. This is particularly true where the allusions for being functionalist in theoretical orientations are made in case of the studies of the rural and urban social systems by the social anthropologists and sociologists in India. We have tried to demonstrate the inconsistencies in such allusions and have highlighted as to how most theoretical orientations in such studies remain diffused or metaphoric rather than qualifying as theory based on the principle of logical closure.

Comparatively, the sociological studies in India, which have followed the Marxist theoretical orientation, seem to be grounded in more systematic and logically consistent foundation. This is so in particular reference to their operationalization of conceptual categories and methods of observation. Its weakness, however, is reflected in the extent to which the conceptual categories and modes of their operationalization are ideologically closed as it were. The basis for this flaw rests not only in epistemology of Marxist discourse as it is operationalized but also in its ideological antecedent in the contemporary Indian history. We have reviewed some of the theoretical and ideological issues raised by sociologists in India in the rest of the essays in this volume. These refer to the debates on the relationship between sociology and the Indian traditional philosophy and the need for the grounding the sociological categories and methods in the Indian philosophical and epistemological traditions. While reviewing the developments in the Indian sociology, our focus primarily is to demonstrate the philosophic and epistemic tensions between the Indian quest for its own sociological paradigm and the compulsions of the universalistic imperatives in sociology to go beyond the boundaries of societal or cultural particularism. The roots of this tension go far back in the history of the British colonialism and the intellectual and ideological response to it by the Indian intellectuals. It has survived even after India gained independence. One may notice that even though the challenges of colonial domination over India have come to an end in political terms, the feeling of uneasiness among the Indian intellectuals, sociologists and social anthropologists about the continuation of the western attempt towards cultural, economic and ideological hegemony continues to persist. This is reflected in the sociological debates in India on the processes of globalization and its impact on cultural identity and development.

The ideological issues in the Indian sociology are deeply influenced by the anxieties about the cultural, social and political encounter of India with the western civilization. This is reflected in the pre-sociological writings of the Indian social thinkers and leaders of national liberation movement. The ideology of the Indian nationalism or nation-building has provided a great impetus to sociologists and social scientists in India. Its reflections in the Indian sociology can be seen in the contributions of founder sociologists such as G.S. Ghurye, Radhakamal Mukherjee, N.K. Bose and their contemporaries. After India gained freedom, the sociological and social anthropological studies have shown a deep concern with the issues of economic, social and cultural development of India, and they have collaborated with the state through their studies in providing data and insights about formulation of strategies of development in a variety of sectors of society. No doubt, this trend was dominant in sociology from 1950 to 1970, but from 1970 onwards sociologists assumed a role of informed critics of state policies of development. It was also a period which saw increased popularity of the Marxist and the neo-Marxist theoretical orientations in sociological studies. Since 1970's onwards Indian sociology has developed towards a multiplicity of discourses in theories and methodologies. Its ideological discourse ranges from being 'consensual' to 'dialectical-historical' to 'critical' and 'symbolic-phenomenological' in orientations. There are also occasional attempts to ideologically anchor sociology in the Indian philosophical tradition. These multiple theoretical and ideological paradigms are by no means logically or substantively exclusive as a great deal of integrative tensions among these paradigms persists in the theoretical analysis and operationalization of methods in the studies of individual sociologists.

Reference

Bourdieu, Pierre, 2000, *Pascalian Meditations* (translated by Richard Nice), Cambridge: Polity Press.

1

Worldview of Sociology and the Challenge of Post-Modernity

For me it is a precious moment; a real privilege to be called upon to dedicate these thoughts to the memory of late Professor A.R. Desai. He, as a person and as a scholar, was the embodiment of the worldview of sociology. Marx and Marxism were not only his lifetime commitments, but also his own response to how sociology or social sciences in general should strive to seek convergence between theory and praxis.

I have chosen the theme of post-modernity and the worldview of sociology because of its contemporaneity, and also because of its great relevance to our comprehension of the normative and philosophical contexts which influence our choices of theory and methodology. This subject assumes significance also because, the philosophy of post-modernity, even though several decades older in its evolutionary voyage, seems to have had a very close relationship with the emergence of social and cultural institutions, values and practices which contributed to the cognitive restructuring or a virtual decomposition of the epistemology, ontology and ethics, on which the paradigm of conventional philosophy was positioned. It challenges the postulates of rationality on which most social science categories of structure, system and change have been formulated; it

A.R. Desai Memorial Lecture, delivered at the University of Bombay, 1999.

also attempts to invalidate the notions of actor or the subject within the social science discourse and its moorings in the structure of social values. Baudrillard articulates this view when he says that, in matters of social discourse, "things have never functioned socially, but symbolically, magically, irrationally" (see, Baudrillard, 1981). Social systems are, according to the post-modern reckoning, illusionary facades characterized by 'micro-orders of domination'.

It is necessary at this stage to make a clear distinction between the notion of worldview and sociological theory or methodology on the one hand, and on the other, between the worldview of sociology and post-modernity. I believe that sociologists who maintain a distinction between theory and methodology in sociological practice are moved by factors which go beyond the essence of praxis and reflexivity, which the acts of scientific objectivation in the production of sociological knowledge implies. The rigidity in the distinction between theory and methodology in social anthropology and sociology is a historical product of its uses for the pursuits of the power by political regimes, and other structures of domination. It reached its peak during the Second World War. It was during this period that large-scale funding of researches by sociologists, social psychologists and other social scienusts was undertaken by the allied nations, led by USA, to generate insights and information helpful for war efforts, field management and morale of soldiers, counter-insurgency operations in countries hostile to the big power interests, etc. No doubt, such researches gave opportunities to academics to innovate upon their research tools and techniques, add sophistication in the scientific models for measurement of social attitudes, values and levels of group integration and its subjective and objective contexts. This investment in research has been of much utility for the application of sociological knowledge for planning and development undertaken for rehabilitation of economies and societies destroyed by the war. The movements for political liberation from the colonial control soon followed all over Asia, Africa and Latin America, and in these countries too, the skills generated in the tools of research during the war were put to uses for undertaking researches to augment planning and development efforts on a massive scale.

But, the disenchantment was not far away. As I am going to argue, the social and cultural developments in the following decades contribute to the movement against 'abstracted empiricism' and positivism in sociology. All of which materially affected, not only the worldview of sociology, but also led to a widespread discontent among philosophers and social scientists, particularly in Europe, which seem to have culminated in the burst of post-modernity. It is not without social and historical reasons that the works of Nietzche, Freud and Marx became increasingly attractive to sociologists of the critical school in Germany and in other European nations right from 1950's onwards. There was a resurgence of interest in the phenomenological philosophy, and the works of Husserl and Heidegger. This development coincided with the disenchantment of youth and intelligentsia in mid-1970s from the values of the emergent post-industrial capitalism which were rooted in consumerism and rise in personal and social alienation and in the dehumanized bureaucracy and public life. Husserl's direct attack on the assumption of universality for the arithmetical or mathematical structures conceptualized in the abstract was also a rejection of positivism in sociology so rampant following the Second World War. Derrida articulates this when he says:

> "In *Philosophie der Arithmetik* (of Husserl), the objectivity of a structure, that of numbers and arithmetical series—and, correlatively, that of the arithmetical attitude—is tied to the concrete genesis which must make it possible. From the start, Husserl refuses, and will always refuse, to accept the intelligibility and normativity of the universal structure as manna fallen from a heavenly place, or as an eternal truth created by an infinite reason. To seek out the subjective origin of arithmetical objects and values, here, is to turn back toward perception, toward perceptual ensembles, and toward the pluralities and totalities found in perception in a premathematical organization" (see, Derrida, 1978: 157).

This, and many other related movements in theory and method in sociology, challenging the paradigm of universal reason and the practice of measurement of cultural and social forms, reinforced the philosophical foundation on which post-modernity entrenched itself. Its genesis, and its sudden growth, do not merely rest on the irrefutability of its epistemology or ontology, but also as Durkheim postulated so convincingly, in the genetic anchorage of philosophy in sociology and as he wrote in his *Elementary Forms of Religious*

Life, its rootedness in the social structure itself. It is, therefore, necessary to explore the concrete social and cultural foundations of the contemporary society and its processes both at the meta-theoretic level, which we designate as the worldview of sociology, and its grounding in theory at a more operational level of sociological praxis, in order to understand the challenges that post-modernity has presented for sociology both at the general and specific levels of its representation.

Worldview of Sociology

Sociological categories have their basis in meta-theoretical normative constructions. The worldview of sociology represents these normative or ideological constructions about societal reality. Edward Shils rightly maintained that sociological worldview, which he broadly defines as the 'calling of sociology', emanates from a historical development in societal structures and consciousness in which it is possible for the individuals to empathize with societal self-awareness. The coming into being of the industrial society, following the social, structural, cultural and the technological revolution in Europe during the 16th century, inaugurated this possibility. This 'great transformation' in the European society, following through the footsteps of Enlightenment and Reformation, made it possible to conceptualize and normatively empathize with values of universalism, humanism, freedom of conscience and political liberty. It marked a turning point in the relationship between consciousness and society, a stage where it was possible for individual members of a society to reflexively comprehend the totality of structural and normative aspects of human engagement in society, despite social differentiation and division into regimes and classes. Durkheim refers to it as the birth of 'individual representation' which not only symbolizes itself, but has the capacity to comprehend the totality, through the enhancement of the 'psychic mobility' in the individuals to comprehend the collective consciousness, and Max Weber locates it in the Calvinistic reformation which broke through the chrysalis of traditionalism, and introduced a notion of predestination which endowed the believer with freedom of moral choice and as an individual, commitment to social responsibility.

Anchored within a normative context, the sociological worldview marks a departure from traditionalism. It has been variously described as 'disenchantment' from the past reckoning of moral order, as Charles Taylor would like to describe or even as a sense of 'resentment' towards it in the Neitzchean formulation. Weber's view that this process implies continual rationalization of values, beliefs and institutions of society can be located within this domain. Its important features as Taylor has recounted were: individualism, utilitarian rationality, particularly its instrumental manifestation in science and technology and the ambiguity of political rights and freedom, even though celebrated outwardly with the fear of looming 'soft despotism' of modern economic and political order (see, Taylor, 1992). In its very beginning, these changes augured well for humanity and contributed to the paradigm of modernity, but their de-ethicization in course of time turned them into an 'iron cage', the metaphor so aptly used by Max Weber.

It would be an oversimplification of reality, however, to locate the worldview of sociology entirely in the paradigms of modernization that it no doubt inaugurated. The more essential contribution that the beginning of disenchantment or resentment from the traditional worldview made to the growth of the worldview of sociology rests in the cognitive and cultural legitimation that it provided to focus on the ordinary, the marginalized and the oppressed. For the times that sociological worldview articulated this perspective, both through impetus to new theorizing and innovations in methods and tools of analysis, its contribution was indeed revolutionary. The recognition of the existential and moral significance of the underclass and the underdog, and the moral and social legitimacy that it gave to the understanding and explanation of their human condition, caught as they were, in the throes of the incipient yet heartless industrialism, is an essential feature of the worldview of sociology. Its contemporary articulation may be found in Pierre Bourdieu's statement: "The power of a mode of thinking never manifests itself more clearly than in its capacity to constitute socially insignificant objects into scientific objects (as Goffman did of the minutiae of face-to-face interaction), or what amounts to the same thing, to approach a major socially significant object from an unexpected angle... The sociologist could well make his or her's Flaubert's motto, 'To write well about the mediocre' " (see, Bourdieu, 1992: 221).

This realization, no doubt, establishes a close linkage between the worldview of sociology and its perspectives on the notions of self, identity and dignity. It contributed to the valourization of ethical and social principles which did not perceive the notion of dignity or identity in the legitimation of hierarchy, prevalent in the traditional societies. Neither did it accept the legitimacy of the pretexts which formalized the notions of status, power and social mobility through a historically established form of feudal or industrial-capitalist social and economic order. As a consequence, "the previous 'higher' forms of life were dethroned, as it were. And along with this went frequently an attack, covert or overt, on the elites which had made these forms their province. I believe, says Charles Taylor, that this affirmation of ordinary life, although not uncontested and frequently appearing in secularized form has become one of the most powerful ideas of modern civilization" (see, Taylor, 1989: 13–14). I would add, that it goes to the heart of the normative principles and practices which constitute the worldview of sociology.

Thinkers, such as Pierre Bourdieu, Charles Taylor and Alain Touraine, seem to identify these normative principles in the feeling of disillusionment with either the practices of social scientists, mired in the monomania of methods and models, or in their realization of the progressive effacement of the subject in the contemporary post-modern, post-industrial society, propelled as it is by values of consumerism and instant gratification. But, for record, it may be reiterated that sociology from its early days (late 19th and early 20th century) had shown an acute concern with the studies of the underclass and the marginalized. This could be easily noticed in the massive documentation and surveys of the work-houses, factory labour, the poor, the uprooted and the migrant communities during the inception of the industrial economy. Marx has extensively annotated the findings of these studies to argue forcefully his case in favour of revolution. This would be evident in all his writings from 1844 onwards. Among the sociologists of his generation, Marx alone seems to have had anticipated the agonies of human condition inaugurated by industrial capitalism which was, as he predicted with so accurate farsight, bound to culminate in the crisis of contemporary post-modern capitalist society.

The early American sociology shows even greater recognition of the significance of studying groups and communities which were uprooted, marginalized and alienated, both by the processes of industrialization-urbanization as well as by in-migration to the continent from the overseas. One could refer to the studies of the hobos, ghetto-dwellers, delinquents, uprooted peasants, sub-cultures of crime and violence and the enclaves of poverty and alienation among the blacks, ethnic migrants and working classes. Extensive studies were conducted on the patterns of urban settlement and its social and cultural consequences to the integration of family, neighbourhood, community life, etc. These studies led to rich innovations of research techniques and methods and also gave sociology a high degree of legitimation in formulation of social policy, planning and execution of strategies of social and economic welfare and development. The worldview of sociology represents these normative concerns which constitute the 'domain assumptions' of theorizing and designing of research. The distinct manner in which the values of Enlightenment and Reformation impacted upon sociology as a discipline rests not so much upon concerns with universalism, humanism, freedom and rationality as general normative goals. But it rests squarely in the successful manner in which sociology could operationalize and internalize these normative objectives in the corpus of its research and theorizing. Slowly, this empathic response of sociology to understanding the conditions of the marginal and less 'significant' categories of society were publicly recognized. For this reason, sociology came to be noticed and was made use of widely by public, politicians, administrators, journalists and media men, as tool of social diagnosis and as a matrix for the definition of social issues of relevance and concern.

Worldview is an 'open concept'; it is defined not by itself but by the context in which it is located. The context was provided by the industrial and republican revolutions in the west and their epistemological and ethical imperatives; it was provided by the urgency of praxeological concerns in the production of knowledge by sociologists and also by the commensurate innovations in their tools and techniques of research. This historical and pedagogic situation of sociological worldview links sociology deeper with the 'language of the sources' which public articulate as well as the design and play of the artist, the literati and the philosophers which mirror sociological concerns in a generalized, cognitive and evocative form. There is, and there has always existed, as says Bourdieu, a closer relationship of correspondence, both cognitive and appreciative between the 'spontaneous sociology' of the literary forms and the 'scientific sociology' resulting from 'socio-analysis' of reality by sociologists.

Sociological Theory and Worldview

Worldview constitutes the domain in which the differentiation in the ways of sociological theorizing has taken place throughout history. It may be noticed, however, that for a time, the theoretic concerns overwhelmed the sociological practices in teaching and research, and as sociology gained recognition from the public, the ruling elite and the intelligentsia, its orientation became more formal than normative. To some extent, this dilemma is inherent in the very principles and operations which distinguish theory from the worldview of sociology. Theory, despite its range of variations from phenomenology-ethnomethodology to nomological formulations, involves a degree of axiological constructions and analytical reasoning which cannot be avoided. Even the best examples of phenomenological theorizing or in the efforts to 'ground' theory in the concrete realities of 'here and now' have imperatives which cannot do without logical and analytical differentiations of concepts and their operationalization. The predominant inclination in theoretic efforts is essentially to postulate analytical distinctions whereas sociological worldview forms a synthetic domain of values, norms and ideologies.

The historicity of the location of social processes, values and institutions constitutes the foundation on which sociological worldview is grounded. Theory, on the other hand, cannot avoid making some kind of analytical abstractions to overcome the problem of solipsism. Because of this difference, a tension has always existed in the task of a sociologist, as between the grounding of his conceptual and theoretical formulations in the domains of values, articulated by sociological worldview, and his need to understand and explain the nature of social realities. Even the most ardent proponents of phenomenology have not been able to fully rid their researches from this inner tension.

Sociological theories, as they interface with sociological worldview and its historicity, reflect in their orientation the changing social and cultural conditions. The cumulative effect of the changes in social conditions impacts on the worldview itself. It would be worthwhile to examine, as to how far the contemporary wave of post-modernity in philosophy, humanities and social sciences is indicative of the alienation of theory from the worldview or it reflects the tensions of supersession of one worldview by another which is not yet born, but exists in the womb of time. This temporality, however, merits our attention.

There is a widespread feeling among sociologists that a crisis prevails in sociological theory. This has persisted during the past several decades following the Second World War. The disenchantment from nomologism, functionalism, survey research or abstracted empiricism signifies this tension. No doubt, historical developments in the western society during the ensuing period may partly explain this situation. From 1940's to 1950's, the western sociology saw the golden age of formalization of sociological theory, cognitively as well as in operationalization of concept and methods. The war experiences, the holocaust perpetrated by Nazism and Fascism, robbed western sociologists of the belief that the worldview of sociology would by itself take care of the monstrosities of state, power elite and the privileged classes. It also created a deep skepticism about the universality of reason in human action or its manifestations through public policy, social organization and institutional structures and values. Marxism, Freudianism, existential phenomenology and historicism were revived, were innovated upon and integrated with new paradigms of theory and protocol of research. With hermeneutics, discourse analysis, cultural analysis and ethnomethodological orientations in sociological theorizing, all of which added up to the epistemological and ontological tensions of post-modernism, challenges both to the theory and worldview of sociology have emerged.

A look at the contemporary efforts of sociologists to meet with these challenges reveals two types of responses. First, there is wider acceptance of inter-paradigmatic fusion or integration in theorizing. Ideological and theoretic exclusivism has rapidly given way to liberalism and creative interpretations. A second and more powerful response to these challenges comes from sociologists, who remain committed to sociology as an exercise in scientific objectivation of social realities, not from the positivistic perspective of a system which implies inter-subjective interaction among individual actors, but as a 'field' which Bourdieu defines as "the locus of relations of force—and not of meaning—and of struggles aimed at transforming it, and therefore, of endless changes" (see, Bourdieu, 1992: 103). Bourdieu rejects the viability both of Parsons' systemic theoretical approach as well as Luhmann's notion of 'apparatus' since both these views are ultimately mired in the fallacy of nominalism. He writes: "The notion of field reminds us that the true object of social science is not the individual, even though one cannot construct a field if not through individuals, since the information necessary for statistical analysis is generally attached to individuals or institutions... This does not imply that individuals are mere 'illusions', that they do not exist: they exist as *agents*—and not as biological individuals, actors, or subjects—who are socially constituted as active and acting in the field under consideration by the fact that they possess the necessary properties to be effective, to produce effects, in this field" (p.107). Further, "the real is the relational: what exist in the social world are relations—not interactions between agents or inter-subjective ties between individuals, but objective relations, which exist 'independently of individual consciousness and will' as Marx said" (p. 97).

There are equally strong alternatives for preserving the worldview of sociology through its commitment to scientific theorizing by Ernest Gellner, Jurgen Habermas, Alain Touraine and Anthony Giddens to name a few. All of them have responded to the challenge of post-modernity to the theory and practice of sociology. They review the challenge differently than Bourdieu, since they do not totally reject either the utility of the notion of system or that of the actor, or the 'subject'. We see it in the writings of Touraine. Habermas attempts to synthesize the phenomenological category of 'lifeworld' with 'social system' and accords important role to the 'communicative action-system'. The goal remains that of 'methodological objectivation' as that of Bourdieu, but unlike Bourdieu, the relevance of the problematic of modernity and post-modernity is accepted as an extension of the capitalist-market linked mode of social transformation. It is indeed curious, how both

Habermas and Bourdieu, despite having made radical departure from original Marx, enthusiastically make use of his contributions: Bourdieu, by his inversion of Marxist categories of material conditions, relations of production, market, capital and profit and class, etc., by his own notions of 'field', 'habitus', 'capital', 'profit', 'market', 'class', and 'power or domination', etc., as products, though not of material but cultural-ideological conditions. And, Habermas does the same by confession that his "theory of capitalist modernization developed by means of a theory of communicative action does follow the Marxian model" (see, Habermas, 1987: 375).

Another issue which lies at the heart of the relationships among sociological theory, its worldview and the process of post-modernization, and is linked deeply with the ideas of actor-system relationship has been raised by Alain Touraine (1995) and Charles Taylor (1989). Touraine finds in the contemporary debate on post-modernity and its accompanying social and cultural conditions a tendency towards rejection of sociology. He affirms that "at a more abstract level, we find that sociology too is being rejected. Sociology has always been a disturbingly critical analysis of modernity, but it was also a positive critique. This was as true of Durkheim and Weber as it was of Tocqueville and Marx before them, and it was also true of Parsons and the Chicago School. Sociology talked about industrialization and social classes, about political institutions and social conflicts; and it asked how economic innovations could be reconciled with majority access to the fruits of sources of growth" (see, Touraine, 1995: 196–97). No longer so now. The new found liberal appeal transcends the sociological response to the issues of exploitation and inequalities. It denigrates the role of instrumental rationality, but offers no substitutes to replace it.

Both Touraine and Taylor propose that in order to overcome this crisis in sociological worldview and its theory it was necessary to restore the actor-subject relationship as the point of centrality to the paradigm of sociology. To overcome the limitations of heartless and mindless instrumentality of reason, postulated as essential to modernity, it is necessary to ethicize the role of actor as a subject. This may be our only hope to escape from the iron cages of modernity and post-modernity. Touraine characterizes it as the centrality of the subject-reason in the societal paradigm, comprising 'life', 'consumption', 'nation' and 'company' (1995: 219). This he offers as a model of 'new modernity'. According to him, "actor-system correspondence no longer seems 'natural', and we are no longer convinced that a universalist reason should triumph over particular interest" (p.353). Yet, "there can be no modernization without rationalization, but that modernization also means the formation of subject-in-the-world who can take responsibility for themselves and for society. Modernity must not be confused with only capitalist mode of modernization" (p. 203). Individual becomes subject through the process of subjectivation which is anti-thesis of individual's surrender to transcendental values. Man once projected himself on to God; in the modern world, man becomes the basic value. The central ethical principle has now become freedom" (p.209). Subject is, therefore, to Touraine, an individual as well as a social movement, which he later defines as project for action.

For Taylor, the subject is essentially a moral entity. Sociology, either of the variety of Enlightenment naturalism, as of Marx, or critical tradition of Adorno, Horkheimer or Habermas, he contends, tends only to make compromises on ethical issues by hanging on to a "notion of integral expressive fulfilment, in which the demands of sensual particularity would be fully harmonized with those of conceptual reason, and in which the domination and suppression of the former by the latter would be overcome. This remains the ethical standard, even where it cannot be integrally realized" (Taylor, 1989: 506). It seems obvious, therefore, that despite new movements in sociological theories and methods, some of the core issues, such as those related to its domain, individual versus social system, rationality versus ethical responsibility, and structure or social order versus social movement, remain central to its contemporary theoretical discourse.

Post-modernism and the Worldview of Sociology

We may now shift our discussion towards post-modernism. Does post-modernism have a worldview? What possible relationship does it have with sociological practices and methods? Can post-modernism be located within the discourse of sociology on social structure, culture and change? What type of relationship could be established between the worldview of sociology and the repertoire of post-modernity? Fredric Jameson mentions two important features of post-modernism: first, 'transformation of reality into images' and secondly, 'fragmentation of time into a series of perpetual presents' (see, Jameson, 1988: 28). The birth of post-modernism, he says, could be traced to the 1960's, when "the position of high modernism and its dominant aesthetics become established in the academy and are henceforth felt to be academic by a whole new generation of poets, painters and musicians" (p. 28). It is no doubt the product of a social condition of late consumer and multinational capitalism riding the tide of media-technology revolution. Its celebration of the 'present' and the 'instant' adds up to the 'disappearance of the sense of history' and the 'inability to retain the past' as it applauds 'perpetual change'. It seeks to efface linkages with tradition which most earlier social formations had. Post-modernism presents an epistemology which abolishes the role of normal language, language of speech and eschews most linguistic norms. It celebrates 'pastiche' instead of parody, a neutral practice of mimicry of style, which as Jameson writes, is "without that still latent feeling that there exists something *normal* compared to which what is being imitated is rather comic" (p.16).

A more serious discourse on post-modernism is witnessed in the philosophical contributions of Jacques Derrida and its social science interface in the writings of Michel Foucault, Jean Baudrillard, Jacques Lacan, etc. Derrida, amongst them, is in the forefront in contributing to an epistemological-ontological perspective of post-modern philosophy. Language or text forms its point of beginning, 'differance' or 'difference' its elemental structure, through which, Derrida weaves an epistemology of multidirectional usages of text and meanings. In his, *The Margins of Philosophy*, he uses the metaphor of a sheaf, since "the word sheaf seems to mark more appropriately that the assemblage (of the text) to be proposed has the complex structure of a weaving, an interlacing which permits different threads and different lines of meaning—or of force—to go off again in different directions, just as it is always ready to tie itself up with others" (p. 3). He is able to integrate in his notion of 'differance' the Freudian distinction between the 'pleasure principle' and the 'reality principle' innovatively used by Lacan, as also the notion of 'force' basic to Foucault's archeology of knowledge. Here, as also in the artistic style, the projected image of being and substance, whether ontological or epistemological, is that of impermanence or flux.

No doubt, post-modernism manifested itself first in the domain of art, literary styles and philosophical discourses. Its impact on the social sciences spread out slowly as sociologists increasingly had to cope up with the emergence of new social and cultural movements and institutional practices, which gained momentum from 1960's onwards. This was manifested in student movements, their disenchantment with consumerism sponsored by post-modern capitalism and supported by state, by revolution in sexual mores, new awareness about gender issues and its ideology, multiculturalism and movements for ecological protection from mindless and self-centred industrialization. The post-modern challenge to sociology has its root in the post-modern social conditions. There seems to exist a clear relationship between philosophical articulation of post-modernity and the social changes that took place in society in its post-industrial phase.

Some of its obvious indicators are: the breakdown of community values and its structures due to high levels of social and psychological mobility of members in society; the revolutionary changes in the gender relationships and emergence of new family norms about marriage, childcare and conjugal responsibilities; and erosion in the participatory behaviour of individuals in the affairs of society and community, due to the legitimization of self-referentiality in individual ethic. Alienation and anomie, which classical sociology held as problems created by the industrial society, cease to be so perceived in the post-modern society. On the contrary, the borderline between freedom and alienation is so narrowed as to render the distinction infructuous. Mass media, hyperconsumerism and the supremacy of images over values downgrade the role of the subject in the manifestation of post-modernity. David Reismann's paradox, of the 'lonely crowd', ceases to be a problem. It is legitimated or even applauded.

The post-modern society also brings about radical changes in the infrastructure of the economy. If the industrial-capitalism, which inaugurated the phase of modernity, was based on the centrality of 'wage labour', and its accompaniments in the commodity-factory mode of production, the post-modern society, as Bauman writes, is generated by 'consumer conduct', which implies "consumer freedom geared to the consumer market". Individuals are engaged (morally by society, functionally by social system) first and foremost as consumers than producers. Consumer freedom, which was a mere 'squatter' in the era of modernity, moves over to a central position of 'legitimate resident' (see, Bauman, 1989: 46) The substitution of consumer freedom as the hub around which the life-world rotates, now changes the Freudian assumption of the antagonistic relationship between the 'pleasure principle' and the 'reality principle'. For the consumer, the reality is not the enemy of pleasure.

These processes also bring about rapid changes in the notions of state, nation, democracy and territory. Economic and cultural globalization, emergence of global diaspora, expansion of market, financial capital and banking, revolution in the technology of communication through telephony, internet, fax, e-mail, etc., are increasingly abridging the power of the state. These have also rendered the classical ideas about nation-state and territory highly elastic and subject to external and internal factors often beyond its control. The imperatives of high technology uses in affairs of public administration, and in strategic planning and execution of matters related to economy, defence and international relations, radically alter the autonomy and power of political leadership, and change the context of political responsibility. This partly explains the recent debates in political science and public administration about the 're-invention of democracy' and 'the state' (see, Singh, 1999). These substantive changes in the social structure and values of society in the post-modern phase have a very close linkage with the beginning of the cultural and philosophical debate in sociology.

Sociology and Post-modernity

This brings me to the last question in this regard. How does post-modernity affect the theory and worldview of sociology? How is it influencing the praxis and contemporary discourse in sociology? How valid is the distinction being made between, what is called a 'post-modern sociology' and the 'sociology of post-modernity'? Here, we may begin with a quote from Zygmunt Bauman:

> "Indeed, if postmodernity means what the current concepts imply, a reform of culture, of world-perception, of the intellectual stance—then sociology faces the task of an essentially strategical adjustment. It must make itself resonant with new, postmodern culture, and break its links with the ontological and epistemological premises of modernity. It must transform itself into a postmodern sociology. In particular, it must follow other elements of postmodern culture by accepting (in theory as much as in practice) the self-containment and self-grounding of the production and reproduction of meanings. It must abandon its traditional identity of a discourse characterized by an attempt to decode such meanings as products, reflections, aspects or rationalizations of social figuration and their dynamics. If, on the other hand, the self-containment of contemporary culture, and the associated implosion of vision, signal processes which reach beyond the realm of culture proper (if they accompany transformations in, say, principles of systemic organization or power arrangements)—then it is not the traditional strategy of sociology which calls for revision, but a new focus of inquiry is needed, and a new set of categories geared to the changed social reality. In this case—without resigning its formative questions—sociology must develop into a sociology of postmodernity. In particular, it must accept the distinctiveness of the postmodern figuration, instead of treating it as a diseased or degraded form of modern society" (see, Bauman, 1989: 35).

Obviously, during the past few decades, sociology has been attempting to come to terms with post-modernity. Its substantial representation is where post-modernity is treated as a symptom of a crisis brought about by the post-industrial economic, cultural and technological challenges. This has contributed to creative innovations in methods and concepts, or even in theoretic paradigms of sociology, such as we witness in the cases of phenomenological, ethnomethodological and dramaturgical sociologies. Attempt is made to render sociology more relevant to comprehend the post-modern social and cultural conditions. In this process, sociology has faced challenges, which have led it to be subsumed in the cultural hubris of post-modernity, particularly, in its epistemological and ontological assumptions, whose instances we may find in extreme applications of Garfinkel's ethnomethodology or in Goffman's dramaturgy, both of which question the authenticity of meanings in sociological discourse. But, in these instances too, the extent to which their paradigms imply the necessity to decode meanings or demystification of sociological stances, they continue to accept the validity of social reality as an ontological presence and as an objective reality.

The focus on sociology of post-modernity is, otherwise, pre-eminent in the works of other mainstream sociologists, such as Bourdieu, Giddens and Touraine. Bourdieu may not have anchored sociology primarily in the notion of a social system or social order; he prefers to use the concept of a 'field' but field is a social-cultural arena where agents enter into relationships and form strategies as per their 'habitus' to augment access to social, economic and cultural capital, to position themselves in society. Although, the role of the individual is denied, the concept of habitus still links Bourdieu's sociology to culture-society-personality matrix, which is central to a theory of social order and social change in the classical sociology. Similarly, Touraine's emphasis on social movement and social action gives centrality to the place of 'rational-subject' in the processes of configuration of society, thus, it rescues sociology denying its 'rejection' implicit in most post-modernist philosophy. Touraine writes: "there can be no modernization without rationalization, but that modernity also means the formation of the subject in the world who can take responsibility for themselves and for society" (see, Touraine, 1995: 203). Anthony Giddens too reiterates the significance of the subject and the formation of 'self-identity' in the post-modern society in order to establish protective relationships to safeguard against the uncertainties of this society. Society constitutes a social order in a process of change whose direction remains uncertain and the identity of individual problematic (see, Giddens, 1990 and 1992). He defines structure as a process which constitutes itself through motivated agents and their interaction, and exists through, what he terms as 'structuration'. The concept of structuration, according to him, adds dynamism in social analysis of systems that are increasingly flexible, open to influence of plurality and have loosely coordinated power centres. Evidently, the sociology of post-modernity continues to make strategic conceptual and methodological responses to the challenges of post-modernity.

It is, therefore, essential that sociology as it encounters post-modernity remains consistent in its commitment to studying order and change by adopting strategies of innovative exegesis and extension in its conceptual and methodological repertoire. The imperative of studying post-modernity itself as a product of the post-industrial phase of global capitalism should continue to engage sociologists. Among the classical sociologists, Marx, more than Max Weber or Durkheim, was able to anticipate the cultural and structural logic of transformation of the industrial capitalism to its next phase of post-industrial evolution—a phase in which the inner contradictions of the processes of rationalization would yield to forces of perpetual impermanence and estrangement of human consciousness. The social and cultural attributes of the post-modern society confirm this in large measure. We may thus conclude:

> "Proper analysis of postmodern condition brings us, therefore, back into the orthodox area of sociological investigation (though an area now structured in an unorthodox way). This means that rather than seeking a new form of a postmodern sociology (a sociology attuned to its style, as an 'intellectual genre', to the cultural climate of postmodernity) sociologists should be engaged in developing a sociology of postmodernity (i.e., deploying the strategy of systemic, rational discourse to the task of constructing a theoretical model of postmodern society as a system in its own right, rather than a distorted form, or an aberration from another system" (see, Bauman, 1989: 61).

It seems to me to have a great relevance for the Indian sociologists who are observing a slow but inevitable process of movement towards modernization or even post-modernization of society. Here, the persistence of the cultural and structural features of multiple and mixed historicities constitutes a very relevant framework for comparative analysis at the substantive level of social realities. It should also be interesting to evaluate as to how the Indian sociology and social sciences have perceived and encountered the challenges of modernity and incipient post-modernity.

References

Baudrillard, Jean, *Simulacres et Simulation*, Paris: Galilee, 1981.

Bauman, Zygmunt, "Sociological Response to Postmodernity", *Thesis Eleven*, 1989.

Bourdieu, Pierre and L.J.D. Wacquant, *An Invitation to Reflexive Sociology*, Chicago: University of Chicago Press, 1992.

Derrida, Jacques, *The Margins of Philosophy*, Sussex: Harvester Press, 1982.

—, *Writing and Difference*, Chicago: Chicago University Press, 1978.

Giddens, Anthony, *Consequences of Modernity*, Cambridge: Polity, 1990.

—, *Modernity and Self-Identity: Self and Society in a Late Modern Age*, Cambridge: Polity, 1992.

Habermas, Jurgen, *The Theory of Communicative Action*, Vol. 2, Cambridge: Polity Press, 1987.

Jameson, Fredric, "Postmodernism and Consumer Society", in *Postmodernism and its Discontents: Theories and Practices*, by E.A. Kaplan (ed.), New York: Verso, 1988.

Singh, Yogendra, "The Desired Role of Political Leadership in Economic Reforms" in *Indian Economy and the Institutional Set-Up*, by J.L. Bajaj (ed.), Delhi Policy Group, 1999.

Taylor, Charles, *Sources of the Self: The Making of the Modern Identity*, Cambridge: Harvard University Press, 1989.

—, *The Ethics of Authenticity*, Cambridge: Harvard University Press, 1992.

Touraine, Alain, *Critique of Modernity*, Oxford: Blackwell, 1995.

2

The Concept of Man in Sociology

Indeed, there is poetic justice in sociologists' writing on the concept of man. Did not sociology in several ways attempt to abolish man from its theoretic constructs? The exhortation for 'bringing man back-in' (Homans, 1964), the nostalgia for the 'lost science of man' (Becker, 1971), and the research of the 'images of man' in the traditions of sociological theorizing (Mills, 1960) represent both, a feeling of guilt among sociologists as well as the deepening crises in the paradigms of sociology. Central to this is the debate in sociology on the ontological and ethical nature of man. The crisis is both epistemic and historical. Epistemologically, the emergence of sociology as a discipline marked a degree of obsolescence of the traditional cognitive categories, philosophical premises and worldviews for the understanding of human condition. Historically, the process of this obsolescence was immanent in the material conditions and social forces generated by the western society, which gave birth to sociology following industrial revolution. Sociology to this extent assumed the role of a demystifying discipline for which it was a matter of course to call into doubt or even to reject many traditional categories and value premises about the nature of society and man. But paradoxically, sociology could not, despite this radicalism of its premises and categories, disburden itself from its past.

The past of sociology, as of most other social sciences, lies in meta-physical-philosophical traditions of the Graeco-Roman origin, theological meta-physics of the middle ages and the social philosophical contributions of the periods of Renaissance and the Enlightenment. It is indeed a highly burdensome heritage of paradigms. In many ways sociological concept of man was a deliberate refutation of the notion of man as projected through purely rationalistic theory of man in metaphysics and the hierarchical theory of man in theology. Nevertheless, many critical tensions in the notion of man in sociology did survive because sociology's meta-theoretical separation either from philosophy or theology has never been complete. On the contrary, during the past few decades, one could discern tendencies of differentiation in sociological paradigms which are indeed rooted directly in philosophy. There has particularly been a revival of interest in neo-Platonic ideas in sociological constructions in the writings of sociologists like Max Horkheimer and Theodore Adorno (1973) and a resurgence of linguistic philosophical approach in sociology (cf. Gellner, 1965; Winch, 1951; Cicourel, 1973, etc.).

The reason behind these developments bears close connection with the concept of man in sociology which in course of its classical commitment to positivistic theory and emphasis on raw empiricism fragmented and intrumentalized the notion of man. It also led to a refraction in the vision on man and society with the loss of the critical (moral) perspective. This perspective existent in ethics and philosophy had thus to be reinstated. Horkheimer and Adorno write:

> Thus, the fundamental difference between what since Comte we have become accustomed to call 'sociology' and the philosophic doctrine of society of Plato—as well as that of Aristotle or even Hegel—is no longer merely one of subject matter, but a profound difference of conception and method. The great philosophy had as its ideal the development of a doctrine of society derived from the absolute principles of Being. Sociology, however, ever since it bore that name, prided itself on precisely the opposite: like the natural sciences it wanted to emancipate itself from any sort of teleology and to be satisfied solely with causal relations formulable by laws ... From the very beginning of the new science the joy in progress was muted: its thought on society took pride in not transcending that

> which was. The impulse of philosophy, to transform the Ought into the Is readily gave way to the sober acceptance of the Is as the Ought. And so it has remained from the days of Comte down to most famed teachers who founded the schools of the new sociology, Max Weber, Emile Durkheim, Vilfredo Pareto. Whenever the voice of this science is raised in the greatest pathos, one can be sure that it is proscribing something for itself, and precisely that essential for the sake of which men reflect about society. Equivocation often has very sound reasons: sociology has remained 'positive' not only because it desires to keep to the given and wants to extirpate the wish as the father of thought, but also because it takes a positive stance towards that which exists. It has enjoined itself to refrain from treating that which exists critically (Horkheimer and Adorno, 1973: 7).

Sociology in its voyage of self-discovery from the time of Comte to this day has not succeeded into realizing a unity of its paradigms. Its strength lies on the other hand in projecting a worldview which sets into perspective the vital relationships between man and society. This worldview is characterized by a dual quality: it is *synthetic* and *substitutive*. These two aspects of sociological worldview pull this discipline into two different creative directions. The synthetic element in sociology tends to infuse in its worldview values and categories with roots in multiplicity of paradigms on man, nature and society. This explains the pulls and creative tensions that are continually generated in sociology towards other sciences. It is also explicated by the facts that writings of the few of the founders of sociology contained a singularity of paradigms. Comte, Pareto, Marx, Weber and Durkheim, all of them show tensions of competing paradigms in the structure of their ideas, and project a synthetic worldview of sociology. The substitutive character of sociological worldview sets it apart, sharpens its self-awareness, draws conceptual and methodological boundaries that separate it from other sciences. More often, it is based on the elaboration of a single paradigm and its operationalization.

That sociological worldview is synthetic as well as substitutive adds a dialectical quality to its cognitive structure. It lends a critical attribute to its formulations on man and society, and more specifically endows sociology with qualities of objectivity and apperception to understand the reality and problem of man. The question, however, considering the great variety of paradigms in sociology and the synthetic yet substitutive character of its worldview is how to review the concept of man so that the two major contributions made by sociologists in the understanding of man, first, the social structural bases of human problematic and secondly, innovation of conceptual theoretical categories and systems to diagnose and explain this problematic, are adequately explicated.

Treatment of the concept of man in sociology should proceed in two directions: it should explicate the theoretic contingencies in sociology to the concept of man. In addition to this, it should highlight contributions made by sociology to the understanding of existential dilemmas and problems of man in changing social structure, its historical dialectic and direction. History and theory should thus offer two complementary frames of reference for treatment of man in sociology. Its significance rests also on the fact that sociology as it emerged as a discipline in the west, it carried with it the imprints of western civilizational ethos, its ideational patterns and its social structure. Sociological worldview, even its cognitive categories, thus tend to be culturally relative rather than universal. In treatment of concept of man in sociology, it would be, therefore, not possible to detach the issue of historical particularities of social structure and culture from theoretic constructs for the understanding of the problem.

Concept of Man and Sociological Theory

There are two meta-theoretical assumptions in sociological theories which bear directly on the concept of man. The first set of these assumptions relates to the conception of the relationship between man and society and the place of man in society. There are sociologists who construct a model of society in order to derive from it the sociological model of man. Contrariwise, the step is reversed by other sociologists who first construct a model of man in order to understand societal reality. Society as a category indeed occupies central place in thinking and investigation in both frames of reference. Philosophically, the two positions correspond closely to 'realism' and 'nominalism' in meta-theory. The ground for debate on the abolition of man as an active concept in sociology was primarily a reaction against certain radical theories based on sociological realism. The second meta-theoretic component in sociological theory has its anchorage in the dichotomy between positivism and idealism. Indeed, it is rare to find sociologists taking radical stances in respect of positivistic or idealistic positions but all forms of sociological theories bear the imprint either of the one or the other in their meta-theoretic orientation. Realism-nominalism and positivism-idealism thus constitute ideal typical meta-theoretic dimensions in the matrix of sociological categories. Within each meta-theoretic position there have emerged variations and sub-variations but broadly these two frames of reference do have a place in all varieties of sociological theories, and the concept of man that each theory posits is influenced by the nature of these assumptions.

Concept of Man in Positivistic Sociological Theory

Comte and Spencer whose names are associated with the origin of sociology were both staunch positivists. Positivism, in fact, represented the ethos of Enlightenment period which also dominated the sociological theory. It was normal at this time to borrow models from the natural sciences, physics, biology and chemistry and to employ them analogically as it were for the understanding of sociological realities. Spencer borrowed his model from biology and Comte from physics. Spencer also took a clearly 'realist' position in regard to the relationship between man and society. In his *Principles of Sociology* (1898) he wrote:

> Carrying the controversy between nominalism and realism into another sphere, a nominalist might affirm that just as there exist only the members of a species, while the species considered apart from them has no existence; so the units of a society alone exist, while the existence of society is but verbal... But without disputing the other steps of his argument, the last step may be denied. The arrangement temporary in the one case, is permanent in the other, and it is the permanence of the relations among component parts which constitutes the individuality of a whole as distinguished from the individualities of its parts. A mass broken into fragments ceases to be a thing; while conversely, the stones, bricks and wood,

> previously separate, become the thing called a house if connected in fixed ways. Thus, we consistently regard a society as an entity, because, though formed of discrete units, a certain concreteness in the aggregate of them is implied by general persistence of the arrangements among them throughout the area occupied. And it is this trait which yields our idea of a society (pp. 447–48).

Spencer's concept of man, following the rational utilitarian tradition of positivism, is that of an abstraction and not an existential reality. He formulates his idea of man when he begins to describe 'social types' in his *Principles of Sociology.* Here, he develops both a quasi-racial theory of man and differentiation of personality types in types of societies—militaristic and industrial. In his distinction between these two societal types and their processes of 'metamorphoses' he posits the concept of man through analyzing the relationship between the state and citizen and through his formulation how the idea of voluntary cooperation and civil ties, rights and duties only develops in an industrial society. He writes: "The regions whence changes towards greater political liberty have come, are the leading industrial regions ... Where industrial activities and structures evolve, this branch of the regulating system, no longer as in the militant type, a rigid hierarchy, little by little loses strength, while there grows up one of a different kind: *sentiments* and institutions both relaxing. *Right of private judgement in religious matters gradually establishes itself along with establishment of political rights.* In place of uniform belief imperatively enforced, there come multiform beliefs voluntarily accepted" (ibid.: 567). The will of the citizens is thus possible only at the stage of industrial society.

In August Comte's sociology we find another expression of the positivistic approach to the concept of man, once again very dimly visible to perception. In his *Philosophie Positive and Polity* (cf. Barnes, 1961), one would find formulations of the relationship between the individual and society and individual and the state respectively which very closely forerun that of Spencer. In *Polity* he particularly establishes the similarity between individual and social organism. "The difference between the individual and the social organism in Comte's opinion are only that the latter is essentially immutable while the social organism is capable of immense improvement. Similarly, the individual is capable of lesser degree of differentiation of functions than the social organism. Society is governed by the law of scientific progress which to individual is denied. This position completes what has been described as Comte's sociologistic positivism.

More dynamic conception of societal processes and implicitly also that of the concept of man, however, one may find in Comte's theory of social progress, particularly in his theory of positive religion. Unit of society to Comte is not individual but the family which is based on the feeling of affection; on this rest the superstructures of state, or city and church, the state representing the principle of action, and the church synthesizing all the action processes of the former two. These institutions evolve slowly with the evolution of *cerebral system* (based essentially on Gall's phrenological principle of psychology). The church has thus to enforce universal surveillance. Comte's concept of man is reflected in the postulate of cerebral system from which the essentials of personality system can be derived. The cerebral system comprises of feeling, action and intellect; feeling is the basis of morality which passes according to Comte into three stages in which man's nature finds its expression: the family, the state and finally the race. Man's highest moral height, altruism, finds its origin in family; during the Middle Ages it took the shape of civic culture, and in the 'positivistic' period morality should become universal. These three stages also represent advancement in sympathetic capacities of man, of attachment, of veneration, and finally of benevolence. These emotional stages in the evolution of the dominant drives of man also coincide with periods of religious institutionalizations; fetishism which is linked with the origin of family is dominated with attachment; polytheism, which is at the root of the origin of state is based on veneration principle and finally, monotheism, with its universality favours the sentiment of benevolence.

Comte builds into his theory of positive religion also his scheme of positive social reconstruction. Its philosophy also rests on three-fold division of human personality: action, intelligence and feeling. Material forces, wealth and social classes are based on the principle of action. Intellectual force, founded on speculation, is considered in idealistic and aesthetic expressions and moral force based on affection is expressed in command, prompted by character and obedience, and inspired by the heart. Women represent the principle of heart, also they symbolize the highest feeling of affection and tend to be the embodiment of moral principle compared to classes which affect action and represent materialistic forces or leaders who direct our activities. The principle of social hierarchy should be based on this hierarchy of affection intellect and feeling in which the new priests of the positive religion of humanity—sociologists—would occupy the highest position without an iota of temporal power. Their function would be directive, moral and universalistic based on the principles of positive science.

Comte's conception of man could be deduced from his formulation of structure of human nature and its derivative expressions both societal and cultural. One would also notice a faint resemblance in his formulation of human nature with later-day postulates of personality system in the functional theories of sociology, especially Parsonian three-fold modes of orientation. Only, Comte's postulates are not logically exclusive, have no roots in dynamic psychology and his sociology is completely devoid of concept of man as a unit of actors in the social system. What exists is mere social category and not man. Only a faint shadow of man, if not his ghost, hovers over Comte's sociology.

Pareto is another classical positivist in sociology who pushed man far back into the dark corner in sociology. This is so despite two major innovations in Paretian sociology which distinguish it from that of Comte and Spencer: a theory of social action as component of social system and a theory of the structure of sentiments. Since sentiments occupy an infrastructural place in Pareto's sociology, and provide the building blocks for his sociology of action, it needs explanation. Unlike Comte, Pareto's formulation of sentiment does not have a psychological connotation at all. It is an abstract hypothetical notion, which in itself is neither true nor false, but assumes a form only through social acts. The social act has reality but the sentiment has none. Thus, Pareto's famous distinction between the 'residue and derivatives' which lay the foundation for his social system and action frame of reference is mechanistic rather than normative or existential (cf. Henderson, 1937: 63–64). Pareto's concept of social system is more formal than sociological. A 'residue' is the manifestation of a sentiment. A 'derivate' is non-logical argument, explanation, assertation, appeal to authority, or association of ideas or sentiments in words. Of about fifty residues, the important ones are: residues of combination, of persistence of aggregates, of manifestation of sentiments through overt acts, of sociability, of integrity of individual and finally of sexuality. Among the important 'derivations' are: affirmation, authority, accord with sentiment or principles and verbal proofs.

The concept of man in Pareto's sociology is linked with his theory of elite to which the notions of residues and derivatives are organically linked. He divides population into the categories of elites and masses based on the predominance of residues of combination, action and integrity of individual in the former and of persistence of aggregate, sentiment and sexuality and sociability in the latter. He further divides the elites into two categories, viz., governmental and non-governmental, based on the same two types of dominant residual tendencies, of persistence among the governmental elites and combination among the non-governmental elites which in course of time leads to the petrification of the elan of the governmental elites and their eventual replacement by the non-governmental. History thus to Pareto is not only a cemetery of aristocracies but also of the governing elites.

The concept of man that emerges from these formulations of Pareto is not existential but categorial, a characteristic of all positivist sociologists of the 19th century. Man, as a being, remains in the background, and in the forefront of their treatment is man as a member of class or mass. Inferentially, notion of man is non-dialogical (cf. Casslerer, 1948) and is based on a typification which renders man into a form of abstraction. Pareto's own deductive logic in the formulation of the 'abstract man' emerges sharply when seen negatively, in contrast to that of Marx than when seen positively, in terms of his own constructions. Unlike Marx, whose notion of man we shall discuss later, Pareto denudes man completely of his existential being as well as his structural being or species being. His distinction of human action into the categories of the logical, where means are commensurate with ends and the non-logical, where means are not commensurate with ends, and his justification of these by 'derivatives' of various sorts, does introduce a partial dynamic element in the existential component of man; these also introduce an element of demystification of man, a challenge to the positivistic progress ideologies rampant at his time. His notion of elite as a foxy, brutish and opportunist being, out always to use 'ideologies' of various sorts to beguile the gullible masses, his faith in the susceptibility of masses to fall victims to such vulpine tactics are indeed counterpoints to Marx's notion of 'proletariat' basically revolutionary, praxeological and humistically transcendent. It is in this contradistinction between Marx and Pareto that one can get, though negatively, a glimpse of Pareto's notion of man.

The positivistic sociology slowly undergoes critical tensions from within its cognitive structure. The writings of Emile Durkheim symbolize this turning point. In his writings, utilitarian positivism of Spencer and Pareto is replaced by a sociologistic positivism, which later imbibes many attributes of symbolic interactionism. Sociology, as a truly mature and systematic discipline, owes much to the contribution of Durkheim. He also makes far more significant contributions to the concept of man.

Durkheim's concept of man emanates from his concept of society. Through his notions of societal structure, function, its differentiation and evolution, Durkheim develops theories of knowledge, ethics and education, normal and pathological modes of behaviour, crime, suicide and religion. His concept of alienation and alienative forms of division of labour are also organically linked with his treatment of society, and social facts. Defining social facts as 'things' having attributes of exteriority and constraint, slowly Durkheim builds a theory of society which is essentially symbolic and immanent in nature. Society is defined as a reality *sui generis;* it renders man a product of societal processes and his freedom a resultant of progressive differentiation, of societal roles, forms and institutions. In his *The Division of Labour in Society* (1933), Durkheim states his conception of man as he develops his theory of social differentiation. He posits two states of societal evolution through changes in the structure of its solidarities: the mechanical and organic. Visible symbol of social solidarity is law: with repressive sanction in mechanical solidarity and restitutive sanction in organic solidarity. Man does not have a personality of his own in a society in the state of mechanical solidarity, as it is a solidarity through likeness. Personal or civil rights, contractual obligations do not exist at this stage. Man as a person is only endowed with psychic images of the collective and not of their representations or symbolic forms. The latter does not have a differentiated structure in mechanical solidarity. With organic solidarity coming into being owing to the growth of population, clustering populations in townships, etc., there is increase in the volume of social interaction as the 'dynamic density' of society increases. Correspondingly, there is increase in the 'moral density' of society.

At this stage of societal development from the chrysalis of the solidarity emerges the individual representation; collective representation is thus differentiated, functional specialization follows not because of man's inherent rationalism, his hedonistic urge or heredity but because of the fundamental fact that societal structure itself has undergone a basic transformation. Durkheim writes:

> Collective life is not born from individual life, but it is, on the contrary, the second which is born from the first. It is on this condition alone that one can explain how the personal individuality of social units has been able to be formed and enlarged without disintegrating society... It is not the absolute personality of the monad, which is sufficient unto itself, and could do without the rest of the world, but that of an organ or part of an organ having its determined function, but which cannot, without risking dissolution, separate itself from the rest of the organism. Under these conditions, cooperation becomes not only possible but necessary. Utilitarians thus reverse the natural order of facts, and nothing is more deceiving than this inversion. It is a particular illustration of the general truth that what is first in knowledge is last in reality. Precisely because cooperation is the most recent fact, it strikes sight first (ibid.: 279–80).

Increasing division of labour in society, its role structures and functions not only bring into being the notion of man as a separate existential reality but it also leads us to diagnose the sociological problematic of man in modern industrial society. Alienation of man from society as a result of the progressive complexity and specialization of functions is a theme which Durkheim for the first time introduces in sociology. He has in this respect been a forerunner among sociologists on the concept and the problematic of man.

Alienation of man in societies with progressive organic solidarities results, according to Durkheim, for two reasons: first, due to the state of anomie in society, a condition in which the differentiated elements of social structure cease to be at the requisite level of interaction essential in organic solidarity, and secondly, because of the normative erosion in society following anomie. When components of social system that require continual interaction of higher intensity and coordination, as the parts now have attained autonomy, are not able to do so, as 'opaque environments' interpose between them, the solidarity of the whole is transformed into the alienation of the parts. This also results from the rapid rate of changes that follow the industrial revolution in society; this introduces realms of autonomy in social structures much faster than the generation of the sociological and moral forces in society to coordinate the level of interaction.

Under these circumstances, man is caught in a moral vicious circle, because to Durkheim, the source of morality also lies in the self-same societal processes which give birth to anomie and alienation of societal forms. He writes:

> Society is not then, as has been thought, a stranger to the moral world, or something which has only secondary condition of its existence. It is not a simple juxtaposition of individuals who bring an intrinsic morality with them, but rather man is a moral being only because he lives in society, since morality consists being in solidary with a group and varying with this solidarity. Let all social life disappear, and moral life will disappear with it, since it would no longer have any objective (ibid.: 399).

Linked with questions of anomie and morality is the notion of the normal and pathological social facts and behaviours that assume significance in Durkheim's formulation of the concept of man. In his *The Rules of Sociological Method* (1950) and *The Suicide* (1951), he has developed the notion of man to a new existential level, a forerunner of contemporary cognitive sociology (cf. Cicourel, 1973). Traditionally, the idea of human responsibility and free will had dominated the notion of man both in utilitarian philosophy and medieval Christianity. The distinction between normal and pathological was made on the grounds of man's choice of his deeds and his consequent responsibility; the normative judgement by society of the human deed was not put into question at all, Durkheim has almost radicalized the notion of human responsibility and free will by rendering them obsolescent. He postulates that normal action cannot be judged on the basis of *normative* frame of reference of a particular society which would elude detection without a scientific indicator. Normal behaviour would itself prove the reality of the existence of a particular form of normative structure; this behaviour can be judged only through the generality of the forms of social actions. This generality would further be specific to societies, and normal and pathological cannot be formulated for all societies for all times to come.

In terms of human condition, it revolutionizes the relationship between the judge and the judged. Men commit suicide not because of a monomania—a taint of free will or personal sin—but because of interposition of socially 'opaque structures' between their individual representations and images and that of society, and between their definition of the reality resulting from this interposition and that of the society. So, suicide is sometimes reflection of man's overconformity to societal ideals, it is altruistic; sometimes it results from underconformity, it is egoistic; and at other times it is because the norm of conformity is itself in a flux, in the processes of rapid social change, then suicide is anomic. Hence, pathological and normal are not categories to be defined by a transcendental normative principle but through essential reflexivity of human situation in society and its social processes. It has a deeper significance to the concept of man; it gives man a moral reprieve not available to him in the past.

These ideas of Durkheim on the concept of man find their final expression in his later work *The Elementary Forms of the Religious Life* (1961) and his famous essay on "The Dualism of Human Nature and Social Condition" (1914). He uses the theme of religion to explicate his sociology of knowledge, but in the centre of this problem is the concept of man. Religion has its basis in the bipartite division of all phenomena "which embraces all that exists, but which radically excludes each other. Sacred things are those that interdictions protect and isolate; profane things, those to which these interdictions are applied and which must remain at a distance from the first. Religious beliefs are representations which express the nature of sacred things and the relations which they sustain, either with each other, or with profane things" (ibid.: 56). This realm of the sacred is further divided into the personal and collective, which in two opposite forms manifest the same reality. Man as mere body is profane; he ascends in status as he imbibes more and more of the sacred through his proximity to religious symbols or gods. Yet, gods also need man to sustain them.

Durkheim writes: "If it is true that man depends upon his gods, this dependence is reciprocal. The gods also have need of man; without offerings and sacrifices they would die" (ibid.: 53).

Durkheim now treats the concept of man in extension of, as well as, in contradistinction with the concept of god. The separation between soul and body, the basis of animistic beliefs in primitive religions, he maintains, is not born of irrationality but a quantum jump of human consciousness to conceptualization and self-objectification from the levels of mere sensate awareness. He says:

> The fact is that man is not merely an animal with certain additional qualities: he is something else. Human nature is the result of a sort of recasting of the animal nature, and in the course of the various complex operations which have brought about this recasting, there have been losses as well as gains. How many instincts have we not lost? The reason is that men are not only in relation with the physical environment, but also with a social environment infinitely more extended, more stable and more active than the one whose influence animals undergo. To live, they must adapt themselves to this. Now, in order to maintain itself, society frequently finds it necessary that we should see things from a certain angle and feel them in a certain way; consequently, it modifies in ideas which we would be inclined if we listened only to our animal nature; it alters them, even going so far as to put the contrary sentiments in their place. Does it not even go so far as to regard our own individual lives as something of little value, while for the animal this is the greatest thing? (ibid.: 83).

Religion is thus a symbolic externalization of societal reality through human consciousness, which in the first instance had subjectively internalized it through societal interaction. It is the source of formation of conceptual world, its universal as well as specific manifestation. Man attains his human qualities, his selfhood and identity through the mediation of his psyche with society; in the process societal objective reality gets internalized into his psyche, qualitatively transforming it and endowing with new capacity for its symbolization and externalization. It is this form of societal self-externalization through man that offers us the objective reality of social phenomena. Universal categories, therefore, for ever remain in the realm of the ideal possibilities since the very process of mediation through which the symbolic universe of man projects societal self-awareness is never fully complete; it is always partial, dialectical and critical. Durkheim writes:

> ...it is rather at the school of collective life that the individual has learned to idealize. It is in assimilating the ideals elaborated by society that he has become capable of conceiving the ideal. It is society which, by leading him within its sphere of action, has made him acquire the need of raising himself above the world of experience and has at the same time furnished him with the means of conceiving another. For society has constructed this new world in constructing itself, since it is society which this expresses. Thus both with the individual and in the group, the faculty of idealizing has nothing mysterious about it. It is not a sort of luxury which a man could get along without, but a condition of his very existence" (ibid.: 470–71).

In his essay following the *Elementary Forms of the Religious Life*, Durkheim further crystallized his views on man and nature of man. He now clearly formulated the concept of man as *homo-duplex*. Man, at the same time, he said, is both I and We. There is a dialectical relationship between these two dimensions of human nature which grows constantly with growth in societal self-awareness. Summarizing the ideas on Durkheim's notion of homo-duplex, Tiryakian writes:

> Durkheim states that the body-soul dichotomy is echoed in the human psyche itself. The mind is a composite of sensation and feelings, as well as intellectual and moral activity. Our bodily appetites are self-centred but our mental activity very often seeks impersonal ends or disinterested pursuits. Physical sensation cannot be transferred to others; nobody can perceive or have the same sensory experiences of the same phenomenon as I do. On the contrary, concepts are always common to a plurality of men and can always be shared, even if they are initially the product of one person; our intellect functions by means of impersonal concepts which are by nature universal. According to Durkheim, these considerations verify the old notion of *homo-duplex*.

> Our inner life has what might be called a double centre of gravity: there is an awareness of our own proper individuality, which is grounded in our biological nature, and there is also an awareness of an extra-individual component of the self. I perceive and react to the world in terms of both my own personal experiences, localized by my body in space and time, and also in terms of a much greater, impersonal sort of knowledge about the world. In man, then there is a being which sees everything in the light of its own self and which in its activity has no other end but itself; but there is also another being which knows things *sub specia aeternitatis*, as if it participated in a mental activity other than its own, and which tends in its actions to realize extrapersonal ends. Between these two aspects of man there is a fundamental and irreconcilable opposition. How could we belong, asks Durkheim, completely to ourselves as well as completely to others? The ego (the conscious self) cannot be completely something other than itself, for then it would dissolve (as in ecstasy). In order to think, one must *be*, one must have an individuality. But from another perspective, the self cannot be wholly or exclusively itself, for then it would become void of all content. If being is necessary for thought, thought is equally necessary for being (1962: 47–48).

Durkheim thus not only consolidates the position of sociology as a discipline in its own right, beyond an analogical extension of the other social sciences, but he laid down the foundation of most ideas and issues on the concept of man which remain live and valid even today. It is indeed significant that in his conception of man one can easily see the mirror image of the contemporary sociological conceptions of man—be it the symbolic-interactionist, phenomenological, structural or ethnomethodological. Even a similarity between the Marxist or neo-Marxist conception of man and the one constructed by Durkheim in his later works can be discerned, especially in the context of structural dialectics (as distinct from historical dialectics).

Concept of Man in Functional Sociology

From utilitarian positivism of Spencer's sociology, mechanistic positivism of Pareto and sociologistic positivism of Comte,

Durkheim's sociological positivism was of a highly transient and critical character; it was, as we have observed, imbued with internal tensions. Sociology following the works of these classicists branched off in two major directions both having a neo-positivistic hue. While the Paretian tradition was extended by Henderson and Homans, the Durkheimian tradition, especially in its early positivistic form, emerged as a new functional theory in social anthropology of Malinowski and Radcliffe-Brown and sociology of Parsons, Merton, Davis and other sociologists, mostly in the United States. It is interesting that the symbolic-interactionist and phenomenological aspects of Durkheimian sociology did not at first develop in the United States, but in the Continent itself, especially in interaction with the immanent interpretive tradition of the German sociology. To this we shall return later.

The metamorphosis of positivism into functional sociology took place under historical circumstances, such as the emergence of Freudian theory of man and society, disillusionment of the west with the negative consequences of industrialization, the two world wars which left an indelible scar on the conscience of European man and the emergence of Marxism not merely as an alternative ideology of science but also as a new state craft in the Soviet Union. All these developments deeply influenced sociology following its classical origin. Functionalism as an approach in sociology has imbibed an empirical orientation, a systemic perspective on structure and function of social entities, mainly role structures or action systems, and an overt or covert psychological dimension depending upon whether the psychological frame is Freudian or behaviouristic.

The concept of man in functional sociology emerges in various forms and at several levels of analysis: personality formation and the role of primary institutions in child-rearing, social structure and characterological forms of men, and alienation of man in the context of structural complexity and contradictions. These are some of the major themes in functional sociology around which the concept of man is postulated. This would be evident from the works of prominent functional sociologists such as Parsons, Merton and Homans.

Parsons has formulated his concept of man synthesizing three major theoretical orientations, viz., sociological, Freudian-psychological and behaviouristic-psychological. In his *Social System* (1972), he treats man as a *plastic* and *sensitive* being; both plasticity and sensitiveness constitute together the sociological nature of man. He defines plasticity as the capacity of the human organism to adapt to infinite variations of the eco-cultures and social situations and sensitivity as capacity of man to learn and internalize values and to institutionalize them into roles and functional skills. The two important dimensions of sensitivity in man are motivational structure and value structure: the former is rooted into the phylogenetic and ontogenetic organic characteristics of man through which Parsons establishes the link between Freudian approach and his own; the value structure, on the other, is primarily sociogenic and its foundation lies in the processes of institutionalization and legitimation at the societal level and socialization at the personality level. Socialization and institutionalization are thus two mutually reinforcing processes.

These processes reflect themselves through system states, socialization in the personality system, institutionalization through the societal and cultural systems, but the linking process between the two are the roles or action orientations of men in society. This action frame of reference at the level of human personality emerges primarily from the critical tensions of motivational structure and not the cultural structure. Parsons, on the basis of the postulates of primacy of 'motivational integration' in the personality system and of the 'cultural integration' in the social system, distinguishes between two problematics of sociology: alienation and anomie. Alienation, according to him, is a state of disorientation in the role structure at the personality level resulting from the internal dislocation of relationships within the components of motivational structure e.g. cathection, cognition and evaluation; it results from imperfections in the introjection and internalization of value orientations through the mechanism of socialization. The mal-integration in the value orientation structure of society, Parsons would define as a state of anomie. Though heuristically or even substantively distinct both alienation and anomie have an interactive character.

In his collaborative work *Toward a General Theory of Action* (1951), as different from his *Social System*, Parsons takes a more overtly psychological approach to personality system. He more explicitly elaborates the structure of human need dispositions, dynamics of motivational orientations and their organization through different psychological mechanisms.

The distinguishing feature of concept of man in Parsons sociology, however, remains the effacement of man as an existential historical being. His, like most other functional approaches in sociology, is a conception not of man but of a personality, not of a being but of an abstract psycho-organic system. He does raise some interesting issues on man in his *Social System* but their significance lies in demonstrating the impact of societal and cultural systems on the role integration of man in society. The most significant notion that Parsons develops in this context is that of 'basic personality structure' which he borrows approvingly from Kardiner and Linton. It represents a form of modal personality through a fit between the dominant cultural values enshrined in primary institutions of a society and the personality systems of the members of that society. Through this notion, Parsons endorses two important trends in social sciences: first, the theory of ontogenetic growth of personality, a neo-Freudian innovation, and secondly, the need to study the variations in modal personality of men in specific techno-ecological and cultural systems through child-rearing and socialization processes. This latter trend in the analysis and diagnosis of human personality, its characterological contours and its processes have since occupied a great deal of attention of functional sociologists (see works of Parsons and Bales, Whiting, Kardiner and Linton, etc.) As the emphasis shifted from man to the concept of personality, the historical and philosophical issues on man and his future were lost to operational and empirical diagnostic concerns.

The main weakness of studying man through mechanisms of personality formation or its characterological variations is that in this perspective the more significant problems of man and his relationship with society, such as his autonomy to reflect critically about societal reality as an object external to him, his power not only to empathize but also to apperceive, and his reflexivity, are lost sight of. It also neglects other existential problems such as man's alienation not merely as a role deviance, the sense in which Parsons uses this term, but as historical evolutionary dialectics of society, as immanently given to it. Paradoxically, Parsons who embarked upon the heroic task of synthesizing and improving upon the theoretical contributions of the classicists, in his zeal for the construction of logically closed and coherent system-categories, emasculated sociology of its more fundamental concerns existent in the works of Marx, Weber and Durkheim upon whose works he tried to build his system theory.

Merton is another important innovator in functional sociology. His impact on contemporary sociology has been as great as that of Parsons even though his contributions are not that architectonic. He is less historical than Parsons, more realistic about theorizing, more lucid in style but essentially in regard to his contribution to the concept of man, he has little more to offer than Parsons. Despite his raising the problem of man in modern society in a changing paradigmatic context, his focus in the study of man is confined to the analysis of deviant modes of adaptation of a person. Merton writes:

> Until recently, and all the more so before then, one could speak of a marked tendency in psychological and sociological theory to attribute the faulty operation of social structure to failures of social control over man's biological drives. The imagery of the relations between man and society implied by this doctrine is as clear as it is questionable. In the beginning, there are man's biological impulses which seek full expression. And then, there is the social order, essentially an apparatus for the management of impulses, for the social processing of tensions, for the 'renunciation of instinctual gratification' of Freud. Non-conformity with the demands of a social structure is thus assumed to be anchored in original nature. It is the biologically rooted impulses which from time to time break through social control. And by implication, conformity is the result of a utilitarian calculus of unreasoned conditioning.
>
> With the more recent advancement of social sciences, this set of conceptions has undergone basic modification. For one thing, it no longer appears so obvious that man is set against society in an unceasing war between biological impulse and social restraint. The image of man as an untamed bundle of impulses begins to look more like a caricature than a portrait. For another, sociological perspectives have increasingly entered into the analysis of behaviour deviating from prescribed patterns of conduct. For whatever the role of biological impulses, there still remains the further question of why it is that the frequency of deviant

behaviour varies within different social structures and how it happens that deviations have different shapes and patterns in different social structures (1968: 185).

Consequently, the concrete outcome of Merton's study of man does not go beyond a "systematic approach to the analysis of social and cultural sources of deviant behaviour". His aim is to "discover how some social structures exert a definite pressure upon certain persons in the society to engage in non-conforming rather than conforming conduct" (ibid.: 186), which he explains through incongruence-congruence between legitimate cultural goals and institutionalized means that individuals adopt in their role performance especially with regard to major areas of choices of goals and means for realization of social objectives. On this basis he formulates two types of adaptations of behaviour, viz., conformity, where there exists a congruence between cultural goals of society and means legitimized by it for their achievement and deviance where this congruence does not exist. On the basis of the variations in deviance either in respect of culturally defined goals, its legitimate or institutionalized means or both, Merton postulates four model adaptations of deviant behaviour: *innovation*, where new means are introduced for realizing culturally defined goals; *ritualism*, where means themselves become all too important to the neglect of culturally defined goals; *retreatism*, where actor is indifferent both to culturally defined goals as well as the means; and finally, the *rebellion*, where both culturally defined goals as well as the means are thrown overboard to be substituted by new ones. Merton views conformity as the trait of persons in stable societies, although he does not rule out overconformity as a deviant form of adaptation homologous to retreatism in the reverse.

All forms of deviant modes of adaptation in behaviour emerge in more endemic form in a state of anomie in a society. Social structures give way to anomie following increase in the deviant modes of personal adaptation as well as they might also generate it. To Merton, anomie is a state of societal malintegration of role structures and their institutionalization and not a state of mind as held by other social psychologists and sociologists (he specially criticizes McIver's definition of anomie as a state of mind (cf. McIver, 1950).

We would notice that Merton like Parsons identifies the concept of man with that of personality system as an integrated system of role structures and role performances. He too concentrates on deviance as the most relevant parameter for analyzing the man-society relationships and more than Parsons he schematizes the notion of man by rendering it an outcome of a 'property-space model' generating logical sets of categories. Similarly, like Parsons, Merton too develops the concept of 'modal personality' or 'status personality' in his treatment of bureaucratic structure and personality. Specialized roles, according to him, expose persons to norms of overconformity, the case in instance being bureaucracy; this generates 'trained incapacities' on the one hand and ritualism on the other. The more a person due to this reason overconforms to his specialized roles, the more he is rendered marginal to the rest of the roles he has to perform and is also thereby exposed to maladjustments.

Both Parsons and Merton, in their treatment of personality and role-specific problems of integration of man in modern society, especially industrial society, raise indirectly questions of alienation, anomie, deviance, overconformity, etc., which do tend, to be significant issues on the concept of man in sociology. They anticipate problems of man in modern society such as those of 'organization man' (cf. Whyte, 1956; Galbraith, 1967), 'industrial man' (cf. Burns, 1969), 'other-ditected man' (cf. Reisman, 1950) and 'one-dimensional man' (cf. Marcuse, 1964) etc., but they do still fail to project a proper concept of man since they look at man primarily as a system of role structures; it is endowed, of course, with socio-organismic dynamics but is devoid of historical-biographic dynamics.

George C. Homans, in this context, raises a pertinent question in his exposure of the limitations of 'functional theory' which led to the exile of man from sociological analysis. He says the functionalist's fundamental unit, the role, was a social fact in Durkheim's sense. And their theoretical programme assumed, as he did, that sociology should be an independent science, in the same sense that its propositions should not be derivable from some other social science, such as psychology. This meant, in effect, that the general propositions of sociology were not to be propositions about the behaviour of individual consciousnesses—or, as I should say, about men—but propositions about the characteristics of societies or other social groups as such (cf. Homans, 1964: 810). This led to the neglect of the concept of man from functional sociological theory (as different from functional analysis which does not imply propositional format for explanations). This critique is indeed symptomatic. One might, therefore, ask about the concept of man that Homans postulates in his sociological theory: Is it the one that restores man really back to his substantive status in sociological analysis? Does it restore back to him his historical and biographical self-awareness?

Indeed, one is disappointed when he takes a close look at the notion of man that Homans develops in his sociology. Despite his plea for 'bringing man back-in' his notion of man is mechanistic; man's all activities result, according to him, from a set of fundamental psychological dispositions or processes. These dispositions can be converted into universal psychological propositions which according to him are at the root of all forms of human activities, social interactions and modes of institutionalization in society. Amongst these, four propositions are crucial: the success proposition, the stimulus proposition, the deprivation-statiation proposition, and the frustration-aggression proposition. Human interaction situation directed by these psycho-behaviouristic propositions is a game of exchange of gratifications and values and it determines its own dynamics. Man operates in society following his personal matrix of exchange with others of gratification-deprivation though rooted these may be in social institutions and contexts (Homans, 1961: 30–78). Obviously, the theoretical framework of Homans' notion of man is in the behaviouristic psychology, particularly in the Skinnerian form. It is psychological, reductionistic and completely ahistorical as well as non-biographical. It also does not recognize human problems of alienation and overconformity in modern societies since all such modes of human conditions can always be explained by interposing one or another set of psychological propositions. Its orientation on the concept of man thus remains empirical and operational in a mechanistic sense.

It would thus appear that functional sociology both in its systematic postulates such as those of Parsons and Merton or in its micro-systematic form as in Homans has rendered man a peripheral concept. Man is treated not in the fullness of his existential being, but as an abstraction or as a process; in the former sense it is equated with role or constellations of value patterns in the personality system and in the latter merely as a by-product of imputed psychological dispositions. It is indeed paradoxical that functional sociology which claims its development from Durkheim failed completely to develop the concept of man as postulated in his notion of *homo-duplex*. It thus failed to notice the most creative as well as critical aspects of the concept of man, the substantive issues of man's growing self-estrangement and his growing self-awareness as dialectical processes in contemporary industrial and post-industrial societies.

The loss of this critical perspective on man has been primarily due to a certain scientific notions of sociology which these sociologists wanted to develop. Consequently, we find more wholesome treatment of man in those sociologists, even though they have some orientation of functional variety (in Kingsley Davis' sense; cf. Davis, 1955), who were less overwhelmed in establishing a homologous relationship between science and sociology. David Reisman, Lewis Mumford, Daniel Bell, Wilbert Moore and several other sociologists who fall under this category; were not so self-conscious about the nomological aspect of sociology, but have contributed deeply to the understanding of the relationship between modern industrial society and man. Reisman and Glazer in *The Lonely Crowd* (1950) make a characterological assessment of man's changing nature, motivational orientation and value syndromes from the traditional to modern society. It passes though three stages: 'tradition-directed' in traditional societies to 'inner-directed' in transitional societies to 'other-directed' in the modern societies. In the inner-directed syndrome, the dominance is of the "drive to live upto an ideal"—a phenomenon which according to Reisman and Glazer was pervasive in the 19th century-United States, whereas in the other-directed type, the dominant value syndrome is of "making good through making friends"—a tendency which reflects the problem of alienation of man in modern societies. Lewis Mumford in his *Condition of Man* (1944), Wilbert E. Moore in *Man, Time and Society* (1963) and Daniel Bell in *The Coming of the Post-Industrial Society* (1914) have analyzed the implications of the modern technological, media-explosive post-industrial society to the being and consciousness of man. If Mumford analyzes it from diagnostic and prescriptive points of view, Moore and Bell delve deeper into the mystery of fundamental structural revolution that modern society is undergoing today—a change which basically alters man-society, man-nature relationships by introducing the imperatives of re-scheduling and re-synchronization of 'time' in ordering human activities (Moore, 1963). This need gets acute since post-industrial society also introduces contradiction of *New Societies* amidst plenitude or affluence that it generates.

Daniel Bell postulates that post-industrial society is primarily an information society; the industrial society is goods-producing society. The primacy of information creates new problems. These are: inadequacy and hypertechnicality of information, new problems of coordination, marginality of participation and feeling of powerlessness, constriction of social interaction, and social 'diremption of time'. It creates new cultural dilemmas for society which introduce new elements in the definition of man. Bell writes:

> I have attempted to suggest the agenda of issues which emerge with the onset of post-industrial society: the new hierarchies of technical elites and the bureaucratization of science; meritocracy and equality; the antinomian thrust of an adversary culture, the communal society and the difficulty of consensus. These run the gamut from ethos and value to politics and social organization. Yet, in an intangible way, there may be more—a change in consciousness and cosmology, the dark tinge of which has always been present at the edge of man's conception of himself and the world, which now moves to the phenomenological centre.
>
> In existentialist terminology, man is 'thrown' into the world confronting alien and hostile powers which he seeks to understand and master. The first confrontation was with nature, and for most of the thousand years of man's existence, life has been a fight against nature to find shelter. Man as *homo faber* sought to make things and in making things he dreamt of remaking nature. To rework nature, to make fabricated things, was to enhance man's power. In the industrial society, the cosmological vision was the game against fabricated nature. The post-industrial society turns its back on both. In the salient experience of work, men live more and more outside nature, and less and less with machinery and things; they live with and encounter one another ... In the daily round of work men no longer confront nature, as either alien or beneficent, and fewer now handle artifacts and things. The post-industrial

> society is essentially a game between persons. Will this changed experience create a change in consciousness and sensibility?
>
> For most of human history, *reality was nature* and in poetry and imagination men sought to relate the self to the natural world. Then *reality became technics*, tools and things made by men yet given an independent existence outside himself, the reified world. Now *reality is primarily the social world*—neither nature nor things, only men experienced through reciprocal consciousness of self and other. Society itself becomes a web of consciousness, a form of imagination to be realized as a social construction. Inevitably, a post-industrial society gives rise to new utopianism, both engineering and psychedelic. Man can be re-made or released, their behaviour conditioned or their consciousness altered. The constraints of the past vanish with the end of nature and things. But what does not vanish is the duplex of man himself—the murderous aggression, the primal impulse to tear apart and destroy; the search for order, in art, and life as the bending of will to harmonious shape. It is this ineradicable tension which defined the social world and which permits a view of utopia that is perhaps more realistic than the here-and-now millennium on earth that modern man has sought. Men in their imagination will always seek to make society a work of art; that remains an ideal. Given the tasks that have to be solved, it is enough to engage in the sober construction of social reality (1974: 481–88).

This reflection on man in post-industrial society represents the peak of maturity in line with the tradition of Durkheim we analyzed above. It is also noteworthy that it raises more fundamental phenomenological issues on man in modern society than could be possible within the framework of functional theory of Parsons, Merton or Homans.

Concept of Man in Dialectical and Interpretive Sociology

Dialectical sociological theory owes its origin to a tradition altogether different from that of positivism or functionalism. It is rooted in philosophy and history and has always been skeptical of the varieties of raw empiricism. Its emphasis is on immanent law and meaningful relations in social systems rather than on external causal relationships. Karl Marx represents a tradition of sociology with focus primarily on the immanent laws and on social dialectics. Max Weber, responding indirectly to Marx, shifted the emphasis from immanent laws to meaningful systemic understanding of social reality. Both drew their inspiration from philosophy—Marx from Hegel and Weber from Kant. Both as they developed their ideas, transformed the philosophical constructs of their predecessors. Marx not only inverted but also transformed the tenets of Hegelian philosophy. Weber rejected the Kantian dissociation between phenomenon and noumenon and tried to synthesize it through sociology.

But the most distinctive mark of the dialectical and interpretive theories in sociology has been their recognition of the problematic of man in modern society. It constitutes the central problem of their sociological theory.

Alienation of man is central concern in Marx's sociology; to this end his analysis of stages of revolutionary social transformation provides answer to the puzzle of human condition. Similarly, for Weber, modern capitalist society, its rational bureaucratic organization and legal rational forms of authority assume relevance as these inaugurate new concept of man and new sets of relationships between man and society.

Marx develops his concept of man in his *Economic and Philosophic Manuscripts of 1844* (1974) on which the impress of Hegelian philosophy though in an inverted form is at its highest. He locates the critical element of human destiny in the species character of man; man is a body and also a member of a collectivity which is carrier of his accumulated historical endowments, his past and his future potential. The uniting link between the organic and species levels of his being is *labour*—a typically human attribute. It is human attribute because man alone is capable of confronting through mastery over nature the objectified product of his labour, labour *estranged* from him as a product of history. Man makes history through progressive stages of estrangement of his labour and by giving it species form. It is an immanent law of social life but its validity lies not in the *principles* but in the material conditions, modes of production of concrete men in concrete societies. Since man alone is capable of self-reflection on the product of his estranged labour, that represents most of the societal phenomena that surround him, he alone is a candidate for freedom.

The notion of freedom which Marx develops in his later works through his emphasis on revolutionary praxis marks the culmination in his concept of man. In his manuscripts, however, he deals primarily with the historical conditions of human estrangement. Marx writes:

> What then constitutes alienation of labour? First, the fact that labour is *external* to the worker, i.e., it does not belong to his intrinsic nature. Its alien character emerges clearly in the fact that as soon as no physical or other compulsion exists, labour is shunned like the plague...We have considered the act of estranging practical human activity, labour, in two of its aspects: (1) The relation of the worker to the *product of labour* as an alien object exercising power over him. This relation is at the same time the relation to the sensuous external world, to the objects of nature, as an alien world inimically opposed to him. (2) The relation of labour to the *act of production* within the *labour* process. This relation is the relation of the worker to his own activity as an alien activity not belonging to him; it is activity as suffering, strength as weakness, begetting as emasculating, the worker's own physical and mental energy, his personal life—for what is life but activity?—as an activity which is turned against him. Here we have self-estrangement, as previously we had the estrangement of the thing (1974: 66–67).

Apart from these two levels of estrangement, Marx also visualizes a third form of estrangement of man, at the level of his species being, and it is in this context that he raises the concept of freedom and alienation. He writes: "Man is a species being, not only because in practice and in theory he adopts the species (his own as well as those of other things) as his object, but—and this is only another way of expressing it—also because he treats himself as the actual, living species; because he treats himself as a *universal* and therefore a free being" (ibid.: 67). Man proves his species character through his work which is objectification of man's species life, "for he duplicates himself not only, as in consciousness, intellectually, but also actively in reality, and therefore, he sees himself in a world that he has created" (ibid.: 69). Man's physical existence is thus rooted in his degradation of spontaneous free activity and its enthrallment "in such a way that species (life) becomes for him a means; estranged labour is thus turned through man's species-being, both nature and his spiritual species-property, into a being alien to him, into a *means* for his *individual existence*. It estranges from man his own body, as well as external nature and his spiritual aspect, his *human* aspect. An immediate consequence of the fact that man is estranged from the product of his labour, from his life activity, from his species-being is the *estrangement of man from man*" (ibid.: 69).

The notion of man in the *Economic and Philosophic Manuscripts* is essentially phenomenological, the emphasis being on existential problems of man. Marx in his later works moves from this position to overwhelmingly praxeological concept of man. It is indeed not absent from his early works, but later on it becomes paramount in his treatment of man. In *The German Ideology* (1968), Marx and Engels give a much fuller treatment to the concept of man from this perspective. Emphasis now is on sociological analysis of structural differentiation of human society, its historical basis and its impact on the consciousness of man. Interestingly, in this aspect of sociological analysis, one could discern some faint resemblances between Marx and Engels and Durkheim. The statement that "as individuals express their life, so they are. What they are, therefore, coincides with their production, both with *what* they produce and with *how* they produce. The nature of individuals thus depends on the material conditions determining their production. *This production only makes its appearance with the increase of population. In its turn this presupposes the intercourse* (Verkehr) of individuals with one another. The form of intercourse is again determined by production" (1968: 32, italics added). Increase in population as a causal factor in social differentiation was also emphasized by Durkheim; he called it the increase in the dynamic density of society, but unlike Marx and Engels he did not attribute this change directly to the existential and historical nature of man. Marx and Engels attribute growth in population through a chain of sequential developments at the basis of which lies the being of man. They write:

> The first promise of all human history is, of course, the existence of living human individuals...The writing of history must always set out from these natural bases and their modification in the course of history through men. Men can be distinguished from animals by consciousness, by religion or anything else you like. They themselves begin to distinguish themselves from animals as soon as they *produce* their means of subsistence, a step which is conditioned by their physical organization. By producing their means of subsistence men are indirectly producing their actual material life (ibid.: 31–32). Men thus construct their own social reality; they produce their ideas, concepts and consciousness through their material intercourse with men, 'real, active men'. Consciousness can never be anything else than conscious existence, and the existence of men is their actual life-process. If in all ideology men and their circumstances appear upside-down as in a *camera obscuro*, this phenomenon arises just as much from their historical life-process as the inversion of objects on the retina does from their physical life-process (ibid.: 37).

Evidently, now, emphasis shifts from existence to consciousness and on history as mediating process for man. History is not given to man, but man makes history. He makes it by his first historical act of production and reproduction to satisfy his needs. "The production of life, both of one's own in labour and of fresh life in procreation, now appears as a double relationship: on the one hand, as a natural, and on the other, as a social relationship. By social, we understand, Marx and Engels say, the cooperation of several individuals, no matter under what conditions, in what manner and to what end...Thus, it is quite obvious from the start that there exists a material connection of men with one another, which is determined by their needs and their mode of production, and which is as old as men themselves" (ibid.: 41). Marx and Engels draw a sharp distinction on this basis between man and animal: the animal does not enter into 'relationship' with anything, it does not enter into any relation at all; relationship as also consciousness are entirely human attributes. "Consciousness is from the very beginning a social product, and remains so as long as men exist at all. Consciousness is at first, of course, merely consciousness concerning the *immediate* sensuous environment and consciousness of the limited connection with other persons and things outside the individual who is growing self-conscious. At the same time, it is consciousness of nature, which first appears to men as completely alien, all powerful and unassailable force, with which men's relations are purely animal and by which they are overawed like beasts. It is thus purely animal consciousness of nature (natural religion)" (ibid.: 142). Nature at this stage of growth of consciousness is hardly modified historically; man is less advanced praxiologically and herd consciousness prevails. This consciousness grows further with division of labour following increase in population. "From this moment onward consciousness can really flatter itself that it is something other than consciousness of existing practice, that it *really* represents something without representing something real; from now on consciousness is in a position to emancipate itself from the world and to proceed to the formation of 'pure' theory, theology, philosophy and ethics, etc. But even if this theory, theology, philosophy, ethics, etc., comes into contradiction with existing relations, this can only occur because existing social relations have come into contradiction with existing forces of production" (ibid.: 43).

This linkage between history (mode of production and its relationships) and consciousness immanently inheres contradictions so long as the resulting division of labour is governed by moments of forces of production, the state of society and consciousness in a manner that "intellectual and material activity—enjoyment and labour, production and consumption—devolve on different individuals and that only possibility of their not coming into contradiction lies in the negation in its turn of the division of labour". Indeed, "division of labour offers us first example of how, as long as man remains in natural society, that is, as long as a cleavage exists between the particular and the common interest, as long, therefore, as activity is not voluntarily, but naturally, divided, man's own deed becomes an alien power opposed to him, which enslaves him instead of being controlled by him". This structural contradiction is result of assignment of exclusive sphere of activity for each individual which he cannot escape. This could only be abolished in a communist society which according to Marx and Engels will resolve the contradictions of division of labour and consequent fragmentation of human consciousness by abolishing the exclusive sphere of activity to each individual, rendering possible the emergence of a whole man. They write: "In communist society, where nobody has one exclusive sphere of activity but each can become accomplished in any branch he wishes, society regulates the general production and thus makes it possible for me to do one thing today another tomorrow, to hunt in the morning, fish in the afternoon, rear cattle in the evening, criticize after dinner just as I have a mind, without ever becoming hunter, fisherman, shepherd or critic" (ibid.: 45). Achievement of this ideal is possible only through revolutionary praxis. Two conditions are necessary for this according to Marx and Engels: first, great mass of humanity must be rendered propertyless accompanied by great increase in productive power of society, and secondly, a universal intercourse between men in their *world-historical* rather than local being (rendered possible only through increase in productive power and universal propertylessness) which brings about the universal individual into being.

It is at this level that Marx combines in his notion of universal man or whole man (cf. Fischer, 1973: 15–30) the theory of revolutionary praxis. He also in the same process postulates his theory of human nature. The *universal man* emerges through the evolutionary dialectics of the *historical man* and the *natural man.* The natural man is a sensuous man, a passionate man who enjoys interpersonal relationships. Erich Fromm equates Marx's emphasis on passion in human relationship with Freud's libido and treats it as the elemental factor in his theory of human nature (Fromm, 1973: 80–81) but he does also see a progressive evolution in his concept of man. He writes: "Speaking of psychology as a 'a natural science of man' (identical with 'a human natural science'), Marx starts out with a concept of human nature that runs through his whole work until the last pages of *Capital*, where in the third volume he speaks of working conditions—'most adequate to their human nature and most worthy of it'. While in the *Economic and Philosophic Manuscripts* of 1844 Marx speaks of 'essence of man' or the 'species life' of man, in *German Ideology*, he qualifies the use of essence by stating that this essence is 'no abstraction' and in *Capital* he replaces the concept of 'essence' with that of 'human nature in general', to be distinguished from 'human nature as modified in each historical period' (ibid.: 70). These variations in the concept of Marx also represent the progressive growth in his paradigm as it changes from philosophical to sociological orientations. His sociology of man emanates logically from his critique of the modern industrial society and its series of transformations over the primordial form.

Max Weber postulates the concept of man from the same structural perspective but with a contradistinct paradigm. He rejects positivism and treats social phenomena as meaningful symbolic realities, but his approach to sociological analysis is formal and schematic and not dialectical. He uses history but for comparative schematization and not as an instrument of social transformation. His value judgement, however, on industrial society as well as on capitalism does give a ring of resemblance with that of Marx. The concept of man in Weber's sociology can be constructed from his analysis of *The Protestant Ethic and the Spirit of Capitalism* (1965), his *Sociology of Religion* (1966) and his *Essays in Sociology* (1952). His theory of division of labour as formulated in *The Theory of Social and Economic Organization* (1964) is an indirect reflection on the forms of rationality in social action; it implicitly touches upon the notion of man.

In the *Protestant Ethic and the Spirit of Capitalism*, Weber develops his concept of man through his analysis of ethical transformation in society resulting from Protestant reformation. Traditionally, man did not have autonomy of choice in action or freedom of initiative to alter his life situation in this world or the other world. Even redemption of man could not be individual but only collective. Emphasis was on other-worldly asceticism, negation of self, and conformity to collective ethical norms. Man as a free actor did not exist at this stage of religious belief. Even in Lutherian reformation and the notion of 'calling' that he introduced, Weber says, the individuality of man was circumscribed: "the individual should remain once and for all in the station and calling in which God had placed him, and should restrain his worldly activity within the limits imposed by his established station in life. Thus, for Luther, the concept of calling remained traditionalistic" (Weber, 1965: 85). Man's liberation from this Providential bondage was possible only through ethical revolution of Protestantism which shifted the emphasis from of other-worldly asceticism to this-worldly asceticism. The idea of collective redemption was now replaced by individual piety and ethical responsibility. This brought into being a new spirit, the spirit of capitalism, as also the notion of man as an ethically responsible being.

This new ethic imposed on man a moral imperative to "establish kingdom of God on earth", to practise frugality, self-denial and productively use time towards progressive accumulation and investment of material and intellectual resources. This led to the productive rationality of man in the capitalist society. Thus, man as a responsible being comes into existence. Weber is, however, skeptical whether this creative responsibility goes always with rationality of man. He postulates that man's rationality is only partial, since its critical boundary lies within the influence of traditional 'affect' and transcendental 'charisma'. The interplay of tradition and charisma renders man's rationality always problematic. This also happens to the capitalist society and its ethic of this-worldly asceticism. He evaluates the capitalist ethic in these words:

> In fact the *summum bonum* of this ethic, the earning of more and more money, combined with the strict avoidance of all spontaneous enjoyment of life, is above all completely devoid of any eudaemonistic, not to say hedonistic, admixture. It is thought of so purely as an end in itself, that from the point of view of the happiness of, or utility to, the single individual, it appears entirely transcendental and absolutely irrational. Man is dominated by the making of money, by acquisition as the ultimate purpose of his life. Economic acquisition is no longer subordinated to man as the means for satisfaction of his material needs. This reversal of what we should call the natural relationship, so irrational from a naive point of view, evidently as definitely a leading principle of capitalism, as it is foreign to all peoples not under capitalist influence (ibid.: 53).

Another dimension of Weber's concept of man can be found in his treatment of 'legitimate order' and its exemplification in his sociology of religion. He particularly makes use of the concept of 'charisma' to add a creative transcendental element in the existential character of man. In his sociology of religion the manifestation of charisma is located in the prophet or prophecy. Even Protestant reformation had its share of prophets. Social systems change only through prophecy either of the 'exemplary' character or of 'imitative' character. Charisma endows a legitimacy to prophecy in society which sets into motion a new wave of reform and change. In course of time charisma is routinized and rationalized. Man, to Weber, is thus simultaneously an 'affective being,' a 'rational being' and above all, he is a 'charismatic being'. Charisma effaces traditional interpretation and adds innovative elements to rationality and affectivity. "The charismatic quality of an individual as perceived by others, or himself, lies in what is thought to be his connection with (including possession by or embodiment of) some *very central* features of man's existence and the cosmos in which he lives. The centrality, coupled with intensity, makes it extraordinary... The centrality is constituted by its formative power in initiating, creating, governing, transforming, maintaining or destroying what is vital in man's life" (Shils, 1966: 201). This charismatic quality of man though not equally available to all human beings is yet a universal qualitative resource in man, because charisma involves intensity of contact to the followers as it means intensity of cognitive upsurge to the prophet.

Weber is a systematic sociologist. He proceeds in his formulation of the concept of man also of other sociological categories through a scheme of typifications. The components of tradition, rationality and charisma are principles on the basis of which man's existential character and his sociological roles are typified. The extent of freedom and unfreedom that a man may enjoy would depend upon as much the growth of social structure as on his individual typification. This links Weber's concept of man on the one hand with phenomenology and on the other with symbolic interactionism.

Concept of Man in Critical and Phenomenological Sociology

Sociology, both of the Marxist and Weberian theoretic traditions, underwent major changes and syntheses following the holocaust of the Second World War. Critical theory and neo-Marxist theory in sociology emerged as a direct consequence of this. Max Horkheimer, Jurgen Habermas, Theodore Adorno, Erich Fromm and Herbert Marcuse initiated theoretical and empirical studies from a new synthetic framework on the basic existential character of man. One finds a creative mix of neo-Platonism, Marxism, neo-Freudianism and phenomenological ideas of Edmund Husserl, Max Schiller and Mannheim in the paradigms of critical theory. The aim is to bring back the essential dialogical and dialectical character of man's existential being. It is clearly evident in the writings of Horkheimer and Adorno. They observe:

> The most important consequence to be drawn from insights into the interaction of the individual and society—and, to be sure, just that which positivistic sociology avoids—is that the human being is capable of realizing himself as an individual only within a just and humane society. This insight is already contained in the Platonic theme, that functional social coherence is the precondition for the actualization of the idea implanted in every human being. Only the just society will permit the human being to realize his idea. *The more concrete his thought becomes, the more it becomes one that is critical of society* (italics added) (1973: 46–47).

It is in this critical perspective that Horkheimer and Adorno see inherent instability in the 'bourgeois man' who is tyrannized by oppositions, such as between the bourgeois particular existence and politically general existence, as well as between the private and professional spheres.

Critical theory combines empirical understanding with theoretical constructions that lead to praxis. *The Dynamics of Prejudice* (1950) by Bettelheim and Janowitz, *The Authoritarian Personality* by Adorno and his associates (1950), *Prophet of Deceit* (1919) by Lowenthal and Guterman, etc. have gone into the analysis of the pathology of man, his ideological self-rationalization and negative projections in modern industrial society. The central theme of the *Authoritarian Personality* is a relatively new concept—the rise of an 'anthropological' species which Adorno would call the authoritarian type of man. "In contrast to the bigot of the older style he seems to combine the ideas and skills which are typical of a highly industrialized society with irrational and anti-rational beliefs. He is at the same time enlightened and superstitious, proud to be an individualist and in constant fear of not being like all the others, jealous of his independence and inclined to submit blindly to power and authority" (Adorno et al, 1950: ix). The portrayal of the authoritarian personality based on intensive empirical investigations and clinical analysis proceeds on the logic of 'character typology' which Adorno's theory of negative dialects refutes. In his work *Negative Dialectics* (1973) Adorno writes:

> Contradiction is not what Hegel's absolute idealism was bound to transfigure it into: it is not of essence in a Heraclitean sense. It indicates the untruth of identity, the fact that the concept does not exhaust the thing conceived. Yet the appearance of identity is inherent in thought itself, in its pure form. To think is to identify.
>
> Conceptual order is content to screen what thinking seeks to comprehend. The semblance and the truth of thought entwine. The semblance cannot be decreed away, as by avowal of a being-in-itself outside the totality of cognitive definitions...
>
> Contradiction is non-identity under the aspect of identity; the dialectical primacy of the principle of contradiction make the thought of unity the measure of heterogeneity. As the heterogeneous collides with its limit it exceeds itself. Dialectic is the consistent sense of non-identity. It does not begin by taking a standpoint. My thought is driven to it by its own inevitable insufficiency, by my guilt of what I am thinking (1973: 5).

Critical theory, in its epistemological postulate, was, according to Adorno, negative dialectical in nature. It rendered norms of validity of concepts inherently dissoluble and problematic. In his empirical study of the authoritarian personality, the use of character typology introduces thus a logical contradiction. The non-identical element of the identity of authoritarianism get neglected. Adorno anticipates this criticism. He writes:

> The reason for the persistent plausibility or the typological approach, however, is not a static biological one, but just the opposite: dynamic and social... The marks of social repression are left within the individual soul ...Individualism, opposed to human pigeonholing, may ultimately become a mere ideological veil in a society which actually is inhuman. Thus typification is linked with the theory of negative dialectics (1950: 747).

Adorno's concept of man is both phenomenological and clinical. Where phenomenology sharpens the understanding of human situation, the clinical analysis, its negative dialectics offers scope for praxis. It is this constant tension between theory and praxis that informs critical theory.

Erich Fromm and Herbert Marcuse have, though in a less epistemologically sharp manner, used a similar problematic for the understanding of man. There is, however, a difference. The attempt in the works both of Fromm and Marcuse to integrate Freudian notion of man and society with the Marxist one is central and direct. Fromm deliberately breaks away from the meta-psychology (death and life instinct and primal consciousness) of Freud and builds primarily on his theory of instinctual drives, which he finds has close resemblance with Marx's emphasis on man as a sensuous being. He also rejects Freudian theory of phylogenesis, especially his universal Oedipal complex. He, on the contrary, postulates that each society governed by its socio-economic and material conditions develops its own pattern of libidinal structure which shapes man's character structure—a basically ontogenetic process. Indeed, this led to his differences with Adorno, Horkheimer and Marcuse.

In his *Man for Himself* (1964) Fromm develops a dialectical concept of man, linked with his species-nature. It is endowed with internal dichotomies, both existential and historical. Man is different from animal rather negatively, by "the relative absence in man of instinctive regulation in the process of adaptation of the surrounding world"; "self-awareness, reason and imagination have disrupted the 'harmony' which characterized animal existence. Their emergence has made man into an anomaly, into the freak of the universe. He is part of nature, subject to her physical law and unable to change them, yet he transcends the rest of nature" (ibid.: 40). Man has no innate drive for progress, says Fromm; it is the contradictions of his existence that goad him to proceed onwards. The fundamental existential contradictions of man are life and death. Death is an unalterable destiny for man, hence he puts all he has for life. With this is also related another contradiction: man is alone, he is alone as much as he is unique, not identical with anyone else. His lifespan being short, his capacity to bear loneliness being susceptible, he seeks compensation in social solidarity. Man is a social being. But this also leads to contradictions—historical contradictions in individual and social life "which are not necessary part of human existence but are man-made and soluble, soluble either at the time they occur or at a later period of human history"(ibid.: 43). Man can annul historical contradictions by his own action, but he cannot annul existential contradictions. He may try to sublimate it by pursuit of pleasure or business but the tension in human life remains.

Man can resolve this dilemma, according to Fromm, only through commitment to ideals. He says: "Man is not free to choose between having or not having ideals, but he is free to choose between different kinds of ideals, between being devoted to the worship of power and destruction and being devoted to reason and love" (ibid.: 49). This is the basis of his 'humanistic ethic', its basis in contradistinction to authoritarian ethics lies in the affirmation of life, the unfolding of man's power, (where) virtue is responsibility towards his own existence.

In *Escape from Freedom* (1942), Fromm deals with the general problems of man's existential conditions. "The main theme of this book is that man, the more he gains freedom in the sense of emerging from the original oneness with man and nature and the more he becomes an 'individual', has no choice but to unite himself with the world in the spontaneity of love and productive work, or else to seek a kind of security by such ties with the world as destroy his freedom and the integrity of his individual self" (ibid.: 18). Alienation of man is a result of his feeling of isolation and powerlessness which can be resolved only through enrichment of interpersonal relationships; to realize this, the negative condition of man through his atomization or isolation as 'freedom from' should be transformed into the positive activity of the integrated total personality or 'freedom to'. This would entail structural as well as ethical changes in society.

In *The Sane Society* (1955) Fromm again reiterates his humanism, now called 'normative humanism' as a solution of the problem of man's self-alienation and its societal concomitants. Theoretically, he covers almost the same ground he explored in *Escape from Freedom*, but he now shifts his emphasis to the needs of man, both material and psychic. The impress of Marx is now more prominent, as he says, "the species man can be defined not only in anatomical and physiological terms: its members share basic psychic qualities" (ibid.: 121). He also analyzes the structure of the capitalist society and the state of human situation, anonymous authority, anonymous institutions and progressive alienation of man from his own objective reality and the progressive schism in his psyche. The 'road to sanity' that he suggests is once again the reiteration of his normative humanism which implies societal structural changes to reinforce this value system.

Marcuse's position basically differs from Fromm's. First, Marcuse does not reject Freudian presuppositions of meta-psychology. He retains the postulate of Thanatos—the death instinct and reiterates the Freudian hypothesis of intensification of destructive activity in the wake of civilizations. In his *Eros and Civilization* (1955) he gives a positive interpretation to Thanatos whose aim was not aggression only but also end of tension in life—the '*Nirvana* principle'. Civilization no doubt enslaves and alienates man owing to its 'performance principle' and Marcuse approvingly quotes Schiller that in such a society "...enjoyment is separated from labour, the means from the end, exertion from recompense. Eternally fettered only to a single little fragment of the whole, man fashions himself as a fragment; ever hearing only the monotonous whirl of the wheel which he turns, he never develops the harmony of his being, and, instead of shaping the humanity that lies in his nature, he becomes a mere imprint of his occupation, his science (Schiller in Marcuse, 1955: 135).

How could man redeem himself from this fate that modern industrial society imposes upon him? Marcuse's answer is that since it "was civilization itself that 'dealt modern man this wound', only a new mode of civilization can heal it. The wound is caused by two polar dimensions of the human existence...sensuousness and reason, matter and form (spirit), nature and freedom, the particular and universal". To overcome this contradiction it would be necessary that the 'play impulse' of man is reinvigorated through creating in him mental faculty to exercise his freedom through *imagination*. "Once it has gained ascendancy as a principle of civilization, the play impulse would literally transform the reality. Nature, the objective world would then be experienced primarily neither as dominating man (as in primitive society), nor as being dominated by man (as in the established civilization), but rather as an object of contemplation" (ibid.: 137). Very much like Marx, Marcuse reiterates that realm of freedom and non-repression lies in abundance, "freedom is not within but outside the struggle for existence". The realm of necessity is the realm of unfreedom. This state of man's liberation from alienated labour (non-aesthetic work imagination) is the state of *Nirvana*.

At this level of analysis Marcuse's *Eros and Civilization*, which starts primarily as a neo-Freudian construction, takes on a purely sociological dimension. It is this idea that he further develops in his *One-Dimensional Man* (1964). In this work, his diagnosis of modern industrial society remains more or less unchanged but his agenda for social change undergoes some basic changes. It moves towards social nihilism of a kind. One-dimensionality is a characteristic of the overconformist industrial society. He writes:

> *One-Dimensional Man* will vacillate throughout between two contradictory hypotheses: (1) the advanced industrial society is capable of containing qualitative change for the foreseeable future; (2) that forces and tendencies exist which may break this containment and explode the society (ibid.: 13).

Marcuse diagnoses the problem of one-dimensionality in modern society in such processes as complete information and media control and its standardization, closing of the political universe through anonymity of relationship between the rulers and the ruled, containment of change and conquest of the unhappy consciousness through 'repressive desublimation'. This last element Marcuse defines as, "flattening out of the antagonism between culture and social reality through the obliteration of the oppositional, alien and transcendent elements in higher culture by virtue of which it constituted another dimension of reality". This liquidation of two-dimensional culture, he says, takes place not through the denial and rejection of the 'cultural values' but through their wholesale incorporation into the established order through their reproduction and display on a massive scale" (ibid.: 57). The result of all this is the emergence of one-dimensional thought, the triumph of positive thinking.

Marcuse is hopeful to resolve this contradiction in social life and the life of man through the abolition of reified nature of institutions and human relationships that one-dimensionality introduces. It would call for release of repression both in conceptual and experiential realms. Emphasis should shift from abstract general categories, mass production of culture to specific experiences and meanings. He says, "the philosophic concept 'man' aims at the fully developed human faculties which are his distinguishing faculties which appear as possibilities of the conditions in which men actually live. The concept articulates the qualities which are considered 'typically human'. The vague phrase may serve to elucidate the ambiguity in such philosophic definition—namely, they assemble the qualities that pertain to all men as contrasted with other living beings, and, at the same time, are claimed as the most adequate or higher realization of man" (ibid.: 169). The alternative that Marcuse suggests for the solution of this dilemma of modern man goes beyond the aesthetic and becomes revolutionary nihilism, especially in his *Reason and Revolution* (1960) and other essays, Marcuse even pleads for a violent revolution to throw away the one-dimensionality of the society and man. He justifies it on the basis of his construction on the Freudian theory combined with Marxism.

Phenomenological sociology which emerged as a reaction to the idealistic epistemology and social philosophy has contributed richly to the concept of man. Its roots could be found both in classical phenomenologists like Edmund Husserl and Max Schiller (whose concept of man we have already discussed) as well as in classical sociologists like Marx, Weber and Durkheim. Its concept of man also overlaps the works of C.H. Cooley and George Mead—the symbolic interactionists. Among the prominent phenomenological sociologists who have synthesized the paradigms of Husserl with Weber is Alfred Schutz. Husserl wanted to create presuppositionless philosophy by rejection of assumptions about the generality of categories and by founding them on experiences of conscious human beings who live and act in the 'world' and apperceive and interpret it. To him, forms of consciousness are tied to experience, which is man's attention directed on objects both real and imaginary, material or ideal and which constitutes object of his 'intentionality'. This reality can be grasped only after elimination of all preconceived notions concerning reality and through initial suspension of beliefs in the 'outer world'. Reality of the outer world is neither confirmed nor denied; it is 'bracketed' in an act of phenomenological reduction. What is left after elimination of all ontological assumptions is "inner world of conscious individual", the concern of phenomenology.

Husserl also formulated a theory of transcendental phenomenology where one could 'bracket' not only outer world but also individual consciousness. Much of Husserl's formulations thus relate to problems of inter-subjectivity and individual consciousness in the life-world. It does not grapple directly with the problems of social structure and the situation of man. Alfred Schutz, has, therefore, rightly criticized Husserl for his lack of social science concern and in his own phenomenological formulations drawn heavily from Weber, especially his interpretive paradigm and emphasis on typification as a process of social construction and management of meanings and experiences. He formulates his concept of man through his treatment of the 'cognitive setting of the life-world' where he states that each individual constructs his own 'world'. The life-world is a social world which one finds pre-structured but the essence of human identity or self lies in mediating between the pre-structured life-world that he inherits through existent typifications and the exercise of his own intentionality. He particularly deals with this problem in the context of the 'stranger' who being raised in his community finds himself in an outside culture; the stranger has to reconstruct the reality of the host community piece-by-piece through *rules* of the community (Schutz, 1970). Schutz constructs the existential structure of man combining the perspective of social psychology; he treats man's motivation as anchored in two-fold directions: first, future-oriented, goal-directed motives which constitute 'in-order-to' motives; and secondly, motives concerned with reasons of their action, based on past experiences; these constitute 'because motives'. The problem of relevance in human action, the problematic of man is rooted into the structuration of human motives in the life-world. Man makes dramatical rehearsal of future action, he is capable of 'motivated phantasying' which serve both as cushions and crises in the being of man. Borrowing from Weber, he also classifies social action as rational and non-rational, but he treats rational action as a mere ideal not realizable in everyday life conduct. Schutz emphasizes the role of symbols in synchronization of the 'shocks' of human experiences of everyday life; man proceeds through manipulating symbolic universe and takes 'leaps' in his consciousness with their help. This ability of symbolic leaps in man is the basis of his humanity.

It is true that Schutz, like most phenomenologists, deals primarily with the structural inquiries; these alone provide the context for the problematic of man. But, in contemporary phenomenological sociology, one may find efforts to grapple directly with the existential problems of man, not to the exclusion of the context of social structure but as its interactive dimension. Berger and Luckmann in *The Social Construction of Reality* (1966) and Berger in *The Sacred Canopy* (1969) and Berger and others in *The Homeless Mind* (1974) portray phenomenologically this aspect of the concept of man. In *The Social Construction of Reality* emphasis is more on man's comprehension and construction of social reality. Sociology of knowledge is not treated as a separate branch of sociology but the very medium through which social reality externalizes from man's subjective experiences. Man is treated both as a body, a phenomenon of 'here', and as existent in time, a 'now'; all social reality is thus here-and-now reality in which man first subjectively internalizes the social reality through his intentionality and then externalizes the same through symbolic typification. "Consciousness is always intentional; it always intends or is directed towards objects." This consciousness progressively expands through hierarchies of typification from the face-to-face experience to remoter levels of interactions and their symbolization. Internalization of objective reality of society through socialization process and its institutionalization later in the form of objective social reality determines the dialectic of social reality. It is mediated through symbols; man constructs social reality both through his personal symbolic manipulation as well as through universal symbolic language which Berger and Luckmann call the 'canopy'. The symbolic universe provides the order and meaning to human life and is the aid to solve the many continual puzzles of human existence. Problems that man faces arise both out of contradictions in the symbolic universe (its malintegration, lack of legitimation or institutionalization) as also through contradiction in the subjective experience of man.

This problem is dealt with more concretely by Berger in his *The Sacred Canopy*, which is a treatment of religion and its existential moorings from a phenomenological perspective. The explication of the phenomenology of man and the dialectic between man and society through religious symbolic universe is its main theme. Berger writes: "Society is a product of man. It has no other being except that which is bestowed upon it by human activity and consciousness. There can be no social reality apart from man. Yet it may also be stated that man is product of society." There is a dialectical relationship between man and society. "The fundamental dialectical process of society consists of three moments, or steps. These are externalization, objectivation, and internalization. Externalization is the ongoing outpouring of human being into the world, both in the physical and the mental activity of men. Objectivation is the attainment by the product of this activity (again both physical and mental) of a reality that confronts its original producers... Internalization is the re-appropriation by men of the same reality transforming it once again from the structures of the objective world into structures of subjective consciousness" (ibid.: 4). Also, "man does not have a given relationship to the world. He must ongoingly establish relationship with it. The same instability marks man's relationship to his own body. In a curious way, man is "out of balance with himself. He cannot rest within himself, but must continuously come to terms with himself by expressing himself in activity" (ibid.: 5). Formulated in this term, sociological concepts of man, according to Berger, is essentially humanizing, it refers back the imposing structure of social reality to the living human beings. Man also produces values and "discovers that he feels guilt when he contravenes them". Alienation of man emerges as a result of conflict between identity as socially assigned and the identity as subjectively appropriated by man; there is internal confrontation that man faces between the socialized and non-socialized self and external confrontation on account of maladjustment between society and individual. When consciousness is alienated, it ceases to be dialectical. To resolve it, man depends upon 'recipes' of symbolic systems, religion is one such system, but even secularization keeps the problematic intact.

The theme of secularization and human situation is discussed by Berger and his colleagues in *The Homeless Mind* which is a critique of modern society and man. Modern society introduces the phenomenon of 'componentiality'—a process in which man's life experiences are fragmented and he is alienated from himself. This happens through the very institutions that modernization is supposed to bring about, modern technology, bureaucracy (which lead to multi-relationality), pluralization of interactions and emphasis on taxonomic order. The solution of this problem lies in the creation of adequate symbolic system or value systems and not in taking recourse to a 'counter culture', as the ideology of modernization. Without adequacy of values none of these structural changes would solve the problem of man.

Berger has formulated his phenomenology after duly synthesizing in his work the postulates of Durkheim, Schutz and also Mannheim. Specially Mannheim's diagnosis of our time as a phenomenon of 'contemporaneity of non-contemporaneous', or the lack of it between values, psychological orientations and structural changes in society, especially the changes in the elite structure. In his Man and Society in *An Age of Reconstruction* (1940) Mannheim suggests the need for creation of a psychological response to structural changes of modern time commensurate with the new challenges. It should neither be bourgeois-oriented in ideology nor should it be total planning-oriented. It should follow a middle path between the two based on pragmatism. Freedom of man should be combined with new planned social order. Only this type of social construction will be able to transform man equal to the challenges of the contemporary society.

Closely related to the phenomenological approach to the concept of man is that of symbolic interactionism in sociology, led by George H. Mead, elaborated by Herbert Blumer and given a new form by Erving Goffman. Mead, in his *Mind, Self and Society* (1934), formulated a dynamic interactional theory of the relationship between self and society. Self develops in society from the ego principle 'I', with the help of social interaction in family setting. The human child internalizes society in his self-objectivation into 'me', through 'conversation of gesture', in play and in primary group interaction. His consciousness is also formed in the same process. Mind, self and society are thus products of the same interactional process and bear a dynamic relationship. Man's self and his consciousness are thus creators as well as products of society. This defines the contingency of human problem. The notion of *praxis* in Mead is that hand mediates both with nature as well as in relation with other men. Labour has played a great role in evolution of man from the ape; speech and hand go together to shape the history of human evolution.

In his *The Philosophy of the Present* (1932), Mead says that "the past (or the meaningful structure of the past) is as hypothetical as future", the past is involved in the present, hence successful policy on man should recognize this truth and evolve conscious responses to be able to deal with "several things at once". He is a relativist through and through since he believes in the capacity of man to be at home with two or more exclusive systems. His dialectical approach to self, and society, bears close resemblance to Martin Buber's approach in *I and Thou*, his philosophical anthropology that sociality results only from social interaction. Only Buber's approach to man's existential problems is ethical whereas Mead's is relativistic rational.

Herbert Blumer states the premise of his theory as: "Human society is made up of individuals who have selves (that is, make indications to themselves); the individual action is a construction and release, being built up by the individual through noting and interpreting features of the situations in which he acts; that group or collective action consists of the aligning of individual actions, brought about by the individual's interpreting or taking into account each other's action" (quoted in Zeitlin, 1973). Blumer, in his emphasis on the interactional dimension, neglects completely the role of social forces in defining the role of men in society.

From the viewpoint of the concept of man in sociology the contribution of Erving Goffman is really original. His is not only a dramaturgical but also a debunking notion of man. Man as actor, he postulates in his *Presentation of Self in Everyday Life*, presents a front; his real self is never in judgement because we infer meaning from others, action based on the impressions that we register about him. Men, therefore, try consciously to manage impressions. There is thus a discrepancy between the human self and social self. Man deliberately creates 'front regions' to project those aspects of his self which he wants to be noticed and 'back regions' for those that he wants to conceal. Apart from these two regions is the 'outside' sphere, the goings on of the establishment outside the walls. Groups in which actors act have their secrets, 'dark' and 'strategic', and in each of them gets introduced what Goffman calls 'discrepant roles', the role of informer posing as a member of the team. Each organization creates its social world and its inmates experience this world subjectively through slow formation. In *Asylums*, the study of hospital inmates, Goffman makes this analysis of subjective structure of the inmates and its dynamics. Hospitals which are based on professional knowledge "present a partisan view" of themselves to the non-professional inmates. This is the demand of the impression management.

Through these and various other studies on the role structure and subjectivity of members in small groups, Goffman brings to bear upon us the tension inherent in human interaction and social actions. He also in this process projects a concept of man which is totally demystifying and marks the end of an illusion.

The Problematic of Man in Sociology

In what way does a sociologist distinguish himself from other social scientists when he talks of man or of concept of man? Answer to this question would lie primarily in the worldview that sociology has been able to project as its own. This worldview, a product of structural transformation in society following industrial revolution, was basically of positive humanism—a humanism which sometimes blended with rationalism as in Comte and Pareto and sometimes transcended it to reach a new apperceptive level of empathy and critical view of societal processes as in Marx and Schiller. It was also a demystifying worldview, a perpetual challenge to the conceptual superstructure of the establishment and its ideology. Peter Berger remarks that "sociology is essentially a debunking discipline. It directs, uncovers only rarely inspires. Its genius is very deeply negative, like that of Goethe's Mephistopheles who describes himself as a 'spirit that ever says no'. To try to change this character is to destroy whatever usefulness sociology may have— especially its moral and political usefulness, which comes from being held in balance, simultaneously and within the mind of the same person, with the affirmation of moral passion and humane engagement. Therefore, we offer no apology for the negative tone to our argument" (Berger et al., 1974: 207).

It is indeed true that sociological concept of man in most of its treatment is diagnostic, tends to focus upon problems such as alienation, anomie, deviance, diremption and contradictions of human life. As we found in the treatment of Goffman it also tends to be highly cynical and truly debunking. Berger has, therefore, a point when he caricatures the role of sociology in the interpretation of human condition. But he pays little attention to yet another dimension of sociological concept of man—its substitutive normative structure. Sociology is not merely an art of apperception to demystify and debunk, but it also offers an alternative worldview. As C. Wright Mills postulates, sociologist observes, empathizes and portrays with understanding every 'worry' of man in private and public situations when it becomes 'trouble'. He does so by linking biography of man with his history. This effort indeed belongs to the truly constructive contribution to the understanding of the problem of man. Once sociology was deeply involved with this type of understanding. The lament of Ernest Becker for the *Lost Science of Man* refers particularly to this creative period of sociology, when it was less cynical more humanistic and purposive. It is true that Spencer's sociology was a "a perfect compliment to the narrow classical economics", but even though classicists like Ward and Small treated sociology as a "science of purposive mind, not passive matter. Sociology is a 'telic' science, a science in the service of human well-being and progressive development" (Becker, 1971: 16). Critical and humanistic concern was predominant in Karl Marx; praxeological orientation was his main contribution not only to sociology but also to the concept of man; Durkheim was not morally neutral, he had not only a substitutive ethic but also its commensurate epistemology.

Negativism in sociology is indeed a phase in its development when the western society faced peculiar problems of a post-industrial society. The obsolescence of the liberal capitalistic worldview and ideology, disenchantment of youth from the establishment culture and their search for a 'counter culture', and distrust in formal methodology were at its root. Most cynical expression of this pressure in sociology one could find curiously among those who still believe in an alternative. John O'Neill writes: "Sociology owes its fortune to the fact that nothing occupies man like himself. We are amazed by the misfortune of others as by our own good fortune... Sociology is a study of people. It is a human pastime with pretensions to science", but despite this extreme cynicism, O'Neill does not loose hope, he believes in redemption and exhorts: "In calling sociology a skin trade, I want to restore its symbiotic connection with the body politic and to situate it in relation to the exchange of organic needs and utopian celebration of the libidinal community which surpasses all understanding. This means that the rhetoric of scientism in sociology as well as its humanism must be tested against commonsense relevance of everyday life" (1972: 10). The alternative in this case is reflexive sociology.

The proponents of reflexive sociology, however, omit the fact that what they call reflexivity of sociology, the quality of cognitive and emotive rapport between the sociologist and the subject of his study was for ever the basic theme of phenomenological sociology; it epitomized Schiller's thesis on the nature of sympathy and Husserl's transcendental phenomenology. What it really represents today is symptomatic. It is not a crisis of universe of discourse or method of sociology but of the value system of society which has been rendered obsolete. This indirectly reflects the responsive nature of sociological paradigms to social issues and social change.

There is yet another level—the moral level—in which sociology's contribution to the concept of man has been indeed revolutionary. It emanates from its analysis of deviant behaviour and 'deviant roles'. Sociology by locating the source both of the cognitive categories and moral structure of society in the society itself and in its dynamic processes has abolished at least in moral sense the dichotomy between the normal and pathological, the deviant and the conformist, the retreatist and the revolutionary. This development is not new since the beginning of the wave of 'cognitive sociology' as Cicourel thinks but its roots lie in Durkheim's theory of ethic and epistemology. Cicourel, while portraying the approach of cognitive sociology, writes: "Our description of social structure, therefore, must always incorporate the ways in which normative accounts presuppose an unstated reliance on thought processes, socially organized memory, selective attention, and several sensory modalities. *Rather than viewing the blind or the deaf as social problem, we can reconceptualize our feelings and treatment of such persons by recognizing that they develop special strategies for dealing with their lack of modality* (italics added; Cicourel, 1973: 9). This reiterates in another form the humanistic and substitutive worldview of sociology and its continual reassertion in different forms in its treatment of man and the problematic of man in society.

References

Adorno, T.W., *Negative Dialectics*, London: Routledge and Kegan Paul, 1973.

—, *The Authoritarian Personality*, New York: Harper, 1950.

Barnes, H.E., *Social Thought from Lore to Science*, New York: Dover Publications, Inc., 1961.

Becker, E., *The Lost Science of Man*, New York: George Braziller, 1971.

Bell, D., *The Coming of Post Industrial Society*, London: Heinneman Educational Books Ltd., 1974.

Berger, P.L., *The Sacred Canopy*, New York: Doubleday and Company, 1969.

Berger, P.L. and Luckmann, *The Social Construction of Reality*, U.S.A.: Doubleday and Co., 1966.

Berger et al., *The Homeless Mind*, Pelican Books, 1974.

Bettelheim, B. and Janowytz, M., *Dynamics of Prejudice: A Psychological and Sociological Study of Veterans,* New York, 1950.

Burns, Tom, *Industrial Man*, London: Cox and Wyman Ltd., 1969.

Cicourel, A., *Cognitive Sociology*, London: Cox and Wyman Ltd., 1973.

Davis, K., "The Myth of Functional Analysis as a Special Method in Sociology and Anthropology", *American Sociological Review,* 1951.

Durkheim, E., "Le Dualisme de la nature humaine et ses conditions sociales", *Socientia XV* 1914.

—, *The Division of Labour in Society*, New York: Macmillan Company, 1933.

—, *The Elementary Forms of Religious Life*, New York: Macmillan Company, 1915.

—, *The Rules of Sociological Method*, New York: The Free Press of Glencoe, 1950.

—, *Suicide*, New York: The Free Press of Glencoe, 1951.

Fischer, E., *Marx in his Own Words*, Pelican Books, 1973.

Fromm, E., *Escape From Freedom*, London, 1942.

—, *Man for Himself*, New York: Holt Rinehart and Winston, 1964.

—, *The Crisis of Psychoanalysis*, Pelican Books, 1973.

—, *The Sane Society*, New York: Holt Rinehart and Winston, 1955.

Galbraith, J.K., *The New Industrial State*, U.S.A., 1967.

Gellner, E., *Thought and Change*, Chicago: The University of Chicago Press, 1965.

Goffman, E., *Asylums*, New York: Doubleday and Co. Inc., 1961.

—, *Presentation of Self in Everyday Life*, London: Penguin, 1971.

Henderson, L.J., *Pareto's General Sociology*, Cambridge: Harvard University Press, 1937.

Homans, G.C., *Social Behavior: Its Elementary Forms*, New York: Harcourt, Brace and World, 1961.

—, "Bringing Men Back In", *American Sociology Review*, December 1964.

Horkheimer, Max and Adorno, T.W., *Aspects of Sociology*, London: Heinemann Educational Books, Ltd., 1973.

Lowenthal, L. and Gutman, R., *Prophets of Deceit*, New York, 1949.

Mannheim, Karl, *Man and Society*, London: Routledge and Kegan Paul Ltd., 1940.

Marcuse, H., *Eros and Civilization*, London: The Beacon Press, 1955.

—, *Reason and Revolution*, Boston, 1960.

—, *One Dimensional Man*, London: Sphere Books Ltd., 1964.

Marx, Karl and Engels, F., *The German Ideology*, Moscow: Progress Publishers, 1968.

Marx, Karl, *Economic and Philosophical Manuscripts of 1844*, Moscow: Progress Publishers, 1974.

McIver, R.M., *The Ramparts we Guard*, New York: The Macmillan Company, 1950.

Mead, G., *Mind, Self and Society*, University of Chicago Press, 1934.

—, *Philosophy of the Present*, The Open Court Publishing Co., 1932.

Merton, R.K., *Social Theory and Social Structure*, The Free Press of Glencoe, 1968.

Mills, C. Wright, *Images of Man*, New York: George Braziller Inc., 1960.

Moore, W.E., *Man, Time and Society*, New York: John Wiley and Sons, Inc., 1963.

Mumford, L., *Conditions of Man*, London: Martin Secker and Warburg, 1944.

O'Neill, John, *Sociology as a Skin Trade*, New York: Harper and Row Publishers, 1972.

Parsons, T., *The Social System*, New Delhi: Amerind Publishing Co. Pvt. Ltd., 1972.

—, *Toward a General Theory of Action*, New York: Harper and Row, 1962.

Reisman, D. et al., *The Lonely Crowd*, New York: Yale University Press, 1950.

Schutz, A., *On Phenomenology and Social Relations*, London: The University of Chicago Press, 1970.

Shils, E., "Charisma, Order and Status", *American Sociology Review*, 1965.

Spencer, H., *Principle of Sociology*, New York: D. Appleton and Company, 1898.

Stark, W., *Social Theory and Christian Thought*, London: Routledge and Kegan Paul Ltd., 1958.

Tiryakian, Edward A., *Sociologism and Existentialism*, New York: Prentice-Hall Inc., 1962.

Wagner, H.P., "The Scope of Phenomenological Sociology" in *Phenomenological Sociology* by George Psathan (ed.), New York: John Wiley and Sons, 1973.

Weber, Max, *Essays in Sociology*, London: Routledge and Kegan Paul Ltd., 1952.

—, *Sociology of Religion*, London: Methuen, 1966.

—, *The Protestant Ethic and the Spirit of Capitalism*, London: Unwin University Books, 1965.

Whyte, William H., *The Organization Man*, New York: Simon and Schuster Inc., 1956.

Winch, P., *The Idea of a Social Science*, London: 1968.

Zeitlin, I.M., *Rethinking Sociology*, New York: Appleton-Century Crofts, 1973.

3

Ideology, Theory and Methods in Indian Sociology

A review of the growth of sociology in India from the perspective of dominant theoretical innovations, changes in methodology and technique, its interactions with other social sciences, its own infrastructure as a profession, and the contribution that all these tendencies have made to the 'universalization' of this discipline during the period of a quarter of a century—1952–77—cannot be undertaken meaningfully without a framework of analysis that would be of a sociology of knowledge (cf. Singh, 1973; Mukherjee, 1965; Joshi, 1975) within the context of history. Colonialism, and its impact on the intellectual and cultural traditions in India, of which sociology and other social sciences are at a certain level manifestations, provides an important historical backdrop for its theoretic, ideological and professional evaluation. The cognitive and paradigmatic tensions of Indian sociology during 1953–77 bear deep imprints of the socio-historical forces released during the freedom struggle which shaped the responses of Indian intellectuals to the categories and structures of ideas in social sciences and sociology.

The first two decades of the 20th century which mark the beginning of sociology in India set out several of its orientations, such as descriptive and evolutionary studies of caste, social customs, folklore, land systems and the village community; and their comparison with similar institutions in the west (cf. Singh, 1967; Mukherjee, 1965). Its most important meta-theoretic contribution was in engendering an ethno-sociological awareness about Indian sociology which has continued to persist. It needs to be highlighted as the quest for 'universalization' of sociological categories. Indian sociology has significantly been refracted by this cognitive orientation. Whether sociology is a science with accompanying universalistic package of categories and techniques of research or it is a specific cognitive style marked by a mode of apperception or reflexivity in observation and comparison of structures of social relationships and ideas, are questions which have been debated right from the inception of sociology in India.

Sociology was in the beginning less professionalized, most of its patrons came from outside this discipline and were not initiated into its logic or methodology. Most of them treated sociology as a style of cultural critique or reformative ratiocination. Its character was thus defined by its responsive yet critical note on the western interpretations of Indian society, its institutions and cultural patterns. Radha Kamal Mukerjee, B.N. Seal and B.N. Sarkar constantly refuted the efforts of western Indologists and social anthropologists to try to interpret Indian reality in the evolutionary reductionist matrix. Seal thought institutions could only be compared when they were historically coexistent and parallel, and Mukerjee thought Indian social institutions to be unique. He found the sociological categories of the west inadequate for the interpretation (cf. Mukherjee in Barnes and Backer, 1961) of the Indian reality.

From 1920 onwards, sociology slowly became a teaching discipline in universities and its professional character began to emerge. The impact of the British and Continental sociology and social anthropology was very significant in shaping the sociological orientations of researchers and teachers of this time. The teaching of methodology as a separate discipline was still not prevalent; anthropological fieldwork tradition on the British pattern or historical research methods were the two skills which sociologists were generally initiated into for their researches. If they used other empirical devices, these were to be individually fabricated based on the nature of research problem. This trend changed during the Second World War period as sociology declined in the Continent through large-scale migration of scholars. Its centre of gravity shifted to the United States of America where sociology evolved a strong empirical-positivistic orientation, and led to phenomenal innovations of methods and techniques of 'scientific sociology'. At the beginning of the fifties in India, it was this dominant tradition of sociology, with its theoretic package and empirical style, which had made a headway in the tradition of Indian sociology. It also harmonized with the objectives that the national government had for systematic planning and investment of resources for social and economic growth. The need for developmental planning in the villages, cities and tribal areas initiated a series of empirical studies. This became a dominant tradition in sociology, but some philosophical orientations that pre-existed, continued to persist.

The theoretic directions in Indian sociology can be analyzed through the basic tensions which have existed in this discipline since its inception. These tensions are theoretical as well as ideological. Theoretically, the important tension in sociology exists, on the one hand, between the 'master theory' or 'general theory' and 'conceptual schemes' and on the other, between 'universalism' of concepts and propositions and their 'particularism' or contextuality. It would seem that sociologists' commitment to one or the other standpoint about 'theory' in sociology have fluctuated not only because of the nature of its discoveries or successes or failures in theory construction, but also in the light of the changing historical circumstances of the 'calling' of sociology (cf. Gouldner, 1970). This brings sociology face-to-face with another critical tension within its cognitive structure—that of the role of ideology in theory construction. The significance of universalization or particularization of concepts and categories in sociology is derived from the bases of these tensions.

Sociology in India has been experiencing these cognitive tensions from the very beginning of this discipline, but during 1952–77 these tensions have fluctuated significantly in response to the force of history and existential coordinates of knowledge. To review its theoretic directions and its changing structure of ideas, it would be useful to review sociology in four periods: 1952 to 1960, which primarily was a period of adaptive changes and innovations: 1960 to 1965, which was a period of significant shifts in theoretic priorities and the beginning of some critical tensions in theory and ideology of Indian sociology; 1965 to 1970, which was a period of marked sociological self-awareness and growth of new directions in theoretical and substantive contributions; and finally 1970 to 1977, a period when Indian sociology moved towards a new maturity and explored both theoretically and substantively new horizons of knowledge.

The four-fold periodization of Indian sociology, from 1952 to 1977, could probably be identified with certain predominant theoretic and ideological systems for each period, but Indian sociology during this period, like sociology in general, does not show succession of paradigms as we move from one period to another. What obtains is the co-existence of competing paradigms and theoretic orientations. Indian sociologists throughout this period have been less concerned with constructing 'master theories' or general theories, but more prone to using conceptual scheme for analysis of social problems. With the exception of Radha Kamal Mukerjee, who in his *The Philosophy of Social Science* (1960) and his presidential address to the third Indian Sociological Conference in 1958, proposes a general integrated social science model for explanation and understanding of social realities (cf. Singh in Unnithan et al., 1967: 22-23), no other systematic theoretical formulations have been made. Most sociologists have remained satisfied with using conceptual schemes or where they have used general theoretic systems such as in dialectical or Marxist sociology, their writings do not show its awareness, as the emphasis throughout remains on the comprehensiveness of substantive analysis from an ideological position, rather than on the relative power of theoretical systems.

Some of the major theoretic orientations in Indian sociology which have shown varying degrees of ups and downs during the quarter of a century are philosophical, culturological, structural and dialectical-historical approaches. On the formalization criteria of theory none of these orientations has existed in a systematic form. Most of them have operated as styles of analysis or have been evolved into quasi-formal systems of conceptual schemes. All the four theoretic orientations, however, have existed in Indian sociology from 1952 or even before, and have continued to operate in varying forms. Only the philosophical orientation seems to have weakened because it did not have its organic linkages with the substantive problems as domains of sociological enquiry. We shall review, however, the changes in the theoretic structure of Indian sociology during each of the four periods outlined above in terms of innovation and universalization of concepts and categories, particularistic tensions in their formulation and the related interface of ideology, with specific reference to each of these four major theoretic orientations.

Philosophical Theoretic Orientation

The philosophical orientation in Indian sociology is associated with Lucknow School of Sociology, in the contributions of Radha Kamal Mukerjee, D.P. Mukerji and A.K. Saran. Most of its contributions belong to the 1952–60 period, as in the subsequent years only A.K. Saran remains its proponent. It does not seem to have made a major impact on the theoretical nature of Indian sociology. The reason probably lies in the lack of an integrated or unified perspective in the philosophical theoretic contributions of these sociologists. The theoretic tensions in their writings are not homologous. Radha Kamal Mukerjee finds it possible to talk of universal series of concepts and general categories, which not only integrate sociology internationally, but also include other disciplines both in the natural and the social sciences. D.P. Mukerji, on the other hand, is ambivalent about the question of the 'universal' and 'particular' nature of the sociological categories. He is affectively oriented towards Marxism, but leans heavily on the 'particularistic' model of Indian sociology with emphasis on tradition and history. His writings bear deep influence of Dilthey as well as of Marx—the two rather contradictory orientations in meta-theory. Hence, his notion of dialectics, which he recommends as an important analytic device, never takes on the universalistic meaning which it has in popular interpretations of Marxist theory. A.K. Saran, on the other hand, takes a more logically rigorous and consistent stand on the philosophical and ideological nature of the social sciences and sociology. He propounds an approach to Indian sociology which tends to render it entirely particularistic. Hence, one may find that ideologically the three sociologists can be placed on a continuum where Radha Kamal Mukerjee would represent the extreme of universalistic orientation, A.K. Saran the extreme of particularism in sociology, and D.P. Mukerji would fall somewhere in the middle of the two positions.

Radha Kamal Mukerjee's systematic statement about philosophical foundations of sociology and other social sciences is contained in his *The Philosophy of Social Science* (1960). He postulates for each order of reality, from physical to meta-physical, a unified triadic principle of dialectical interaction which links one level of reality with other, and which also renders one level of concepts or categories significant and meaningful to other levels. Hence, his plea for non-compartmentalization of knowledge into the narrow grooves of disciplines. Dialectics, which is a fundamental process linking one level with another and also endowing it with quality and power of self-transcendence, which Mukherjee treats as the essential feature of man as *homo symbolicus*, is not merely a process of conflict and encapsulation but more prominently of harmony and freedom. It is here that he differs from Marxist uses of the notion of dialectics. He writes:

> The philosophy of dialectical materialism today promotes the universal notion of an inevitable pattern of social development through struggles and conflicts of global revolution and war and subsumes all human progress within the dialectic of the economic movement. Modern evolutionary naturalism, Spencerian, Marxian or Bergsonian, reduces man's mind and values as passive entities manipulated mechanically by a vast process that he cannot intelligently direct or control. Evolution as revealed to modern thought has its many levels or dimensions in which persons, values and societies develop in nature. Values are creative and not merely means of adaptation to the environment. The environment also changes, acted upon by human goals, values and ideals (cf. Mukerjee, 1960: 118).

Mukerjee draws from Hegel, Vedanta, Buddhism and Taoism to formulate his notion of dialectics. Not only he says that "man thinks and lives dialectically. All social relations and behaviour and the values that lie deep seated in them embody polar principles and tendencies" but also that "through the dialectic of the Vedantic *neti-neti* Buddhist *sunyata* and Taoist namelessness, the self identifies itself with the reality and the supreme value" (ibid.: 4). He is opposed to all varieties of reductionist logic about human behaviour and values, be it biological, psychological or economic (materialistic). Dialectic means to him capacity of man to transcend through interplay of opposite forces to higher and higher planes of ethical and cognitive awareness. This transcendence is mediated through society. "Man's transcendence is mediated through society which is a constant tension inside", says Mukerjee. He adds: "It is the nature of man to transcend himself because of the immanence in himself of the not-self, the neighbour, the whole universe" (ibid.: 5). In terms of social models of solidarity, Mukherjee finds both the western liberal democratic pattern and the Marxist models inadequate. He suggests the alternative of the 'third way' or the 'middle way'. This imbibes the principles of individual freedom and dignity of common man from the liberal ideology and access to and sharing of societal resources by the working classes, as advocated by Marxism.

The alternative 'middle way' that Mukerjee proposes as a solution for the planning of the future social systems is supported by his postulate for an integrated social science model which will be united at a 'meta-scientific' and 'meta-anthropological' level. It would resolve the conflict between the philosophy of science and philosophy of values, would integrate into one system the diverse formulations in social sciences on the nature of man, values and society and would lead to the construction of a "human general theory of relativity" which "comprises a comprehensive system of universal norms that belong to the nature of existence or reality or eternal goals of the cosmic process, including human history and civilization" (ibid.: 175). Mukerjee's philosophy of social science thus derives its frame of analysis from a notion of dialectics that is meta-physical. As contribution to sociological theory, its place remains very much at the level of axiomatic meta-theory. It is based on a system of deductive reasoning which is exegetic and speculative, hence different kinds of operationalizations of this meta-theory are possible for sociological studies. Attempts to undertake empirical studies on this model have not been made, although Mukerjee has to his credit several empirical studies in the fields of economics and sociology (cf. Bottomore, 1962: 102).

D.P. Mukerji, on the other hand, does not attempt to construct a general system theory or moral philosophy for global social transformation. He uses a notion of dialectics which is Marxist in formulation (he calls it 'Marxological') but still leaves it to individual social scientists to innovate upon its categories commensurate with their own cultural traditions. In his *Diversities*

(1958) which contains most of his theoretical papers, Mukerji strongly pleads for the uses of history in social analysis. For Indian sociological practice the notion of 'tradition' occupies an important analytic place according to Mukerji, because the dialectics of class formation, class conflict and the structural tensions in Indian society bear the stamp of the historical contexts of its traditions and symbols. The sociological model that D.P. Mukerji puts forward is a synthesis between Dilthey and Marx: for him history matters in sociological analysis, the modes of production and related social relationships constitute essentials of historical forces, but its outcome is tempered also by tradition which provides these processes a specific contextuality. To this extent history also does not repeat itself.

D.P. Mukerji prefers historical-dialectical mode of sociological analysis rather than empirical-positivistic one. He rejects the atomism as a relevant notion for sociological analysis on which empiricism is anchored. He specially refutes the values of empirical methods such as surveys and quantitative-mathematical models as they essentially violate the phenomenology of Indian social reality which is devoid of the notion of individual, and has as its unit-category the collectivity or the *sangha*. This renders most models originating from the west, with the exception of an adapted and Indianized version of Marxism irrelevant for Indian sociology. This has a direct implication to the question of the universalism or particularism of categories in sociology. D.P. Mukerji does not rule out the possibility of comparison between historically distinct societal forms or systems or the relevance of objectivity in social sciences, but he strongly pleads for an awareness in formulation and uses of sociological categories which are derived from the native tradition. This introduces a notion of levels in the concept formation in sociology from the contextual to the comparative, from the particular to the universal and from the historical to the general, which has not been systematically dealt with by Mukerji, but is implicit in his sociological formulations.

A.K. Saran, who was Mukerji's student, and later his colleague, though inspired by his writings, takes on a logically more extreme standpoint on the theoretic formulation of sociology and its meta-theory. In his writings (cf. Saran, 1956, 1957, 1961) he proceeds to examine the meta-theory and underlying premises of sociology as a fundamentally western cultural and cognitive response to meet the historical challenges of its own disintegrating worldview, following the industrial revolution and eclipse of its traditional society. Weak and inadequate as is sociology as a cultural alternative, according to Saran, even for the west, to save it from the formidable challenges in the wake of the disintegration of its past traditional sacred worldview, its borrowing by non-western nations, particularly India, amounts to a double self-deception. It first lies in the neo-colonial roots of sociology. Sociology essentially inheres an ideological package which is of the western origin and alien to Indian ethos. Secondly, it is a bad alternative as a worldview to replace the traditional Indian worldview. The solution according to Saran lies in total rejection of sociology. Its concepts and categories, whether formulated in Marxian terms or in positivistic terms (of methodological individualism or social organicism), amount willy-nilly to safeguarding a false proposition—a proposition of naturalistic reductionism and evolutionism.

In critique of D.P. Mukerji's *Diversities*, Saran evaluates the notion of 'planned social order' implicitly equating it with the foundation of sociological theory of knowledge. He writes:

> The historic roots of the idea of a planned social order go back to the breakup of the worldview founded, among others, on the idea of the Great Chain of Being. The immediate positive reaction to the traditional worldview was to substitute the transcendental intuition of order by an immanentist conception of the social system. This was the logic-philosophical basis of the competitive, individualistic society which supplanted the traditional order in the West. ...The implicit auto-apotheosis (of Man) which characterizes modern thought on planned socio-economic systems is the result of this effort. With the addition of the idea of a collective secular Providence to the competitive worldview, there arises an inner tension between the notion of self-adjustment and the notion of planning (Saran, 1965: 129–30).

Saran has continued to develop his ideas in this direction of meta-sociological reasoning since early fifties. In an essay on "Sociology in India", he rejects Radha Kamal Mukerjee's effort towards sublimating social sciences through a dialectical reasoning on to the plane of moral freedom for man in a social system based on the alternative 'middle path'. He characterizes it as logically inconsistent. He also critically assesses D.P. Mukerji and says: "If the implications of his (Mukerji's) largest views are seriously followed up, they will lead us far beyond Professor Mukerji's present position, for its direction is towards *traditional sociology* not far removed from that of Coomarswamy and Schuon" (Saran, 1957). In his writings of the sixties and the seventies Saran has continued to build upon his earlier ideas in two directions. Firstly, he has refuted most western alternative constructions for sociology in India, particularly of Louis Dumont and David Pocock, and secondly, he has more sharply tried to expose the neo-colonial elements in the ties of Indian sociology with that of the West. His contribution of sociological reasoning thus leads directly not only to rejection of universalization of sociological categories but also of sociology.

Saran, along with D.N. Majumdar and other colleagues at the Lucknow University, had come out in the sixties with warning statements about American projects in India to study Indian society as harmful for national security (Saran, 1957). In the mid-seventies, he refuted Edward Shil's 'centre' and 'periphery' thesis on the growth of social sciences, calling it 'magisterial' in style. But his yet sharper comments on Indian sociology can be seen in his observations on Dumont's essay on the "World Renunciation in Indian Religions" (1957: 33–62) where an effort is made by Dumont to show the comparability of fundamental notions of Hinduism, such as *dharma*, *artha* and *kama* with principles of duty, profit and pleasure respectively, each coinciding with the notion of *varna* hierarchy. The particular passage to which Saran takes objection is as follows:

> The analogy with the hierarchy of *varna* is apparent: *dharma* corresponds to be Brahman or priest, *artha* to the king or Kshatriya, the temporal power, and *kama* to the others. This is not all, and one can go further with the help of Talcott Parsons' method of structural analysis. First, *kama* is opposed to the two others as an action flowing immediately from affective impulses is opposed to an action submitted to intellectual and moral considerations. Then, while *dharma* is moral universalism, *artha* is calculating egoism, something after the manner of 'rational action' in our economic theory—but extended to politics, since wealth

> here is little more than an attribute of power. While *artha* is opposed to *kama* as deferred satisfaction to immediate, *dharma* is opposed to both as ultimate ends to particular ends, as the sacred to the profane. In the language of Parsons, *kama* is expressive action, *artha* instrumental action, and *dharma* moral action. The triology gives an exhaustive classification of the types of action and is based upon a system of oppositions (Dumont, 1966: 41).

Saran in his review of Dumont objects particularly to his attempt to interpret the notions of Hinduism, viz., *dharma*, *artha* and *kama* through western categories, especially through the Parsonian transformation, overlooking the antinomy between the two distinctive value systems and worldviews. Dumont defends his effort to compare through outsider's point of view which he postulates, is an essential methodology of social anthropology and is based on the assumption "that man is not a mere word, although men are such through their belonging to one or other particular society or culture" (Dumont, 1966: 23). Saran is basically skeptical of this position when he writes: "...social reality *qua* reality has no 'outside' ... the only outside is its interpretation in terms of an alien culture ..." (Saran, 1962: 68). He further criticizes Dumont for "taking in the name of science, modernity or objectivity, a firmly provincial standpoint for the study of traditional or tradition-haunted societies". Saran has constantly been criticizing western sociology and social science for its 'positivistic' fallacy (cf.Saran, 1962); he finds Dumont too being involved in the same 'positivistic hybris'.

The commentary of Saran has provoked Dumont to write an angry note clarifying his position (Dumont, 1966). He attacks Saran for taking a position which logically forecloses the possibility of a universal language of sociology and leads to a position of cultural solipsism. This controversy has not evoked response from Indian sociologists on a scale that it deserves. Indeed, Dumont-Pocock publication of the series *Contributions to Indian Sociology* (1957, 1960, 1961, 1962, 1964, 1965 and 1966) have evoked rather a self-consciousness among Indian sociologists which has not entirely been in tune with the 'universalistic' postulates they have intended to project. Its main impact has been one of retroactiveness rather than of approval or acceptance. Dumont's *Homo Hierarchicus*

(1970) falls also in the same category. Although *Contributions to Indian Sociology: New Series* organized a high level review symposium on this book, it failed to make an impact on Indian sociology.

On the Saran-Dumont controversy, T.N. Madan, editor of the *Contributions to Indian Sociology: New Series* has this to write:

> But I am not wholly satisfied with the Dumont-Pocock argument regarding the external point of view which they say the sociologist shares with the natural scientist. I am not convinced that such a point of view exists. (If we accept that it exists, then their and Bailey's positions are not opposed to one another). If it did, it should have been possible for us to study social life through observation by communication with the observed people...I want to go further and question if an observer can acquire any understanding of an alien culture, of the context, purpose and meaning of human action, without communicating with the actors through their, his, or some other language, directly or through intermediaries. Once this happens, the external observer ceases to occupy the position of an outsider (Madan, 1966: 12).

The issues raised through this debate which is still going on in Indian sociology have both ideological and theoretic significance. Ever since the issue of the *Contributions to Indian Sociology*—1957, where Dumont-Pocock first formulated the problem of what they called 'For a Sociology of India', through the seventies the debate on this question has been going on. Since its implications are wider and deeper related to several types of theoretic orientations of Indian sociology, we shall examine it at the end of our treatment of various theoretic orientations in sociology.

Culturological Orientation

The most important landmark in the beginning of what we have heuristically called the 'culturological orientation' in the theoretic nature of sociology is Srinivas' work, *Religion and Society Among the Coorgs of South India* (1952). This work led him to formulate the concept of 'Brahmanization' to represent the process of the imitation of life-ways and ritual practices of Brahamanas by the lower-caste Hindus. The concept was used as an explanatory device to interpret changes observed in the ritual practices and life-ways of the lower castes through intensive and careful field study. The notion of Brahmanization, however, had implicit possibilities of further abstraction into a higher level concept, sanskritization which Srinivas introduced because his own field data and those of many others indicated limitations of using only Brahamanic model as frame of reference (see Shahand and Shroff, 1959; Cohn, 1955; Pocock, 1957, etc.). Sanskritization as a concept thus replaced Brahmanization at a more abstract level.

Srinivas achieved this through enlarging the meaning of sanskritization and by distinguishing it from another concept, westernization, using both terms in a systematic manner to explain the processes of social change in India. This conceptual scheme, though referring mainly to the processes of cultural imitation, has a built-in structural notion, that of hierarchy and inequality of privilege and power, since the imitation is always by the castes or categories placed lower in social hierarchy and of castes and categories placed higher up in social and economic status. The concepts sanskritization-westernization soon became a matter of lively debate and exegesis in sociological circles and also of a series of minor innovations by field workers in different parts of the country, as also by historians, political scientists and Indologists.

Though introduced as a heuristic device, the two concepts also implied a systematic logic. Sanskritization characterized a change within the framework of the Indian tradition, while westernization was a change resulting from the contact with the British socio-economic and cultural innovations. Both processes, nevertheless, form a continuous series in terms of relative power of the groups, castes or categories placed within the traditions concerned. The low castes imitate the ritual styles and customs of the upper (twice-born) castes, and sanskritize; the upper castes imitate the cultural styles and institutions of the British or other western traditions, which leads to westernization. We find a systematic formulation of the two concepts in Srinivas' *Social Change in Modern India* (1966) where he defines sanskritization as "the process by which a 'low' caste or tribe or other group takes over the custom, ritual, beliefs, ideology and style of life of a high and, in particular, a 'twice-born' (*dwija*) caste. The sanskritization of a group has usually the effect of improving its position in the local caste hierarchy. It normally presupposes either an improvement in the economic or political position of the group concerned or a higher group self-consciousness resulting from its contact with a source of the 'Great Tradition' of Hinduism such as pilgrim centre or monastery or proselytizing sect" (1966: 67–68).

Along with the concepts of sanskritization and westernization, Srinivas has used the term 'secularization' to denote the processes of institutional innovations, and ideological formulation after independence to deal with questions of religious groups and minorities in India. Secularization is a process which as normatively stated in the Constitution of India and codified through various types of legislations, attempts to stabilize the foundations of religious tolerance and ideological co-existence among sects and communities in India. This, as a national ideology, was given a formal shape after independence.

The conceptual schemes that Srinivas has formulated to analyze the phenomenon of social and cultural change have made the outstanding impact on Indian sociology. It offered an analytic frame to many village studies conducted from 1952 to 1968 particularly (cf. Srinivas, 1955; Marriott, 1955; Majumdar, 1955, 1958; Chauhan, 1974) and later on in the discursive treatment of Indian sociology. It inspired historians and Indologists to re-evaluate their perceptions and premises on the processes in Indian society and culture (see, Raghavan, 1959; Chanana, 1961; Harper, 1959; Staal, 1963) and to critically examine the merits of this concept in the analysis of social and cultural change (Thapar, 1975). It also led some sociologists to study its latent merits which could throw light also on structural changes in India society (see, Gould, 1968; Singh, 1970, 1973) and others to compare it with 'reference group theory' in sociology (see, Damle, 1968; Lynch, 1966). Debate was also generated on Srinivas' concept of 'dominant caste', which, according to him, in most cases, served as reference model for the castes lower in position to borrow or imitate its customs and practices through sanskritization (Dube, 1965; Oommen, 1970). Finally, sanskritization also generated through examination by some sociologists of the structure of traditions in Hinduism which were claimed to be multiple and not unitary in character.

Sanskritization and westernization as concepts and theoretic orientations stirred Indian sociology more deeply than any other conceptual scheme so far. "Here was a concept which had an equal appeal for the Indologists, historians of Indian culture and sociologists and social anthropologists. It also satisfied those who had a special fondness for developing Indian concepts for analyzing national social cultural phenomena" (Singh, 1977: 99). These concepts have been debated in Indian sociology both for their viability as well as limitations to interpret social changes in society. Some debate has also ranged on the possibility of linking these with more abstract concepts such as 'reference group' and 'social mobility' in order to universalize them (Singh, 1973).

Another attempt to analyze the cultural processes of change in India has been made by Milton Singer and McKim Marriott following Redfield's model of 'social organization of traditions and civilizations' based on the dichotomy of the little and great traditions (see, Singer, 1959, 1970, 1972 and Marriott, 1955). The great tradition is that of the elite, urban centres and has a formal character, whereas the little tradition belongs to those of the folk in the villages and the unlettered many. Each tradition has its social organization, and there is a continual flow of themes, ideas or symbols from one to the other level, universalizing some and parochializing other traits of the tradition. This process is triggered both through orthogenetic and heterogenetic factors. Sanskritization as a process could also be incorporated in this process as well as westernization or modernization. Some field studies in villages and cities have been conducted by Singer, Marriott and their colleagues following this model, but it has not made a wide impact on Indian sociology as Srinivas' concepts of sanskritization and westernization. The reason is that except for some advantages of formalization and abstraction this model does not add much to the analytic advantages in studies with uses of its categories. Moreover, sanskritization and westernization can also lend historical and structural-analytic insights whereas the concepts of Singer and Redfield are devoid of possibilities of observing structural tensions in social processes both of modernization and traditionalization.

The major emphasis in study of social change through concepts of sanskritization-westernization and of the levels of traditions is on the changes in cultural styles, customs and ritual practices. There are, however, some presuppositions in the processes both of sanskritization and westernization which do imply precedent or concomitant structural changes, such as improvement in economic position of the sanskritizing caste, superiority and dominance of the caste being emulated and psychological disenchantment among the low castes from their own position in the caste hierarchy. Effort has been made to spell out the presuppositions contained in both the Srinivas and the Singer models and to integrate them on a logical paradigmatic principle (see, Singh, 1973). The two essential coordinates implicit in Srinivas' and Singer's formulations are that of the sources of change—heterogenetic and orthogenetic and the substantive domains of change—cultural structure, comprising the 'little' and 'great' traditions and social structure, comprising of micro-structure' and 'macro-structure'. Placed in a schematic form (of property-space) these lend us typologies of operational concepts in which notions of sanskritization and westernization cannot only be subsumed but also extended to explain also the structural change through generating logically related set of structural concepts of change, such as role differentiation, emergence of new structural forms, bureaucracy and elites through heterogenetic changes and pattern-recurrence, migration, internal social movement, circulation of elites and rise and fall of urban centres and dynasties, etc., through orthogenetic sources. Attempt has been made to analyze processes both of modernization and traditionalization through these conceptual categories based on sociological and historical data.

Structural Theoretic Orientation

The culturological orientation of Indian sociology whose theoretic tendencies we have examined has also been related primarily to studies of the village communities, caste structure, its institutional correlates and family, kinship and religious ideology of the people in villages. .Most such studies being conducted through social anthropological and observational techniques had a holistic character. The social structure was studied at the village level, but it was more descriptive and sociographic than from a theoretical explanatory point of view. The structural orientation differs from culturological because, as Bailey says in structural studies, "we ought not to confine ourselves to the raw material provided by the 'principles that people themselves give', our only task is not to make sense of the flagrant contradictions in popular thought by abstracting out consistent elements that culturological study attempts. A valid sociological understanding can be achieved, given certain problems, by making abstractions immediately from behaviour or from other non-verbal information, and by using our own concepts (Bailey, 1959: 88–101). The pre-eminence of concepts or models is one characteristic of the structural studies. Its other important attributes are related to the nature of problems it undertakes for observation and analysis, such as the processes of structural cleavages and differentiation in societies, problems of equality and inequality, study of power structure, social stratification, social mobility, urbanization-industrialization, changes in the demographic and family structure, etc. Such studies also have a macro-structural and historical perspective.

In the structural studies, one important trend is the focus on comparative categorial relationship, such as caste and class relationship in India and its implication on the nature of the society. This trend has continued since late sixties. In such studies the analysis of social structure is undertaken with the help of two or more conceptual categories. This introduces the element of comparison and generalization in their theoretic power. Bailey's (1960) analysis of structural changes in India with the set of comparative categories like 'tribe', 'caste' and 'nation', Beteille's (1965) study of social structure of a village with analytic categories 'caste', 'class' and 'power' have been forerunners of a whole new series of structural studies. Additional sets of categories that have been used by sociologists for comparative study of social structure are, caste, religion and power (Aggarwal, 1971), caste, race and politics (Verba, Ahmed and Bhatt, 1971) tribe, caste and class (Aurora, 1972), mind, body and wealth (Pocock, 1974) to study the structure of beliefs rather than social relationship caste, class and politics (Bhatt, 1975) and language, religion and politics (Brass, 1975). Several other studies using such comparative sets of categories for analysis of social structure, beliefs, ideologies or cultural systems have been made during the past fifteen years (Thapar, 1977; Fox, 1971). The use of a set of more than two conceptual categories for analysis of social phenomena renders the theoretic elements in these studies not only comparative but also increases their power of generalization. This was not usually a characteristic of holistic studies of villages and tribal social structures conducted in the fifties and early sixties in India.

This tendency of comparison has also coincided with the use of theoretic and conceptual schemes not only to analyze but also explain changes in the social structure. The uses of the terms 'closed' and 'open' stratification (Bailey, 1963; Beteille, 1969; Singh, 1970) and 'harmonic' and 'disharmonic' systems (Beteille, 1971) do constitute attempts towards a new explanatory dimension in sociological analysis. The explanation of course does not reach the level of formal theory, but is a definite advancement from earlier descriptive studies of social structures in India.

The structural theoretic orientation of sociology during the seventies is also reflected in the spurt of urban surveys which were completed from 1957 to 1969 (D'Souza, 1974: 117). These urban surveys, sponsored mostly by the Research Programmes Committee of the Planning Commission, have been analyzed integratedly by Bulsara (1964) for nine cities, though in all more than two scores of surveys have been published. These surveys have dealt with items such as population, language, literacy, occupation and industry, internal migration, income, employment, housing conditions and social life, etc., in the cities. The surveys have used a statistical model for study with the help of schedules and questionnaires on a selected sample fraction. They have mainly generated benchmark data for planners and have occasionally contributed to innovations in methodology through standardization of the tools of research. They have also contributed to the training of a whole batch of researchers in survey type study, who today reinforce many social research organizations in the government and private industry. Cities have also been studied using the culturological model, especially the notion of 'sacred complex' (Vidyarthi, 1961, 1969) or 'cultural configuration'. Some conceptual evaluations of categories used in urban studies have also been undertaken from the criteria of logical adequacy, and principles of verification and validation (Mukherjee, 1965; Berreman, 1972). Studies of urban elite entrepreneurs and other specific structures and categories have been undertaken by several sociologists (Jones, 1975; Rosenthal, 1970; Berna, 1960; Hazlehurst, 1966; Saberwal, 1974). Sociologists have also studied slums in cities from a diagnostic as well as theoretical perspective (Desai and Pillai, 1972). Most of these studies have observed the levels of structural changes and accompanying contradictions in the process of urban growth. Some of them have also innovated upon conceptual schemes, as Saberwal's study of entrepreneurial structure in a Punjab township, which improves upon E. Hagen's thesis on the theory of innovations in developing societies and analyzes the structural notions related to economic and social risk-taking, its absence in the lower classes and its relationship with social mobility.

In the structural theoretic orientation, not only the number of conceptual schemes for comparative studies increases, but also the relationship between concepts and social reality undergoes a new formulation. This is evident in the replacement of studies of villages, so dominant in the sixties, by those of 'agrarian structure' and 'peasantry' in the seventies and eighties. The focus on the study of agrarian structure, and not the village, takes sociology into the macro-analytic domain. It introduces a theoretical rather than a territorial orientation in sociological thinking and also brings the Marxist and functionalist formulations of sociological theory face-to-face challenging each to test and verify their relative theoretic power. It also introduces a new dimension in the study of change, through emphasis on sociology of social movement and revolution. These innovations in concepts and theory have also led to a new methodological awareness in sociology. Sociologists now increasingly use historical method and archival and documentary data to formulate their propositions. This has brought history and sociology closer and there is a possibility of one reinforcing the other.

The interest in agrarian sociology is derived from interest in the study of basic changes in the rural social structure initiated through land reforms after independence. It covers studies of new class formations, social mobility and contradictions arising from these processes, with inter-regional and comparative perspective (cf. Joshi, 1971, 1975; Singh, 1974; Beteille, 1974; Oommen, 1972; Bhalla, 1976).There have also been studies of changes in agrarian relations resulting from 'green revolution' or agricultural prosperity in some regions (see, Ladejinsky, 1973; Oommen, 1977; Mencher, 1974). Many studies on the social movement among the peasantry have also been conducted to analyze historically, as well as in contemporary setting, the contradictions emergent in the agrarian social structure (Dhanagare, 1975; Gough, 1975). Social movements which have their origin either in tribal agrarian problems, or those sponsored by socio-economic reform movements like the Sarvodaya or by the radical movements as those of the Naxalities, have also been studied by sociologists (Oommen, 1977; Desai, 1975; Shah, 1974; Dasgupta, 1974; Mukherjee, 1977). The study of the historical bases of some regional movements like the Siva Sena and the caste movements such as neo-Buddhism have been explored (Gupta, 1977; Rao, 1975; Singh and Singh, 1977; Singh, 1977). The study of social movements has not only added a new methodological orientation but has also led to innovations in conceptualization and formulation of contexts and categories of social change. It makes a significant break from the functional notion of a creative and adaptive change and focuses on those processes of change which have the capacity to bring about a structural transformation in society.

The structural orientation in theory during the seventies has also led to new focus on kinship studies and family sociology (see, Shah, 1964, 1973, 1974; Dube, 1974; Gough, 1975); the emphasis on the diachronic process of changes in family structure, from jointness to nuclearity, has been replaced by that on family cycle studies (Desai, 1964; Nicholas, 1961; Gould, 1968, etc.). Historical studies of family structure and differentiation of its form have been followed by studies in the area of sociology of disputes (Srinivas, 1959) combining in-depth observations with historical social anthropology of villages. Cohn has applied it for macro-analytical study of the Indian civilization (Cohn, 1971). The studies of factional differentiation and conflict in social and political networks have also been conducted to reveal the bases of cleavages in Indian rural and urban society (Nicholas, 1968; Kothari, 1970; Brass, 1965; Weiner and Kothari, 1965, etc.). This has led to historical study of the rise of new elites and changes in their composition and social background (Leach and Mukherjee, 1970; Broomfield, 1969; Rosenthal, 1976). Studies of social mobility and changes in the caste and class structures, both from sociological and historical perspectives, have been particularly emphasized (see, Silverberg, 1968; Bose, 1968; Kothari, 1970; Srinivas, 1968).

An important theoretical insight which dominates the orientation in formulating categories is what may be called, preference for the notion of 'levels' rather than continuum in sociology and social sciences. The conceptual dichotomies through which changes in structure were observed proved too static and inadequate when seen in historical perspective. This was true specially for concepts like rural and urban, caste and class and 'nuclear' and 'joint family'. It also applied in the case of culturological concepts such as 'little' and 'great' tradition and the processes of traditionalization and modernization. Kothari writes: "The prevailing dichotomy between tradition and modernity has created a curious cognitive hiatus—in ideological thinking as well as in much of social science theorizing—between society on the one hand and polity on the other. The former is conceived as if by definition, as 'traditional', the latter as 'modern' and 'developmental'. In reality, however, this is a false approach to the phenomenon of modernization" (Kothari, 1970: 3).

The structural theoretic orientation has not only contributed to deeper insight in the understanding of the basic process in the Indian society but has also led to innovations in conceptual categories, paradigms of analysis and in addition to this brought sociology closer to the work of the historians, political scientists and economists. This has increased the viability of sociological studies and raised new significant professional implications.

Dialectical Historical Orientation

The dialectical theoretic orientation is related primarily to Marxist methods and propositions for the analysis of social reality. We have used the terms dialectical and not Marxist because in Indian sociology, Marxist approaches comprise several adaptive models; many innovations have been made on classical Marxist formulations for the study of Indian society. Also, among Indian sociologists, there is growing awareness that Marxist categories and paradigms will have to be reformulated and tested against societal realities of various historical origins to validate them as universal or particular categories in sociology. In this perspective, when we look at the growth of dialectical-historical orientation in theory, we find that comparatively it is a less developed branch of Indian sociology. Most basic Marxist thinking in India was done in the forties and fifties by non-sociologists (see, Singh, 1973, 1977). Among the early sociologists who emphasized the significance of dialectical model were D.P. Mukerji and Ramkrishna Mukherjee.

D.P. Mukerji, whose contribution to sociological theory we have already examined, continually used the categories of structure, class conflict and the model of socialist society in his analysis of historical social processes in India. Both historical framework and dialectical orientation are essential, according to him, in sociological thinking. He did not conduct any empirical studies using this frame of reference. Ramkrishna Mukherjee made systematic historical as well as empirical studies using dialectical model. His *The Rise and Fall of the East Indian Company* (1958) is a contribution to economic and social history of the institutionalization of colonialism in India through stabilization of economic policies, disintegration of feudalism and aristocratic despotism, and the rise of new middle classes. In his *The Dynamics of a Rural Society* (1957), Mukherjee studies social and economic changes in a set of villages through changes in the structure of classes. He emphasizes the necessity to grasp the systematic and organic character of Indian society for understanding of its social processes. In his later works, Ramkrishna Mukherjee has changed from dialectical historical to a 'probabilistic nomological' approach for the study of social reality. He calls his approach 'inductive inferential' which is neutral to the type of propositions, Marxist or non-Marxist, that one chooses to test and verify. The role of history and dialectics in the sociological thinking and research, according to Mukherjee, stops at the level of formulation of propositions; these may help in even a taxonomic formulation of categories (see, Mukherjee, 1970, 1975) or social indicators, but beyond this the logical principles of test and verification would have to operate independently.

Among Indian sociologists one who has consistently advocated and applied dialectical-historical model in his sociological studies is A.R. Desai. In his studies of nationalism, analysis of rural social structure, the nature of economic and social policies of change in India and the structure of state and society, he has consistently tried to expose the contradictions and anomalies in policies and process of change resulting from the capitalistic-bourgeoisie interlocking of interest in the Indian society (see, Desai, 1959, 1966, 1975). According to Desai, the polarization of class interests, especially of the bourgeoisie in India, is the foundation of modern society in India. It has thus inherent in it the class contradictions and the logic of its dialectics. This has been thoroughly exposed by Desai in his several writings.

The dialectical theoretic orientation has subsequently increased in the studies of political structure, agrarian formations and social movements. The contradictions in Indian political, economic and social structure, and in its development programmes, etc., have been highlighted by Bettelheim, who has concluded that although Indian case is one of mounting contradictions, the Indian bourgeoisie has relatively been more responsive to elimination of these contradictions, at least from some of the structures than bourgeoisie in other nations (see, Bettelheim, 1968).The judgement of several other Marxists within India also, however, coincides with these observations. But there is a significant difference of opinion as to the intensity and rate of expansion of contradictions in Indian society that may trigger off revolutionary movements (see, Desai, 1975). The agrarian studies conducted from the Marxist frame of reference have used 'feudalism', 'capitalistic' and 'pre-capitalistic' categories and mode of production frame of reference in the study of the social structures (see, Sau, 1973 Chattopadhyaya, 1972; Bhaduri, 1973; Saith and Tankha, 1972; Patnaik, 1972). Because of the uses of theoretic categories of feudalism, pre-capitalistic structures and capitalism, with accompanying variations in the modes of production and modes of social relationships, these empirical studies assume significance. Theoretically, the contribution of these studies is two-fold: first, these enrich our sociological understanding of the structural tensions or contradictions in the agrarian society and link them with its macro-structures; and secondly, these also lead to innovations in the Marxist sociological categories themselves, as these are put to test in a different socio-cultural and historical context. The need for such innovations in Marxist dialectical paradigm in India has been emphasized both by Indian and foreign sociologists (see, Joshi, 1974 and Thorner, 1973).

In addition to the uses for the analysis of agrarian relations and class structure, the dialectical theory has also been applied to the study of macro-structural social and economic processes in India. Here, the framework of capitalism is further informed by that of 'imperialism' and 'neo-colonialism' for the understanding of the forces of change (see, Patnaik, 1975; Frank, 1970) in society. There have also been some contributions on the exegesis of writings of Karl Marx on India by both Indian and non-Indian sociologists (see, Thorner, 1966 and Joshi, and Damodaran, 1975).

The dialectical-historical theoretic orientation in Indian sociology has grown rapidly in the seventies, when in addition to macro-structural studies of social, economic and political institutions, micro-structural realities at the empirical level have also been submitted to closer observation. This development has also coincided with more analytic sophistication in the study of macro-social problems. In August 1975, a journal *Social Scientist* was also started from Kerala which publishes Marxist-oriented writings by social scientists and political workers on various problems of theory and substantive realities in India. Evidently, studies with dialectical theoretical and methodological orientation have been on an increase in India with innovations in concepts, methods and categories.

For a Sociology of India

Having reviewed the main theoretical orientations in Indian sociology it may be useful to assess its impact on the process of universalization or particularization of categories and theory. This issue is both ideological and theoretical. Since Dumont and Pocock initiated the debate on "For a Sociology of India" in 1957, this issue has been debated in response to their and Bailey's writings and also independently. Dumont's emphasis in the study of Indian sociology is on its fundamental ideo-structural categories from an 'external point of view'. He would formulate his sociology from the language of the sources as it were, from the sentiments and ideas of the people themselves. Bailey finds fault with this model for its indifference towards study of 'relations', which is the main sociological category. With this frame of reference, sociology gets reduced to what Bailey calls 'culturology'. In his statement on "For a Sociology of India" in the final issue of *Contributions*, however, Dumont clarifies that he does not see the possibility of a particularistic sociology even though the substantive reality he would prefer the sociologist to deal with would be ideas and sentiments and not relations. Thus, without taking a structural position as that of Bailey, Dumont sees the possibility of a general sociology as the only way-out.

The debate between Dumont and Bailey led Indian sociologists to think on this problem from an Indian perspective, where the issue was not of two varieties of general sociology, of which the Indian sociology would be a part, but it was mainly whether Indian sociology could be universal or has to be particularistic. A seminar was organized on this problem in 1966 and its deliberations have been published (Unnithan et al., 1967). The conclusion of this seminar was that Indian sociology would have to operate at both levels, the particularistic and the universal. Some concepts or categories as Srinivas' sanskritization-westernization, would be of primarily particularistic and ethno-sociological relevance, but these could be further abstracted for cross-cultural comparisons (see, Singh, in Unnithan et al., 1967).

The debate on this issue has not subsided. It was given a sharper edge by linking the problem both of creativity and categories in Indian sociology to the colonial situation. J.P.S. Uberoi, in his "Science and Swaraj" concluded: "Every swarajist should recognize what are the essential pre-conditions, under this system (structural asymmetries like rich-poor, international-national, white-black), for the advancement of universal science in our environment. Until we can concentrate on decolonization, learn to nationalize our problems and take our poverty seriously, we shall continue to be both colonial and unoriginal" (Uberoi, 1968: 123). This observation of Uberoi has echoes in many quarters. As we mentioned, Saran is its strong exponent. Many others who support it with qualifications, do not see contradictions in methods and categories of the ethnosociology and general sociology. The problem is ideological, and as such it pervades through all levels of sociological thinking in India where normative questions and not merely technology of research are involved.

Even the universality of methods and tools of research is questioned. Most of these involve translation of cultural idioms and symbols from one culture into another. What is more seriously questioned, however, is the choice of problems and research priorities that sociologists undertake for investigation. In a recent debate on this problem which is contained in *Social Sciences and Social Realities: Role of Social Sciences in Contemporary India* (Dube, 1976), such issues have been reopened for a variety of social sciences. The distortions in sociological thinking and practice are created by alienation of the professional sociologist from the other sections of elites and people of the society. This leads to the distantiation of sociologist from the major issues of national concern or with national identity. His uncritical acceptance of models of theory and research tools imported from abroad have come in for thorough examination (see, Singh, in Dube, 1976).

The question of universalization or particularism of sociological categories in Indian sociology or social science as such remains open. A more enduring solution to this issue would probably come from accumulation of empirical knowledge through the findings of Indian sociologists and social scientists from studies conducted with self-awareness and scientific objectivity within their own ideological setting.

Methodological Orientations

Methodology comprises logic of enquiry and philosophy of science, techniques of operationalization of concepts and tools of research, problems of measurement, verification and validation, and finally questions of universality and particularity in tools of research that use symbolic-linguistic categories for measurement and observation. These components of methodology, therefore, at another level raise similar ideological issues that we discussed in the context of theoretical orientations of Indian sociology. Methodological problems also get entangled in the web of ethical questions, of communication of values, preservation of the confidence of respondents or its exploitation. Since social science research implies social interaction, between the researcher and his respondents, the observer and the people he observes, and also the act of cultural interpretation, the likelihood of asymmetry developing in the relationship of researcher and the human subjects of his inquiry is high and also ethically vital. Indeed, the movement of ethnomethodological ideology in research is a result of the dilemmas created by such ethical and structural problems in social research.

The methodological trends and its problems in Indian sociology have been reviewed earlier (see, Madan, 1973). The ethical questions posed by research methodology have also been discussed at philosophical and political levels. Much of the critique of sociology by Saran mentioned in the philosophical orientation belongs to this level of discussion. We could, however, examine the methodological contributions made by Indian sociology at two points of operation. First, with reference to the types of methods and techniques of research that have been used in sociology and the degree of their innovativeness. Secondly, we could also examine the types of reflections that sociologists have made on their own methodological craft, looking at it from a new context of *post-facto* objectivity.

Indeed, in the sixties, Indian sociology underwent a strong change in its orientation towards the tools and techniques of research. The two most common tools used by sociologists during this period were participant observation by social anthropologists and survey research design for urban studies or studies of social categories. Some social anthropologists also used historical methods in their study, but its vogue was muted only to revive more strongly in the sixties and seventies. Sociology teaching by this time invariably included courses in research methodology. Compared to other social sciences, with the exception of economics and psychology, methodological awareness has been higher in Indian sociology. Whereas survey design using statistical model of investigation has been quite common, the use of mathematical models has been rare. The application of cybernetic model, set theory, matrix algebra, etc., in sociological researches have been made only recently and by few sociologists (see, Rastogi, 1976, 1975; D'Souza, 1972, Mukherjee, 1976). As compared to the sociological practice in India during 1952–60, the trend in 1960–70 and 1970–71 has been more towards structural analysis from a historical and comparative perspective. This type of study did use simple quantitative techniques, but relied more on observational, case historical and documentary data. Only the Marxists studies on agrarian structure, we reviewed, conducted mostly by economists than sociologists have used higher mathematical techniques in survey design of research.

With few exceptions, the sophistication of quantitative methods of research in sociology is yet to be a popular movement. Instead, there is some evidence in recent sociological studies of social movements, historical life cycle of institutions that there is reaction against uses of quantitative techniques of research. Srinivas, in a recent article on this problem takes economists and others who devalue documentary and to task observational facts and insights in researches, and attributes this neglect to the many failings of the explanatory models of these sciences (see, Srinivas, 1975). Similar views have been expressed by other sociologists (Singh, 1976). This reasoning is strengthened by studies on the problems of conducting survey researches in India. It is revealed that many tools which take individual respondent's autonomy of views and opinions for granted (as in the west) do not apply in India, because of the different nature of relationship between individual and society in India (Rudolph and Rudolph, 1958). On the other hand, the emphasis on methods and scientific techniques is most pronounced in the writings of Ramkrishna Mukherjee, who insists that explanation of phenomena through research is not possible without the uses of experimental and inductive inferential models in sociology.

The second important development in Indian sociology is in respect of self-reflection by sociologists who have completed studies or major researches on the methodology they have employed in a post-facto exercise of self-critique and self-assessment. Also, there is a tendency to objectively examine some of the subjective and ideological issues which influenced their research strategy and choice of tools and techniques. We have an interesting account of social anthropologists on their own 'encounters and experiences' doing fieldwork in India (Beteille and Madan, 1975). A similar study on the craft of Indian sociology by sociologists, political scientists and psychologists who have conducted major studies in their field in India has been prepared where each social scientist reflects retrospectively on the problems he faced in his field study, the ideological leads that he now thinks had been implicit in his design of research and concepts and categories he has used (Singh and Oommen, 1977).

These reflections on tendencies in methodology and uses of techniques in Indian sociology and social sciences highlight certain common problems. Sociologists have now acknowledged the role of ideology in operationalization of concepts and theories in research designs and its techniques. They at the same time do not reject norms of scientific method or the statistical model in social researching favour of ethnomethodology. About the uses of techniques, however, their values and preferences are tempered by caution and circumspection. Uses of history, documentary data and reflexive insights are preferred in more recent sociological researches to simplistic attempts at quantification ad statistical reasoning. More important areas where such insights have been adequately found useful and innovative are that of family sociology, study of social movements, analysis of problems of inter-group relations and mobility of classes and categories. The utility of survey design and quantitative models has been found to be extremely high in studies with a bearing on applied problems or where generation of benchmark data is essential for implementing public policy. Theoretically challenging uses of mathematical models have, however, not been in evidence in Indian sociology on any significant scale.

Sociology and Other Social Sciences

Indian sociology has interacted closely with other social sciences. The teaching of sociology has indeed differentiated from political science in Bombay University and from economics in Lucknow University—the two centres where its teaching made early impact on the profession of sociology in India. Its conceptual categories have also been influenced by discoveries in other social sciences and have in turn influenced their orientation. Historians have influenced deeply the wider uses of the notions of sanskritization and westernization, the study of middle classes and socio-economic formations in India. They have deeply contributed to the validation of propositions of Marxist and dialectical theoretical orientations in sociology as also offered refutation of some of its hypotheses. Political scientists' contributions through studies of political elites, power structure and political communication and studies of ideology have influenced similar studies in sociology. Rajni Kothari has contributed to the theory of political socialization in India which has enriched studies on the formation of cognitive and value systems in personality. Similarly, studies in political participation, political culture and its systemic treatment have offered new insight to sociologists working in this field (Kothari, 1970). The study of leadership by political scientists has enriched insights of sociologists in their own studies of leadership in rural and urban societies.

The influence of sociology and social anthropology has been considerable in India both on history and political science. History has not only influenced sociology but has been influenced by it, especially in the recent formulations of historical problems, where formation of structures, modes of production and other infrastructural realities of society deeply inform historical analysis (see, Thapar, 1975). Indian history bears the imprint of sociology as it moves from narrative history to problem history. It is evident in economic historical studies, analysis of social movements and agrarian structure by Indian historians. A.M. Shah writes: "During the last fifteen years or so, historians have become increasingly receptive to sociology and social anthropology. This is seen in the works of several historians such as Tapan Roy Chaudhuri, Dharma Kumar, Donald Smith, Robert Frykenberg, Eugene Irschic, Burton Stein, Morris D. Morris, Robert Crane, R. Hardgrave, S.C. Misra, Romila Thapar and A.L. Basham, among others. The new journal *Indian Economic and Social History Review*, founded by Tapan Roychaudhuri, has served to bring history and social sciences, including sociology and social anthropology, in closer relationship. Roychaudhuri has devoted almost the whole of the long preface to the second edition of his book, *Bengal under Akbar and Jahangir* to sociology and social anthropology and their usefulness in history" (Shah, 1974: 453).

While the interaction between history and sociology, and political science and sociology, has been mutually reinforcing and has proved beneficial, the same type of interaction between sociology and economics has not taken place during the past one and half decades. Earlier, sociologists and economists used to interact more purposefully in uses of categories and in substantive studies. The reason for this lag lies in high mathematicalization of economics during the past one and a half decades which on the one hand endows economists with a sense of technical superiority in their researches, and on the other alienates sociologists, who often not trained in mathematical logic, tend to be mystified by economists' works without, however, being impressed by them. On the contrary, sociologists often consider such technological skill of economists rather misplaced and inadequate in capturing the essences of the social and cultural correlates of economic behaviour and its system (Srinivas, 1975) in India. It is hoped that as economists' study of social structures, such as the agrarian and industrial social formations, using their own frames of reference, becomes mature, they would also in the process generate insights other than mathematical which could be meaningful to sociologists.

References

Aggarwal, Pratap C., *Caste, Religion and Power: An Indian Case Study*, New Delhi: Shri Ram Centre for Industrial Relations, 1971.

Aurora, G.S., *Tribe, Caste, Class Encounters: Some Aspects of Folk-Urban Relations in Alirajper Tehsil*, Hyderabad: Administrative Staff College of India, 1972.

Bailey, F.G., "Closed Social Stratification in India", *European Journal of Sociology*, Vol. IV, No. I, 1963.

—, "For a Sociology of India", *Contributions to Indian Sociology*, No. III, 1959.

—, *Politics and Social Change: Orissa in 1959*, Berkeley: University of California Press, 1963.

—, *Tribe, Caste and Nation: A Study of Political Activity and Political Changes in Highland Orissa*, Manchester: Manchester University Press, 1960.

Berna, J.J., 1960, *Industrial Entrepreneurship in Madras State*, New York, 1960.

Berreman, Gerald D., "Social Categories and Social Interaction in Urban India", *American Anthropologist*, 74, 1972.

Beteille, Andre, "Ideas and Interests: Some Conceptual Problems in the Study of Social Stratification in Rural India", *International Social Science Journal*, Vol. 21, No. 2, 1969.

—, "The Future of the Backward Classes: The Competing Demands of Status and Power", *Perspectives—A Supplement to the Indian Journal of Public Administration*, Vol. 12, 1965.

—, "The Politics of 'Non-antagonistics' Strata", *Contributions to Indian Sociology* (New Series), Vol. 3, 1969.

— (ed.), *Social Inequality*, Harmondsworth: Penguin Books Limited, 1969.

—, and Madan, T.N. (eds.), *Encounter and Experience: The Personal Dimension of Social Anthropological Fieldwork*, Delhi: Vikas Publishing House, 1975.

—, *Caste, Class and Power*, Berkeley: University of California Press, 1965.

—, *Castes: Old and New: Essays in Social Stratification*, Delhi: Asia Publishing House, 1969.

—, *Harmonic and Disharmonic Social Systems*, Sydney: Sydney University Press, 1971.

—, *Inequality and Social Change*, Delhi: Oxford University Press, 1975.

Bettelheim, C., *India Independent*, London: MacGibbon and Kee, 1968.

Bhaduri, A., "A Study in Agricultural Backwardness under Semi-Feudalism", *Economic Journal*, March 1973.

Bhalla, Sheila, "New Relations of Production in Haryana Agriculture", *Economic and Political Weekly*, Vol. XI, No. 13, March 27, 1976.

Bhambhri, C.P., "Political Science" in S.C. Dube (ed.), *Social Sciences and Social Relations: Role of the Social Sciences in Contemporary India*, Simla: Indian Institute of Advanced Study, 1976.

Bhatt, Anil, *Caste, Class and Politics: An Empirical Profile of Social Stratification in Modern India*, New Delhi: Manohar Book Service, 1975.

Bose, N.K., "Inequality and Social Changes", *Searchlight*, 68, 1968.

Bottomore, T.B., "Sociology in India", *British Journal of Sociology*, 13(2), 1962.

Brass, P., *Factional Politics in an Indian State: The Congress Party in Uttar Pradesh*, Berkeley: University of California Press, 1965.

Brass, Paul R., *Language, Religion and Politics in North India*, New Delhi: Vikas Publishing House, 1975.

Broomfield, J.H., *Elite Conflict in a Plural Society: Twentieth Century Bengal*, Bombay: Oxford University Press, 1968.

Chanana, Dev Raj, "Sanskritization, Westernization and India's North-West", *Economic Weekly*, 13 (9), 1961.

Chattopadhyaya, Paresh, "On the Question of the Mode of Production in Indian Agriculture: A Preliminary Note", *Economic and Political Weekly*, Vol. VII, No. 13, March 25, 1972.

Chauhan, B.R., "Rural Studies", in *A Survey of Research in Sociology and Social Anthropology*, ICSSR, Vol. I, Bombay: Popular Prakashan, 1974.

Cohn, Bernard S., "The Changing Status of Depressed Caste", in M. Marriott (ed.), *Village India*, Chicago: University of Chicago Press, 1955.

—, *India: The Social Anthropology of a Civilisation*, New Jersey: Prentice Hall, 1971.

Damle, Y.B., "Reference Group Theory and Mobility in the Caste System", in James Silverberg (ed.), *Social Mobility in the Caste System in India*, Hague: Mouton and Co., 1968.

Dasgupta, Biplab, *The Naxalite Movement*, Bombay: Asia Publishing House, 1974.

Desai, A.R. (ed.), *Rural Sociology in India*, Bombay: Popular Prakashan, 1959.

—, *Social Background of Indian Nationalism*, Bombay: Popular Prakashan, 1966.

—, *State and Society in India*, Bombay: Popular Prakashan, 1975.

—, and Pillai, S. Devadas, *A Profile of an Indian Slum*, Bombay: Popular Prakashan, 1972.

Desai, I.P., *Some Aspects of Family in Mahuva*, Bombay: Asia Publishing House, 1964.

Dhanagare, D.N., "Social Origins of the Peasant Insurrection in Telengana (1946–51), *Contributions to Indian Sociology* (New Series), 6.

—, "The Politics of Survival: Peasant Organization and the Left Unity in India 1925–46", *Sociological Bulletin*, 24 (1), 1975.

D'Souza, Alfred, "Dialogue between Religions in India", *Social Action*, XXII, 2, 1972.

D'Souza, Alfred (ed.), *Women in Contemporary India*, New Delhi: Manohar Books Service, 1975.

D'Souza, Victor S., "Caste Structure in India in the Light of Set Theories", *Current Anthropology*, 1972.

—, "Scheduled Castes and Urbanization in Punjab: An Exploration", *Sociological Bulletin*, 24 (1), 1975.

—, "Urban Studies", in *A Survey of Research in Sociology and Social Anthropology*, ICSSR, Vol. I, Bombay: Popular Prakashan, 1974.

—, and Sethi, Raj Mohini, "Social Class and Occupational Prestige in India: A Case Study", *Sociological Bulletin*, XXI, 1972.

Dube, Leela, *Sociology of Kinship: An Analytical Survey of Literature*, New Delhi: ICSSR, 1974.

Dube, S.C. (ed.), *Social Sciences and Social Realities: Role of the Social Sciences in Contemporary India*, Simla: Indian Institute of Advanced Study, 1976.

—, "The Study of Complex Cultures", in T.K.N. Unnithan et al. (eds.), *Towards a Sociology of Culture in India*, New Delhi: Prentice Hall of India, 1965.

Dumont, Louis, "A Fundamental Problem in Sociology of Caste", *Contributions to Indian Sociology*, 9, 1966.

—, *Homo Hierarchicus*, Delhi: Vikas Publishing House, 1970.

—, *Religion, Politics and History in India* (Collected Papers in Indian Sociology), Paris: Ecole Pratique des Hautes Etudes, 1970.

—, and Pocock, D.F., "For a Sociology in India: Rejoinder to Dr. Bailey", *Contributions to Indian Sociology*, 4, 1968.

Fox, Robin, *Kin, Clan, Raja and Rule: Hinterland Relations in Pre-Industrial India*, Bombay: Asia Publishing House, 1971.

Frank, A.G., "The Wealth and Poverty of Nations", *Economic and Political Weekly*, 1970.

Gough, Kathleen, *Class Developments in South India*, Montreal: McGill University Press, 1975.

Gould, H., "Time Dimension and Structural Change in an Indian Kinship System: A Problem of Conceptual Refinement", in Milton Singer and B. Cohn (eds.), *Structure and Change in Indian Society*, Aldine: Aldine Publishing Company, 1968.

Gouldner, A., *Coming Crisis in Western Sociology*, New York: The Free Press, 1970.

Gupta, Dipankar, "The Political Economy of Fascism", *Economic and Political Weekly*, XII, No. 25, June 25, 1977.

Gupta, Krishna Prakash, "Sociology of Indian Tradition and Tradition of Indian Sociology", *Sociological Bulletin*, 23 (1), 1974.

Harper, E.B., "A Hindu Village Pantheon", *South Western Journal of Anthropology*, 1959.

Hazlehurst, L.W., *Entrepreneurship and Merchant Caste in a Punjab City*, Duke University, 1966.

Jones, Rodney W., *Urban Politics in India*, New Delhi: Vikas Publishing House, 1975.

Joshi, P.C., *Land Reform and Agrarian Change in India and Pakistan* (Report), 1971.

—, *Land Reforms in India*, ICSSR Trend Report, 1974.

—, and Damodaran, K, *Marx Comes to India*, New Delhi: Manohar Book Service, 1975.

Kothari, Rajni (ed.), *Caste in Indian Politics*, New Delhi: Orient Longman, 1970.

—, *Politics in India*, New Delhi: Orient Longman, 1970.

Ladejinsky, Wolf, "How Green is the Indian Green Revolution", *Economic and Political Weekly*, Vol. VIII, No. 52, December 29, 1973.

Leach, E.R. et al (eds.), *Politics in South Asia*, Cambridge: Cambridge University Press, 1970.

Lynch, Owen M., *The Politics of Untouchability* (Ph. D. Dissertation), Department of Anthropology, New York: Columbia University Press, 1966.

Madan, T.N., "For a Sociology of India: Some Classification", *Contributions to Indian Sociology*, 1965.

Majumdar, D.N., *Caste and Communication in an Indian Village*, Bombay: Asia Publishing House, 1958.

—, M.C. Pradhan, C. Sen and S. Misra, "Inter-Caste Relations in Godhankallan, A Village Near Lucknow," *The Eastern Anthropologist*, 8, pp. 191-214, 1955.

Marriott, McKim, *Caste Ranking and Community Structures in Five Regions of India and Pakistan* (Ph.D. dissertation), Chicago: University of Chicago Press, 1955.

Mencher, Joan P., "Conflicts and Contradictions in the 'Green Revolution': The Case of Tamil Nadu", *Economic and Political Weekly*, Annual Number, Vol. IX, Nos. 6, 7 & 8, 1974.

Mukherjee, Partha Nath, "Social Movement and Social Change: Towards a Conceptual Clarification and Theoretic Framework", *Sociological Bulletin*, 1977.

Mukherjee, R., in Barnes and Becker (eds.), *Social Thought from Lore to Science*, Vol. III, New York: Dover Publication, 1961.

—, *Social Indicators*, Delhi: Macmillan, 1976.

—, *The Rise and Fall of East India Company*, Berlin, 1958.

—, *The Sociologist and Social Change in India Today,* Delhi: Prentice Hall of India, 1965.

Mukerji, D.P., *Diversities*, Delhi: Peoples Publishing House, 1958.

Nicholas, R., "Economy of Family Types in Two West Bengal Villages", *Economic and Political Weekly*, 1961.

—, "Structure of Politics in Village of Southern Asia", in Milton Singer and B.S. Cohn (eds.), *Structure and Change in Indian Society*, Chicago: Aldine Publishing Co., 1968.

Oommen, T.K., "Sociological Issues in the Analysis of Social Movements in Independent India", *Sociological Bulletin*, 1977.

—, "The Concept of Dominant Caste: Some Queries", *Contribution to Indian Sociology*, New Series, No. IV., 1970.

—, *Charisma Stability and Change*, New Delhi: Thomson Press, 1972.

Patnaik, P., "Imperialism and the Growth of Indian Capitalism", in Robin Blackburn (ed.). *Explosion in a Subcontinent: India, Pakistan Bangladesh and Ceylon*, Penguin Books, 1975.

Patnaik, Utsa, "Economics of Farm Size and Farm Scale", *Economic and Political Weekly*, Special Number, Vol. VII. Nos. 31, 32, 33 & 1972.

Pocock, David F., "Inclusion and Exclusion: A Process in Caste System in Gujarat", *South Western Journal of Anthropology*, 13 (1), 1957.

—, *Mind Body and Wealth: A Study of Relief and Practice in an Indian Village*, London: Blackwell, 1974.

Raghavan, V., "Methods of Popular Religious Instructions in South India", in Milton Singer (ed.), *Traditional India Structure and Change*, Philadelphia, 1952.

Rastogi, P.N., *Cybernetic Analysis of Complex III-defined Problems in Organization* (mimeographed), Kanpur: Indian Institute of Technology, 1976.

—, *The Nature and Dynamics of Factional Conflict,* Meerut: The Macmillan Co. of India Ltd. 1975.

Rosenthal, D.B., *The United Elites: Politics and Government in Two Indian Cities*, Chicago University Press, 1970.

Rudolph, L. and S. Rudolph, "Surveys in India: Field Experience in Madras State", *Public Opinion Quarterly*, 22 (3), 1958.

Saberwal, Satish (ed.), *Towards a Cultural Policy*, New Delhi: Vikas Publishing House, 1974.

Saith, Ashwani and Tankha, Ajay, "Agrarian Transition and the Differentiation of the Peasantry: A Study of a West U.P. Village", *Economic and Political Weekly*, Vol. VIII, 14, 1972.

Saran, A.K., "For a Sociology of India", *Eastern Anthropologist*, 15 (1), 1962.

—, "Sociology of India", in Roucek (ed.), *Contemporary Sociology*, New York, 1957.

—, "Sociology of Knowledge and Traditional Thought", *Sociological Bulletin*, 14 (1), 1965.

—, "The Concept of Social Science", in K.D. Sharma (ed.), *Basic Issues in Social Sciences*, Bombay: Academic Journals of India, 1968.

—, "The Faith of a Modern Intellectual", in T.K.N. Unnithan, I. Deva and Y. Singh (eds.), *Towards a Sociology of Culture in India*, New Delhi: Prentice Hall, 1965.

—, "The Natural Sciences and the Study of Man: The Problem of their Synthesis in Contemporary Culture", *Eastern Anthropologists* 14 (2), 1961.

—, "Theoretical Anthropology and the Cult of Man", *Ethics*, LXVI, 1956.

Sau, Ranjit, "On the Essence and Manifestation of Capitalism in Indian Agriculture", *Economy and Political Weekly*, Vol. VIII, No. 13, March 31, 1973.

—, "Political Economy of Indian Agriculture: What is it All About?" *Economic and Political Weekly*, Vol. VIII, No. 20, May 19, 1973.

Shah, A.M., "Basic Terms and Concepts in the Study of Family in India", *Economic and Social History Review*, Vol. I, 1964.

—, "Historical Sociology (A Trend Report), In *A Study of Research in Sociology and Social Anthropology*, Vol. I (ICSSR), Bombay: Popular Prakashan, 1974.

—, *The Household Dimension of the Family in India*, New Delhi: Orient Longman, 1973.

—, Shroff, R.G. and Shah, A.R., "Early Nineteenth Century Village Records in Gujarat", in Tapan Roychaudhari (eds.), *Contributions to Indian Economic History*, 1963.

Shah, Ghanshyam, "Traditional Society and Political Mobilization: The Experience of Bardoli Satyagraha (1920–28), *Contributions to Indian Sociology* (NS) 8, 1974.

Silverberg, James (ed.), *Social Mobility in the Caste System in India*, The Hague: Mouton Publisher, 1968.

—, "The Great Tradition in a Metropolitan Centre: Madras", in Milton Singer (ed.), *Traditional India: Structure and Change*, Philadelphia: The American Folklore, 1959.

Singh, Rajendra, "Agrarian Social Structure and Peasant Unrest: A Study of Land Grab Movement in District Basti-East U.P.", *Sociological Bulletin*, 1977.

—, "Politicization, Protest and Peasant Movement in Uttar Pradesh: A Study in the Politics of Land Control in District Basti", in M.S.A. Rao (ed.), *Social Movements in India*, 1977.

Singer, Milton (ed.), *Traditional India: Structure and Change*, Chicago: Aldine Publishing Company, 1968.

—, *When a Great Tradition Modernizes*, New York: Praeger Publishers, 1972.

Singh, Yogendra, "Chanukhera: Cultural Change in Eastern Uttar Pradesh", in K. Ishwaran (ed.), *Change and Continuity in India's Villages*, New York: Columbia University Press, 1970.

—, "Role of Social Sciences in India: A Sociology of Knowledge, in S.C. Dube (ed.), *Social Sciences and Social Realities: Role of the Social Science in Contemporary India*, Simla: Indian Institute of Advanced Study, 1976.

—, "Social Anthropology of the Study of Rural and Urban Societies", *Economic Weekly*, reprinted in M.N. Srinivas, 1962, 1959.

—, "Sociology for India: The Emerging Perspective in T.K.N. Unnithan et al. (eds.), Delhi: Prentice-Hall of India, 1967.

—, "The Case of the Potter and the Priest", *Man in India*, 39 (3), 1959.

—, "The Dominant Caste in Rampura", *American Anthropologist* (February).

—, "The Scope and Method of Sociology in India", in T.K.N. Unnithan et al (eds.), *Sociology for India,* Delhi: Prentice-Hall of India, 1967.

—, *Modernization of Indian Tradition*, Jaipur: Rawat Publications, 1973.

—, *Religion and Society among the Coorgs of South India*, Bombay: Oxford University Press, 1952.

—, *Social Change in Modern India*, Berkeley: California University Press, 1966.

—, *Social Stratification and Change in India*, New Delhi: Manohar, 1978.

Singh, Yogendra and Oommen, T.K., *The Craft of the Social Sciences in India,* Centre for the Study of Social Systems, Jawaharlal Nehru University, New Delhi, 1977.

Srinivas, M.N., "Mobility in the Caste System", in Milton Singer and B.S. Cohen (eds.), *Structure and Change in Indian Society*, Aldine: Aldine Publishing Company, 1968.

—, "Social Environment and Managements, Responsibilities", *Economic and Political Weekly*, 10,11: 1975.

—, "Village Studies, Participant Observation and Social Science Research in India", *Economic and Political Weekly*, Special Number, 1975.

Staal, J.F., "Sanskrit and Sanskritisation", *Journal of Asian Studies*, 22, 1963.

Thapar, Romesh, *Tribe, Caste and Religion in India*, New Delhi: The Macmillan Company of India Ltd., 1977.

Thapar, Romila, *Past and Prejudice*, Delhi: National Book Trust of India, 1975.

Thorner, D., "The Peasantry Confronted with Industrial Capitalism", 1777–1970, 1973.

—, "Marx on India and Asiatic Mode of Production", *Contributions to Indian Sociology*, 1966.

Uberoi, J.P.S., "Science and Swaraj", *Contributions to Indian Sociology* (New Series), Vol. 2, 1968.

Verba, S., Ahmed, B. and Bhatt, A., *Caste, Race and Politics: A Comparative Study of India and the United States*, Berkeley Hills: Sage Publications, 1971.

Vidyarthi, L.P., *Conflict, Tension and Cultural Trends in India*, Calcutta: Punthi Pustak, 1969.

—, *The Sacred Complex in Hindu Gaya*, Bombay: Asia Publishing House, 1961.

Weiner, Myron and Kothari, Rajni, *Indian Voting Behaviour*, Calcutta: Mukhopadhayaya, 1965.

4

Indian Sociology: Retrospect and Prospect

Indian sociology, like most other social sciences in India, has grown through an encounter with the western philosophical and social scientific traditions. Its specificity in matters both of the choice of concepts and theories and the substantive coverage of the problems for study bears an imprint of this historicity. Nevertheless, sociology in India has also been deeply influenced by the numerous internal processes which signify the passage of India from a colony of the British to the status of an independent republic. Indian sociology, in various measures, embodies in its theoretic orientations and choice of themes for observation and analysis these historical forces which have constituted its 'social conditioning' (see, Singh, 1986). A sociology of knowledge perspective is, therefore, necessary to constitute and to comprehend the many trends and orientations with which the Indian sociology began its growth in India during the colonial period, the new theoretic, methodological and substantive concerns which emerged following independence, the internal differentiation that sociology has undergone during the past fifty years and the challenges and opportunities that sociology faces in the future in response to the changing 'social conditions' in India and abroad.

The Pre-sociological Beginnings

Sociology, before it took its place as a teaching discipline in the academic institutions in India, had emerged as a generalized social ideology which viewed the social institutions of the societies from a scientific evolutionary viewpoint at a global level. This was particularly so in the case of the societies with a history of past civilization. In the colonial context in which many such societies were ensnared, sociology became for the many intellectuals from these countries an ideology of revolutionary social and political movement for emancipation from the foreign rule. In the Indian case, this is illustrated by the publication of a journal, *Indian Sociologist* by Shyamji Krishna Verma, a non-resident Indian political and social revolutionary in Britain, in 1905. In London, Verma came into contact with Herbert Spencer, the founder of the British sociology. He was so deeply influenced by Spencer's sociological ideas that he established six fellowships for Indian students to study in Britain on the conditions that they would go back to India after completing their studies, would not undertake government job in India and would dedicate themselves to the social services in their country. He also instituted a lectureship in the name of Spencer for which he donated a thousand pounds (see, Chaturvedi, n.d.) The *Indian Sociologist* continued to be published from 1905 until the beginning of the First World War. Despite Verma's closer contacts with Herbert Spencer, it was not a professional journal. It published articles and commentaries on social, political and cultural issues which were of contemporary relevance and which articulated the reformist and democratic revolutionary ideologies. The printer of this journal was sentenced in July 1909 and the journal had to migrate to Paris for its publication. Shyamji Krishna Verma was himself a scholar of distinction in Sanskrit and an established Indologist who was appointed as a teacher of Sanskrit, Marathi and Gujarati at the Oxford University. Even though Verma was deeply influenced by the contributions of Herbert Spencer, his own journal did not focus upon sociology either as a discipline as enunciated by Spencer, nor did it focus primarily on social and cultural issues within the frame of reference of sociological categories, strictly speaking. The emphasis on social and political issues was rather generalized and issues discussed had a mix of the orientations of social reformism and political activism.

This orientation in sociological contributions in India continued during the first two to three decades of the nineties. Many Indian academics, trained in the universities of England, France and Germany, contributed to sociology directly and indirectly through their commentaries and exegeses on the writings of the European sociologists and social anthropologists, particularly with reference to their views on Indian society and culture. In a way, this tradition had its basis in the cultural and intellectual renaissance in India during the middle of the 19th century. We may refer in this context to the contributions of Rammohun Roy (1772–1833), Ishwar Chandra Vidyasagar (1863–1902), Swami Vivekananda (1863–1902), Swami Dayananda Saraswati (1834–1883), Swami Sradhananda (1856–1928), Dadabhai Naoroji (1825–1917), Lala Lajpat Rai (1865–1928), J.G. Phooley (1827–1888) and M.G. Ranade (1824–1901) and several others who through their writings and social movements created intellectual and social self-awareness in the country about India's cultural and civilizational strengths and yet pleaded for radical reforms in society in order to encounter the challenges of the western civilization and its colonial expansionism. This period of Indian history is a precursor to the many forms of cultural and political social movements, and it also coincides with the beginning of the institutionalization of the university and college systems in India based on the western pattern. The disciplinary foundations of the many social sciences including sociology and social anthropology were established during this period.

This period followed the inauguration of the early sociological writings by scholars in India either as a sequel to or in response to the writings by the western sociologists on India or in response to the issues of epistemology and history. Most of this type of writing tends to be dialectical and exegetic. The contributions of B.N. Seal and B.K. Sarkar could be mentioned in this context. In case of former, one witnesses critical and discursive response to the comparative evolutionary treatment of various societies and cultures, including that of India, by the British social anthropologists and sociologists, which often reflected not only the wrong premises in their treatment of other cultures or societies but also carried unjustifiable value loads. Seal refuted attempts to interpret the Indian social and cultural reality from a reductionist evolutionary frame of reference, so common in the early 20th century contributions of the western sociologists and social anthropologists. He maintained that institutions could only be compared if they were historically co-existent. Sarkar wrote extensively in response to the writings of the German Indologists and sociologists in whose writings one could clearly discern biases of the 'orientalist frame of reference'. Particularly, the contributions of Max Weber on Hinduism and the culture and social structure of Indian society came under his very critical analysis (see, Singh, 1983; Mukherjee, 1979). Similarly, many other social scientists such, A.R. Wadia, B.N. Dutta, K.P. Chattopadhyaya and S.V. Ketkar etc., created academic ambience through their writings for the teaching and research in sociology either directly or indirectly. One common stream of consciousness, however, in all these writings was that of historicity of the Indian civilization and its distinct cultural and social identity which was denied the centrality it deserved in most western social science or sociological writings on India. These contributions were not strictly in the domain of systemic sociological analysis of the Indian social and cultural realities but indeed, these had a very high degree of sensitizing effect on the Indian academic scene to provide legitimacy to the teaching and research in Indian sociology.

Early Sociological Beginnings

The teaching of sociology as an academic discipline, though still imbued with deeper humanistic and civilizational orientations, started at the Bombay University with Patrick Geddes joining as professor of civics and sociology in 1919 where he served upto 1924 (see, Mairet, 1957). Formalization of sociology in terms of methods and conceptual framework began with his contributions, but in a much diffuse and generalized form. Geddes' major focus was upon viewing social reality from a moral, communitarian, global and multidisciplinary perspective. He maintained that, "our great need today is to grasp life as a whole, to see its many sides in their proper relations; but we must have a practical as well as a philosophical interest in such an integrated view of life" (Mairet, 1957: xii). Geddes had exposure to various disciplines in sciences and humanities ranging from botany, zoology, mining, engineering to sociology. He was influenced by the works of the biologist Thomas Huxley and through him that of Herbert Spencer, the sociologist. He admired Huxley but disagreed with him on his emphasis to look at science from a purely amoral perspective. For this reason, he also admired the French sociologist August Comte, his positive philosophy and religion of humanity. He used to frequently attend the Comtean Church though it was laughed at by Huxley as 'catholicism without Christianity'. On this issue, Geddes differed from his teacher. Later, he moved to Paris from England and was deeply impressed by the French university tradition; its centrality on the pursuit of what Geddes calls the 'morality of truth', 'morality of action', and the 'spirit of immeasurable literary, scientific and constructive endeavour'. Here, he was influenced by Fredric Le Play's writings on regional and ecological aspects of civilization. Le Play's triadic categories of 'work, place and family' have deeply influenced Geddes' own schematization of conceptual categories for the growth of regional cultures of societies, particularly his schema of 'work, place and folk'. Similarly, one could also witness the impact of Comte in Geddes' formulation of the diagrammatic hierarchy of the sciences, with mathematics and logic being at the base, physics, chemistry and biology in the middle and sociology (not social physics as Comte adumbrated) at the top. Geddes had also schematically worked out the boundary conditions in which sociology could closely interact with other sciences. In this case, he listed anthropology, ecology and statistics as the major disciplines for interactive integration with sociology.

Geddes extensively used the technique of constructing 'property space' (in diagrammatic boxes) for generation of concepts and methods for sociological investigation. He emphasized the need for ethical, regional and communitarian sensitivity in sociological studies, but his primary emphasis was upon practical outcome and social engineering. To this end, we find him in the role of a moral architect along with his focus upon the physical architecture of town planning; he consistently laid emphasis upon the regeneration of city life and ecological self-awareness in the planning of the social and cultural habitats at regional and global levels.

Unfortunately, Geddes' entry into the Bombay University's teaching department was of a very short duration and his sociological approach which had a strong blend of empirical methods with philosophical orientations could not get time enough to be institutionalized. Nevertheless, he was instrumental in his successor G.S. Ghurye going to Cambridge for research in anthropology and taking the charge of the department on his return. Ghurye, a Sanskritist and Indologist of great eminence, brought to bear this scholarship together with that of anthropology in developing the pedagogy of sociological teaching at the Bombay University. This is reflected in the curricula for the teaching of sociology. It is also reflected in the researches that Ghurye himself did or directed his students to undertake. In his own writings we witness a creative blend of historicity with Indology, particularly where studies of social structure such as caste, occupation and race are concerned. One can also easily see his emphasis on comparative historical treatment of the formations of social structure and culture with a unique sensitivity to the notion of civilization. Ghurye contributed to sociological writings over several decades and his works cover a vast range of themes relating to the study of concrete structures such as rural and urban communities, social stratification, comparative cultural behaviours, processes of social change and social conflict, cultural styles (dress and fashion), and traditional social formations and sects such as the *sadhus* and *sampradayas*. He also made use of a multiplex of methodologies in these studies, ranging from diachronic historical observations of rural changes to empirical surveys and uses of historical materials and traditional-Indological texts. Even though empirical studies of micro-social systems do find a place in his sociology, his main focus has always remained on macro-historical and comparative studies. This tradition has been continued by his successors at the Bombay University.

Apart from his individual researches, Ghurye's larger contribution to the Indian sociology lies in the training of a whole generation of very distinguished sociologists who gave leadership to the profession in the country, and contributed to its institutionalization and modernization as a social science discipline. These sociologists led the direction of research and teaching in the field of sociology during the decade of the 1950's which witnessed a massive expansion in the number of universities and colleges in the country.

Another equally important centre for the early growth of teaching and research in sociology has been the Lucknow University, where the pioneering role was played by Radha Kamal Mukerjee and his two distinguished colleagues, D.P. Mukerji and D.N. Majumdar. Radha Kamal Mukerjee established the Department of Economics at the University of Lucknow in early 1930's and introduced the teaching of sociology as a part of economics at the M.A. level. It is of interest to note that both at the universities of Bombay and Lucknow, the teaching of sociology was not imparted exclusively; it was integrated with civics and political science at Bombay and with economics at Lucknow University. This is understandable considering the fact that during the first two to three decades of the 20th century teaching of sociology as an independent discipline was confined to very few universities in England, Germany and France, and its curricular structure had a broad multidisciplinary social science perspective. Some of the major universities in England, such as Cambridge and Oxford, started departments of sociology much later during the1960's.

The contributions of Radha Kamal Mukerjee like that of Ghurye are stupendous and multidimensional. Radha Kamal, unlike Ghurye, however, showed greater sensitivity to issues of sociological theory and methodology. Indeed, he is one of the earliest sociologist-economists in India to not only integrate the western theoretical and methodological paradigms in the studies of social and economic problems and issues in India but also the one who clearly lays down the foundation of a distinctive Indian sociological paradigm and theoretic structure. His contributions range from the study of slums and industrial labour problems, regional economic structures, problems of peasantry and agrarian economy, study of social stratification and caste (particularly using scalar methodology to measure social distance), study of the 'social structure' values and social ecology to a comparative philosophical treatment of civilizations. He undertook a critical and philosophical diagnosis of the emerging crises of human condition in the industrial societies and its civilization. The reach of his sociological and economic concerns and his treatment of these problems is indeed unique among the Indian social scientists. His sociology reflects not only the endogenous consciousness and the Indian civilizational anchorage, rather he continually responds creatively to most of the contemporary philosophical, theoretical and methodological orientations and shifts in the paradigms of the western social sciences and sociology. His lecture tour of the universities in America in 1930's brought him closer to many significant American social science orientations of that time such as the focus on social ecology, problems of urbanization and its morphological character, the importance of regional and institutional economics (such as in the writings of Commons, Veblen and Mitchell etc.) and the utility of empirical survey designs of research etc.

But one of the most significant contributions that Radha Kamal Mukerjee has made to sociology, and the debate on which has since continued in one form or another, relates to his formulation of a general theoretical paradigm of social science and sociology from the perspective of the Indian philosophical traditions. It is a paradigm which attempts to generate a universal general theory for the study of social and cultural phenomena as an alternative to the western theoretical approaches in sociology. He offers an alternative worldview of sociology and social science drawn from the philosophical traditions of the Vedanta, Buddhism and Taoism. These traditions, according to him, are embedded in the values of universal humanism and ethical piety rather than in materialistic rationalism or positivism. Mukerjee is perhaps the only sociologist of his times in India who attempted this ambitious alternative philosophical paradigm for generating a universal theory of sociology and social science both as a corrective and as an alternative to the western traditions of social science theory.

In his presidential address delivered at the Third All India Sociological Conference in 1958, on the theme *A Philosophy of Social Sciences*, he postulates an integral and interdisciplinary view of social sciences (including sociology and social anthropology) and diagnoses the dilemma of the western social science in its one-dimensional focus upon the analysis of human condition and social phenomena from the perspective of rationalistic utilitarianism (product of the Enlightenment period) treating humans as 'homo faber' rather than 'homo symbolicus'. He accepts the relevance of the dialectical method in social science reasoning but refuses to confine it to 'dialectical materialism'. He locates the roots of the dialectical methods in the Indian traditions of Buddhism and Vedanta philosophies. He finds their formulations to be more holistically embedded in logic for the scientific exploration of human realities. He also finds in this context the Taoist conception of being and self-identity to be integrally relevant. He writes:

> "The philosophy of dialectical materialism today promotes the universal notion of an inevitable pattern of development through struggles and conflicts of global revolution and war and subsumes all human progress within the dialectic of the economic movement. Modern evolutionary naturalism, Spencerian, Marxian or Bergsonian, reduces man's mind and values as passive entities manipulated mechanically by a vast process that he cannot intelligently direct or control. Evolution as revealed to modern thought has its many levels and dimensions in which persons, values and societies develop in nature. Values are creative and not merely means of adaptation to the environment. The environment also changes, acted upon by human goals, values and ideals" (Mukerjee, 1960: 118, quoted in Singh, 1986).

Mukerjee says that "man thinks and lives dialectically. All social relations and behaviour and values that lie deep seated in them embody polar principles and tendencies" but also that "through the dialectic of the Vedantic *neyti neyti,* Buddhist *sunyat* and Taoist namelessness, the self identifies itself in the reality and the supreme value" (ibid.: 4). Mukerjee thus refutes the logic of reductionism implicit in the western social science formulations of the human actor and social institutions. He postulates, on the other hand, a view of human actor as an eternal negotiator between the existential (deterministic) the transcendent. This he achieves through "the immanence in himself of the not-self, the neighbour, the whole universe" (ibid.: 5). This ability alone justifies the status of human actor as 'homo symbolicus', as value-creating being rather than one involved in mere innovation of technologies to resolve the daily problems of existential survival and development.

In his later contributions, Mukerjee, like P. Sorokin in the U.S.A., began to focus more on the study of comparative civilizations and his treatment of values and cultural traditions became more diagnostic rather than analytical. But his central concern for rendering the western social sciences free from their positivistic and utilitarian anchorage through integrating in their paradigms correctives from the Oriental, particularly the Indian philosophical and civilizational perspectives, remained intact.

D.P. Mukerji and D.N. Majumdar, both colleagues of Radha Kamal Mukerjee, contributed richly to the teaching and research in sociology and social anthropology. Their approach in some ways could be termed as supplemental to the established orientation. For instance, D.P. Mukerji, like Radha Kamal Mukerjee, acknowledges the relevance of the Indian tradition and philosophy for arriving at valid theoretical and conceptual schemes for the study of the Indian society. He, despite being sympathetic to Marxian method and logic, disputed its categories and conceptual structures which, he thought, were largely western-centric. He could see no relevance for many of its categories, for instance, the notions of class and modes of production as formulated in classical Marxism. Innovations were required in this regard for studying the Indian social realities. Such categories for studying the Indian society, according to him, should be derived from the Indian tradition and history, for instance, the traditional notions of community or *sangha* may be more appropriate to understand the social situation of the rural and urban structures in India rather than the notion of class. We see in this orientation a degree of similarity with Radha Kamal Mukerjee's propositions. But there is a degree of difference, D.P. Mukerji does not totally reject the Marxian contributions, particularly its dialectical logic enunciating the centrality of the processes of conflict and contradiction in the social processes of the society. Similarly, D.N. Majumdar supplements Radha Kamal Mukerjee's contributions to the development of the empirical tradition of research. But, beyond this, we may not find many similarities. Majumdar was a trained social anthropologist, a student of B. Malinowski and an avid field observer of the tribes and tribal cultures in India. His concern was more towards capturing the realities of the tribal cultures and social structure through ethnography and to observe its institutional linkages with the rest of the Indian society. His contribution to the ethnography of the Indian tribes is monumental indeed but his theoretical interests hardly go beyond ethnographic comparisons.

D.P. Mukerji, on the other hand, does reflect analytical-theoretical orientation in his writings, particularly when he uses the dialectical-historical perspective of 'Marxology' as he preferred to describe his approach, for the study of the middle class structure and formation in India. He also examines the processes of social change and planning in the country and demonstrates the relationship between the Indian tradition and the western conceptual frames of analysis. But he does not show the same degree of interest, as Radha Kamal Mukerjee did, about offering a general theoretical paradigm of sociology rooted in the Indian philosophy, history and traditions as a counterpoint to the western theoretical approaches. Trained in economics and history, and being a literary writer and novelist, D.P. Mukerji's approach to the teaching and research in sociology was more innovative and non-conventional. This led him to write on many themes of sociology, such as music, art and culture which were not conventionally popular during his days but assumed greater significance later as sociology began to grow through institutional expansion and disciplinary specialization.

The generation of sociologists from Ghurye to D.P. Mukerji, who led its teaching and research from the 1920's to the middle of the 1950's, laid a very solid foundation of the profession in India. In their own writings this generation was more encyclopaedic and macro-analytic in approach. The period of specialization has yet to begin. But we may have to remember that even in the west, disciplinary specialization and methodological sophistication in researches began to gain momentum following the end of the Second World War. These early beginners of the Indian sociology pioneered the vision of sociology and social science as having a historical-civilizational anchorage; they felt acutely uneasy in accepting the positivistic, utilitarian and the general evolutionary constructions and premises of the western sociology; they consistently introduced the perspectives of historicity, culture and values in the formulation of sociological concepts and their theoretical underpinnings; their sensitivity to the methodological aspect of sociological research was open-ended and broadly inclusive of all available techniques and methods as found appropriate. Research methodology or technique was supposed to be a matter of preference for the individual researcher, who, it was felt, should have maximum flexibility in devising and using tools for the observation, documentation and construction of the social reality.

Institutionalization of Sociology

A new phase for the growth of the Indian sociology was ushered in following independence. Its main attributes were: first, the professionalization of sociology; secondly, the emergence of the new institutional supports for its teaching and research (with the expansion of universities and colleges and funding agencies); thirdly, with such growth a beginning in the specialization in sociological researches in terms of the choices of themes and methods began to take place; fourthly, there was unprecedented growth in methodological consciousness in the discipline, and the teaching of methodology began as a specialized course at most places; fifthly, the emphasis upon the social relevance of the discipline particularly in the areas of development planning and social reconstruction of the society gained greater ascendancy; and finally, a debate on 'a sociology for India' began in a systematic manner. It began to be increasingly felt that the Indian sociology should reflect not only the philosophical, historical and cultural specificities of the Indian society but also it should accordingly improvise and innovate upon the existing sociological concepts and categories largely drawn from the western sociology.

Independence in 1947 released new historical forces and aspirations in the country. The country's political leadership, intellectuals and people were acutely conscious of the challenges of nation-building, development and reconstruction of the Indian society. A constitution reflecting the future vision of India as a republic was adopted. Within the framework of a mixed economy, a strategy for the planned development of the Indian economy and society was worked out. The Planning Commission was set up to formulate the priorities and plans for national development. Within its framework, organizations and institutions were set up for the expansion of higher education in the fields of sciences, technology, management, engineering, medicine, social sciences and humanities. Several research councils were set up to augment its growth. A large number of national laboratories in various fields of science were established; agricultural universities were opened; several institutes of technology came up in different parts of the country and there was an unprecedented growth in university and college education.

The teaching of sociology began to expand as new universities and colleges were set up contributing to the increase in the number of teachers and researchers. In order to provide funds and regulate the standards of teaching and research in the universities and colleges, the University Grants Commission (UGC) was created. Funds for conducting researches on policy related problems were also made available by the Planning Commission. The momentum among the sociologists and social scientists to conduct researches in the areas of greater social and economic relevance was accelerated. The new focus upon researches differed from those of the colonial times. The Planning Commission sponsored a series of studies in the areas of urban sociology, rural and agricultural development, the nature of poverty, the social and economic conditions of the weaker sections, the scheduled tribes and scheduled castes etc. Most of these studies were prioritized on the basis of their relevance for planning and development and in many cases based on the need to generate benchmark data required for development projects.

These processes, together with other developments in the field of education, contributed to the professionalization of sociology and social sciences. Sociology was now taught in various universities and colleges as an independent subject and full-fledged sociology departments were set up in the colleges and universities. Its teaching was no longer clubbed with either economics as at the Lucknow University or with civics and political science as at the University of Bombay in the past. The Indian Sociological Society, which for a number of years had confined its membership to the sociologists of the western India, became an all-India association of the Indian sociologists towards the end of the 1950's. The regional associations of sociology, particularly the one from the northern India, sponsored by the sociologists of the Lucknow University, merged with the Indian Sociological Society. The Society meets regularly and provides a national forum to the teachers and researchers of sociology in the country. It regularly publishes a journal, *Sociological Bulletin*, which is internationally recognized. It networks with the International Sociological Association of which it is an organizational member. These institutional processes of growth have broadened and deepened the national and international concerns of the Indian sociologists towards many sociological issues which may range from the theoretical and methodological to those of choices of themes of relevance in teaching and research.

The professional growth of sociology has contributed to the modernization and standardization of its curricular structure. This has been supported by the UGC which set up subject-wise national panels of professors to periodically review, upgrade and modernize the syllabi in consultation with its teachers. The UGC national panel of sociology undertakes and sponsors research projects, seminars, workshops, etc., to evaluate the state of the discipline and its profession to help in formulation of policies for the upgradation and modernization of the curricular structure of sociology. With the higher degree of the regional diversities in terms of institutional standards and linguistic policies in teaching, effort based is made to evolve consensus on the modernization of curricula by the participation of the teachers of sociology from all regions of the country in the work of the national panel. The empirical researches on the state of teaching of sociology and its profession in the country also help in formulating the issues that deserve discussion at the national level, and where the comparative international level of upgradation of sociology teaching and research is required. So far, the recommendations and suggestions made by the national panels have been widely appreciated and incorporated in the syllabi of sociology in the universities and colleges within the country. This has kept the curricula of sociology in India at comparable international standards.

The UGC's efforts towards modernization of the syllabi in sociology and improvement in the quality of teaching, teaching materials and aids cater mainly to the college and university levels of education. After independence, sociology was also introduced at the secondary level of school education. Even otherwise, the education at the primary and secondary levels of education in various subjects required institutional support for continual modernization of the quality and standard of teaching. The National Council of Educational Research and Training (NCERT) was set up to perform this task. NCERT has significantly contributed to the quality of sociology teaching at the secondary level in India through production of textbooks, training of teachers and conducting workshops and seminars from time to time in the country. The fact that sociology is being taught in India right from the secondary to higher degree levels is a testimony to its professional growth and institutionalization.

Impetus to the growth of sociology, particularly in the field of research, gained new momentum when towards the end of the 1960's the Indian Council of Social Science Research (ICSSR) was established. Its objective is to improve and promote the quality of research in social sciences in the country and to make funds and grants available for this purpose. It is also responsible for setting up research institutes of social sciences in the Indian states and provide them funds to undertake researches. It offers fellowships and grants to the teachers and students of sociology to conduct their own researches. It supplements the efforts of the UGC which mainly looks after the universities and colleges. The ICSSR has made a great impact upon the professional and disciplinary growth of the researches in sociology and social anthropology. So far, it has published three decennial surveys of researches done in India in the fields of sociology and social anthropology.

A significant aspect of the contribution made both by the UGC and the ICSSR to the teaching and research in sociology is that their efforts sharpened the concern for relevance in the evaluation and structuring of the pedagogy of the discipline (see, Singh, 1984). Theoretical researches apart, the focus on relevance tends to be a common value frame promoted both by the UGC and the ICSSR, the former seeks it in the curricula and the choice of the research projects and the latter focuses primarily on the selection of the research themes and methods. This is evident from the reports of the national panels of the UGC in sociology, social anthropology, economics, political science and geography.

We witness in these reports the sense of commitment of the profession of sociology and social sciences to reach higher level of achievement in quality of teaching and research. But we also observe that in matters of defining relevance, most members of the profession show unanimity about the indegenization of concepts and theories. Without erecting walls of separation between social sciences in India and abroad, it is felt that along with creative adaptation of concepts, methods and substantive discoveries made by social sciences in the west and in other countries abroad, the Indian sociologists and social scientists should aim at evolving concepts and methods in tune with Indian historicity, its social and cultural specificity and its goals of social and economic development. For instance, the report of the economics panel says: "the standard economics is supposed to explain the *modus operandi* of an idealized capitalist economy. The Indian economy being any thing but that, the orthodox paradigms must perforce collapse"; further, "most of the theoretical concepts evolved in the context of the developed industrial societies of the west are mechanically doled out to unsuspecting batches of students in this country. Not unnaturally we find these rarefied tools of analysis to be of little avail in comprehending their own situation" (see, Singh, 1979). A similar emphasis on indegenization of concepts and methods in the teaching and research is found in the reports of the panels in sociology and political science. Evidently, the notion of relevance as postulated by the sociologists and other social scientists goes beyond mere indigenization of the concepts or methods. It also covers the choice of problems undertaken for research and enunciation of their research methodology. It is evident from the policies both of the UGC and the ICSSR which aim at promoting researches in priority areas which are of national concern for social and economic development. The ICSSR constituted a standing committee of sociologists to promote studies on the educational backwardness of the scheduled caste and scheduled tribe students in various states of India empowering the committee to commission sociologists from these states to undertake research on this problem. The need for this arose because fewer sociologists were observed to be undertaking research projects of their own choice in this area of national concern. From time to time, the ICSSR in consultation with the social scientists evolves the priority list of the areas of research which are funded on a preferential basis. In this category we may refer to sociology of law, gender sociology, problems of the peasantry, minorities and deprived sections of society. The researches on the problems of health, poverty and malnutrition and of the problems of people in remote and more backward areas of the country also receive priority. These priority areas are continually revised and updated.

Differentiation and Specialization in Sociology

The processes of institutional recognition and professionalization of sociology contributed to the enlargement of the range of research interests of sociologists in India. Its linkage with the policy planning and social and economic development reinforced this process. Historically, the end of the Second World War had shifted the gravity of influence in the world of social sciences from Europe to the United States of America where social sciences and sociology had made unprecedented strides in the applied areas of sociological researches and brought about a myriad of innovations in research methodology. Even otherwise, the American sociological traditions had always had a relatively greater applied and policy oriented direction of growth in comparison to the European sociological tradition. This process of growth in the American sociology logically resulted in the differentiation and specialization in sociology. In fact, America had played a leadership role in this direction.

Thus, we witness a convergence of two types of influences of the American sociology upon the Indian sociology soon after independence. The first relates to the emergence of the American sociology as a domineering influence upon the European or even the global sociology following the Second World War, and secondly, its rich and unparalleled advances in policy-oriented research methodologies and techniques accorded it a leadership role in sociology and social sciences. As a consequence of these developments and also because in India the process of planned development had just started, the influence of the American sociology and social anthropology began to grow. Indian sociology increasingly came under the influence of the American sociological and social anthropological conceptual and theoretical orientations.

The process of differentiation in the Indian sociology at this juncture can be seen growing in two directions: first, in the expansion and diversification of the nature of the social, cultural and developmental problems which sociologists began to study and secondly, in the diversification and differentiation of methodologies and tools of research which were now available to sociologists and which sociologists and social anthropologists used increasingly. It may, however, be also pointed out that the emerging national concern for planned development of the Indian society and economy which ranged from rural development, urban planning, empowerment of the scheduled tribes and scheduled castes, weaker sections and minorities to the industrialization of the economy etc. had opened up a vast vista of researchable problems for sociologists and social scientists. The most urgent concerns in the early 1950's were, however, in the areas of rural development and agricultural modernization to overcome the acute problem of food scarcity.

In thematic terms, therefore, the first major differentiation in sociological studies in India was between rural and urban sociology. The decade of the 1950's witnessed a proliferation in the studies of the Indian villages. The pioneering work in this field was done by S.C. Dube, M.N. Srinivas, Ramkrishna Mukherjee, A.R. Desai and several other Indian sociologists. A large number of American and a few British and French social anthropologists also contributed to the village studies in various parts of the country. The American social anthropologist, Oscar Lewis who studied a north Indian village (and had formerly studied a Mexican village) was also associated with the Indian Planning Commission as an advisor. These village studies overwhelmingly had an anthropological orientation. Most were observational, descriptive and holistic in terms of coverage. They attempted a reconstruction of village social structure, culture and customs, its economy and polity etc. from an ethnographic perspective. Very few of them were analytical.

There were few exceptions; however, M.N. Srinivas, while portraying the caste profile of the village did make analytical use of a set of indicators of the caste status, such as ritual status, economic status, political status and status due to numerical strength to arrive at the concepts of 'dominance' and 'dominant caste'. The dominant caste was defined as the one which enjoyed a high status on all these or a maximum number of these status indicators. Similarly, he used the cultural attribute of the lower castes imitating the ideology and way of life of the upper castes to formulate the concept of 'sanskritization'. The attribute of the upper castes who imitated the lifestyle and values of the western civilization, on the other hand, he termed as 'westernization'. The concepts of sanskritization and westernization were extensively made use of by him and a whole generation of sociologists and social anthropologists to explain the processes of social change in India. Similarly, McKim Marriott used the terms 'universalization' and 'parochialization' to explain the dynamics of cultural values and practices in the 'folk-elite' traditions in villages and towns. This conceptual distinction is based on the Chicago university anthropologists, Robert Redfield and Milton Singer's schematic distinction between folk and elite cultures based respectively on the 'little tradition' of the former based on oral culture and the written or the textual tradition of the elite, called the 'great tradition' of culture. Marriott maintained that continually the elements from the folk cultural tradition were lifted up from its local oral ritual or cultural context and were generalized or 'universalized' in the textual (scriptural) great tradition of India. This process he reported from his observation of the cultural institutions and practices in India. Several studies of the folk cultural traditions soon followed.

Ramkrishna Mukherjee's *Dynamics of a Rural Society* and A.R. Desai's (edited volume) *Rural Sociology in India* could be quoted as studies of the rural society which departed both methodologically and analytically from the above social anthropological treatment of the village studies. The former makes use of statistical data from various sources to generate conceptual categories of the class structure in villages and analytically posits them to unravel the problem of rural social structure and development from a quasi-Marxist perspective. The use of the statistical data makes this study comparable to those in other regions and states of India, although Mukherjee confines his attention to West Bengal. A.R. Desai, in his book-length introduction to the *Rural Sociology in India*, explicitly makes use of the historical-systematic and Marxist methods of analysis for the understanding of rural society and its problems; of course, he also refers to the contribution of a few American sociologists who contributed to the systematic methodology for the study of the rural and urban phenomena.

Quite a few rural studies during this period were also conducted with the direct purpose of reinforcing the policies of rural development; this particularly related to the studies focusing upon the community development and extension services and the local panchayat institutions which were introduced by the government. Many American social anthropologists took part in such studies and in several studies, rural leadership, local political institutions and their historical role in rural self-governance were analyzed. In this venture, a number of political scientists also joined, and in course of time these and related studies contributed to the development of the behavioural school of political analysis and political sociology in India. S.C. Dube made a comprehensive study of the impact of the community development institutions on the rural society in India; among the political scientists the contributions of Rajni Kothari and Iqbal Narain are quite noteworthy.

A differentiation process within rural sociology emerged by the end of 1950's. It was first on methodological lines, between those who used anthropological and holistic method for the study of a single village and those who used statistical-survey data for the study of several villages using selected number of analytical variables. Between these two approaches were also studies of the rural phenomena from a folk-elite cultural perspective. Indra Deva and S.L. Srivastava have made in-depth study of the folk culture of villages not only holistically or within a single village but using a regional comparative perspective. A distinction thus between micro-systematic and macro-systematic studies of rural realities has emerged. Differentiation also seems to have emerged between those who study villages directly with the purpose of impact analysis of rural development schemes launched by the state and those who undertake village studies for understanding its institutional structure and its processes.

A large number of urban studies were also conducted during this period although their scale and coverage could not be comparable to the rural studies. The Research Programme Committee of the Planning Commission sponsored more than a dozen and a half studies of cities in India; these studies with a few exceptions were based on a survey design standardized by the experts in the Planning Commission in order to generate comparable data which could be used for urban planning and development. Not only sociologists or social anthropologists but economists, geographers and other social scientists were also involved. These urban studies did help in generating data about the nature of urban social structure, its institutional organization, the nature of urban services, land use pattern and urban demographic features etc. and only few of them such as the Calcutta survey by N.K. Bose contributed to our understanding of the cultural and sociological profile of the urban life. These studies, apart from contributing to urban policy planning, helped in generating interest among sociologists to study urban phenomena in India from its specific historical, institutional and cultural background. It also led to a number of studies of small towns and their socio-economic structure and processes. The studies which followed began to focus more on the rural-urban linkages in historical, institutional and structural-economic domains rather than studying villages or cities individually as social isolates. G.S. Ghurye's study of the 'urban community' and M.S.A. Rao's study of 'fringe villages' belong to this tradition. The study of the structure and formation of the urban life also underwent change as sociologists began to explore the specific rather than the general features of the urban social structure. A number of urban studies have concentrated upon the nature of the entrepreneurial classes in the cities. Satish Saberwal studied a town in Punjab to explore the structure and social mobility among the entrepreneurs whom he describes as the 'mobile men' and Milton Singer made a study of entrepreneurs in Madras. A number of studies of specific communities of traditional entrepreneurial classes have followed since then. These could be classified both in the categories of the industrial as well as urban sociology.

There is a logical relationship between differentiation and specialization in the growth of the social science disciplines. Of course, scholars also opine that the social sciences follow a cycle of differentiation and synthesis; each period of differentiation is in course of time followed by efforts to synthesize the ideas and substantive findings of the diversified social science contributions into an integrated or general theoretical framework. We find that during the decades of 1960's and 1970's in India pressure did begin to build up towards a need for synthesis particularly in uses of conceptual schemes and methods and also in some measure in the operationalization of the choice of substantive themes for study. Yogendra Singh's *Modernization of the Indian Tradition* (1973) represents an attempt to view sociological studies in India through a paradigm to demonstrate the logical linkages and integrative relevance of various isolated conceptual schemes and categories used by sociologists to analyse social change and modernization in the Indian society.

The differentiation in sociological researches now grew in several directions. One could now talk of sociologies in India rather than a single or synthetic sociology. For example, we begin to find research studies in the fields of sociology of rural and urban life, social stratification, industrial sociology, family sociology, sociology of religion, sociology of caste, scheduled caste/scheduled tribe, sociology of medicine, sociology of profession etc. Without being exhaustive, one could now visualize the theoretical and methodological diversities and tensions of differentiation and synthesis in the conceptual schemes and theoretical orientations of the sociological studies. It increasingly became difficult to have an objective view of social change in India without taking into perspective the various dimensions of the findings of the specialized studies of social phenomena. Their evaluation from a schematic and comparative perspective became necessary both in conceptual terms as well as substantively.

Social Change and Differentiation in Sociology

The process of differentiation and professionalization that we witness during the 1950's–1960's period owed its growth to the institutional expansion of sociology and the increasing contact and interaction of Indian sociologists with the researchers from the west, particularly America. By the decade of 1970's major changes took place both within and outside the country which began to impact upon the paradigms of sociology. The involvement of America in the Vietnam war had created a global disillusionment about that country which began to delegitimize its role and leadership; this process also reverberated in the world of social sciences and sociology. The focus on method and technique in sociological studies, identified singularly with the American influence in sociology, came increasingly under criticism for its emphasis on the premise about social systems being essentially consensual and self-integrative or self-maintaining. Functional theory in sociology, a counterpart of such methods, began to be treated as inadequate in diagnosing or analyzing the significant processes within the social system because it neglected the role of conflict and contradictions in the structure and process of social realities. Consequently, not only in Europe or the developing world, but also in America, many alternate theoretical paradigms, particularly those related to conflict theory, Marxist historical materialism or dialectical materialism, phenomenology, ethno-methodology and critical theories, began to gain acceptance. These developments were not *sui generis* but product of emerging global social situation; they exemplify the close relationship that has always existed between theory and social conditions that influence its orientation and growth.

In India, the results of the planned efforts towards social and economic development during the decades of 1950's–1970's were now visible in many directions. In rural India, green revolution had begun to take root, food self-sufficiency was within reach; the welfare policy of reservation had energized the scheduled castes, scheduled tribes and weaker sections to give impetus to new social movements and a 'limited elite' had arisen amongst them to provide leadership; the expansion of industries, government institutions, educational institutions, expansion of the governing and developmental bureaucracy, technocracy and professional services, law and order agencies, para-military and military forces etc. contributed to the expansion of the middle classes in urban areas; and green revolution, even though it was confined to a limited section of the rural peasantry, brought into existence a powerful rural middle class. These changes in society signified 'success' but also triggered many new dimensions of conflict and contradiction in the society indicating 'failures'. The incidence of inter-caste, inter-class violence in the villages increased; the marginalization of the weaker sections, the dalits, women, landless labourers, minorities, etc., was sharpened creating disillusionment and anxiety.

The impact of these changes in society upon Indian sociology during the 1970's onwards can be very clearly observed. The rural studies now increasingly began to use Marxist categories for sociological analysis; the community development projects and extension services came under severe criticism for their status quoism on policies of land reform and support to rich peasantry to the exclusion of the weaker sections. The contributions of A.R. Desai and K. Gough primarily exemplify this orientation. More than sociologists, a large number of economists conducted studies of the agrarian social structure and its processes of change using the categories and methods of Marxism; they operationalized several indicators drawn from the rural economy and society to measure its socio-economic formations; for example, 'feudalism', 'semi-feudalism', 'pre-capitalism', etc. The debate among the Marxist economists, in which a few sociologists also joined, issues raged as to which type of the above social formation the agrarian social and economic structures (region-wise) could be attributed to belong. But a more significant development in Indian sociology during this period was the recognition of the relevance of the studies of social movements.

From 1970's onwards, disenchantment from the functional explanation of social processes and structures had begun. It was noticed that societies underwent changes not merely through internal differentiation of roles and institutions as they underwent differentiation and growth, a postulate supported by the functional theory, but significant and sudden changes took place in societies through mass mobilization and movements of the people or concerned sections of society. This phenomenon was also recognized by Indian sociologists as they witnessed such changes happening in their own society. Moreover, the cumulative effect of the policies of planned development in India had by this time energized several sections and interest groups to mobilize protest movement to realize their demands which ranged from economic, social to political domains. The approach to the study of social change in India from the paradigm of social movement implied application of the theory of 'collective behaviour' in which the significant variables were: the existing state of disenchantment among the concerned people on a set of issues, construction of new identities, the ideological rationalization of the issues into specific goals, the emergence of a leadership, formation of an organizational base and its institutional networks and formulation of the strategies for articulation of demands through the movement in which not only protest but also its withdrawal or reconciliation played an important role.

Thus, a vigorous tradition of a sociology of social movements started in India. Since the studies of social movements were so far confined only to the historians and political scientists, the contributions by sociologists which introduced several sociological concepts and methods in the studies, particularly in the contemporary times, enriched the nature of the movement studies and also brought about an interdisciplinary orientation in sociology. M.S.A. Rao studied the SNDP reform movement in Kerala and published his findings in a systematic form. He also brought together in several volumes contribution of a large number of sociologists to the study of a variety of social movements in India. Peasant movements in various regions of the country were studied by A.R. Desai, T.K. Oommen, D.N. Dhanagare and Rajendra Singh. P.N. Mukherji made a systemic study of the Naxalbari movement in

West Bengal which had a unique place in social movement as its strategy was based on class struggle and violence. He made conceptual contributions to the study of violent social movements. Similarly, T.K. Oommen's study of the *Sarvodaya* and *Gramadana* movement in Rajasthan makes use of the conceptual-theoretical paradigm of 'charisma' and its sociological dimensions to explain the processes within a movement. Dipankar Gupta has studied the Siva Sena movement in Maharashtra and farmers movement in western Uttar Pradesh. The studies of women's movement through sociology of gender have gained momentum. Among several others, contributions in this field have been made by Neera Desai, Veena Majumdar, Gail Omvedt, Maitrayee Chaudhari, Lindsey Barnes, etc. A large number of studies on the *dalits,* backward classes, tribes and minorities have been completed. The contributions of Gail Omvedt and M.S. Gore can be noted as being rich both in terms of substantive analysis and theoretical contextualization. The second and the third survey reports in sociology and social anthropology published by the ICSSR outline in detail most of these studies as also give full account of the advances made and diversification or differentiation achieved by the Indian sociology.

Apart from the study of social movements, the study of structural and cultural aspects of the society gained momentum. I.P. Desai's study of the family system in Gujarat used a diachronic multigeneration perspective for the study of the family structure. This study has provided empirical evidence to support the theory of cyclical structural changes in the family system (joint-single-joint family structures) in place of the prevailing theory of continuum (change from joint to single family system) based on the western experiences. A.M. Shah made a systematic study of the family system in India using the concept of 'household' as the operational unit of the family. He also contributed to the tradition of historical sociology making use of geneology and local history.

Many studies on the sociology of social stratification in India were made which attempted to synthetically conceptualize the role of caste, class and power and other conceptual schemes to explain the structure and processes of status determination, ranking and differentiation in the Indian society. A major contribution to this field came from Andre Beteille. He used the categories of caste, class and power to analyze the changing principles of social stratification in a village in south India. This study has significant analytical value for general understanding of the changes in the system of social stratification. Notable contributions to this theme have been made by K.L. Sharma, Victor D'Souza, Dipankar Gupta and Yogendra Singh. Sociology of profession has emerged as a separate specialization and many studies of the professions and professionalization processes in India have been made. Lawyers, doctors, nurses, managers, civil servants, academics, etc., have formed the subject of such studies. Substantial contributions have been made by studies related to these new social structural phenomena; among the many sociologists who have contributed to such studies, we may refer to T.N. Madan's study of the medical profession, T.K. Oommen's study of nurses, N.K. Singhi's study of civil servants, J.S. Gandhi's study of lawyers and Yogendra Singh's study of university academics. Contributions have also been made towards the study of culture, leisure, communication and media etc. from the systematic sociological perspective. Yogendra Singh, T.K.N. Unnithan and Indra Deva attempted to evolve a theoretical approach to the study of culture and its changes in India from the perspective of the 'sociology of culture'. Communication system which was earlier studied by Y. B. Damle has now been studied more exhaustively. A systemic and critical study has been done by K. Sondhi. I.P. Modi has contributed to a sociological study of leisure and its changing patterns in one of the cities of Rajasthan.

As these new directions of study in sociology have gained strength, the studies in the conventional areas such as that of religion, caste and rural-urban structures etc. have also continued. Of course, these studies now imbibe new methodological and conceptual sensitivity which was absent during the past.

The decades 1980's–2000's have witnessed further differentiation in the Indian sociology. These refer to the choice of substantive areas of study as well as the theoretical concerns. During these decades, the global developments in sociology have already thrown up and crystallized new theoretic perspectives and greatly enlarged the substantive concerns in sociology. This has coincided once again with the new forms and directions of the structural and cultural changes, particularly in the developed societies of the west, such as Europe and America. These changes have had a bearing upon ideology, theory and issues for sociological explorations. The transition from the industrial to post-industrial phase of development in the western societies, poised as they seem to be on the verge of growing into a full-fledged 'information society', has exposed them to challenges and crises which manifest themselves at the levels of social structure, demography, culture, ideology, economy and polity. The process of globalization which these societies have sponsored worldwide through their technological and economic achievements is a synthetic expression of their successes as well as failures.

The decline in population and the ageing of society in Europe has necessitated the reliance on more and more migrant workers (skilled and unskilled) from the less developed countries. This results into inter-cultural conflicts and challenges of multiculturalism. The technological advancements in the production system make it possible to have economic growth without generating employment; resulting in the end of tenure jobs, job-security and institutions of trade unions and factory mode of production. The production process has moved from the pre-eminence of the commodity sector to that of services. The community and family structures have suffered a great erosion of roles. Computers, telephony and internet have abolished the community's social space which has now been filled up with the individual actor whose sense of freedom may have increased but the resultant individualism breeds subjective alienation and emotional anxieties. The processes of decision-making in the polity and economy have become too complex and faceless to be comprehended by common citizens. Hence, representative democracy, celebrated so far as being a major achievement is seen to be flawed requiring 're-invention'. The political party system is in disarray. Increasingly, the demand is made to move from representative democracy, which in practice is considered to be less accountable, than expected, to a form of participatory democracy through networking of the voluntary associations and decentralization at the grass roots. The industrial production system is also under challenge from the environmentalist movements, and governments are under pressure from the civil rights and human rights organizations. The weakening of the bonds of community and family and the perception that state is too faceless and unaccountable have strengthened these movements which support the causes of the migrants, refugees, women, children, marginalized sections of population and the ever new varieties of the underclass.

These changes in the structure of the societies of the developed world have not only led sociology to study new areas of substantive social concerns, such as the role of communication and media, ecology and environment, human rights, civil rights, multiculturalism and cultural identities, the structure of leisure and lifestyles and the future shape of the civil society etc., but theoretically, sociology has tended to become more reflexive, cognitive and interpretive. The empirical methods of observation and analysis have not been forsaken but the treatment of social realities using tools of empiricism and objectivity have been made responsive to the demands of empathy and reflexivity in the construction of social realities. This has resulted into a large-scale creative inter-mixing and synthesization of theories hitherto considered to be contradistinct.

Indian sociology following the decade of the 1990's has been deeply influenced by these developments in the western societies. Also, it has been influenced by many new processes of change within the Indian society, particularly those which reflect upon the social structure and political processes, issues of sustainability in economic growth, problems of ecological and environmental protection in the process of industrialization, displacement of population, particularly from the weaker sections due to urbanization, setting up of mega-industrial projects of irrigation dams, power units and atomic centres etc. The problems of corruption in public life, the protection of civil rights, reforms in the judicial system and public interest litigation, etc., have emerged as new issues of social concern. Social pathologies of homicide, suicide, dowry deaths, and social depravities and exploitation related to women, senior citizens and weaker sections tend to increase during the new processes of social change. The focus on these and several new social problems gains urgency as the country enters into a phase of change which is characterized by an anomalous growth in which the number of the middle classes and those below the poverty line is equalized. This may trigger many unanticipated social and cultural conflicts. It strengthens the legitimacy of the new social movements for the empowerment of the scheduled castes, scheduled tribes, backward classes, minorities, women and other deprived sections of the society. The third survey of research in sociology and social anthropology is indicative of the type of sociological studies which were conducted during the past two decades. The survey reveals that during this period major areas of research in sociology were science, technology and development, problems of the scheduled castes and protective discrimination, studies of old age, women's studies and women's development, sociology of youth in India, culture communication and development, political sociology and political anthropology, crime, delinquency and correctional methods, social movements: old and new, sociology of religion and rural development (see, The Third Survey of Research in Sociology and Social Anthropology, Vols. I and II, 2000). We may notice that there has been a continuity in certain areas of research from the past, and at the same time new areas of emerging sociological concerns have begun to be investigated. The reports also reveal that even though the areas of study in some instances remain conventional, the analysis and theoretical treatment of the data now invites fresh conceptual and methodological explorations.

An important feature of the sociological researches during the period 1980-2000 is that the institutional context in which these researches are being carried out has differentiated. Formerly, universities, institutes and colleges etc. comprised the institutions from where most sociological researches originated. Now, the country has seen a stupendous expansion of the 'non-governmental organizations' which not only conduct but also fund sociological researches. Most of these researches are in the applied sociological area and cover themes which conventional sociologists are bound to neglect. The studies of human rights, environment and ecology, empowerment of women and children, studies of displaced communities, social forestry, etc., are a host of new areas in which these voluntary organizations have been instrumental in sponsoring or conducting researches.

Towards a Sociology for India

An important area of sociological debate in India which has persisted relates to the quest for a particularistic Indian sociology. As we have noted in the writings of Radha Kamal Mukerjee and D.P. Mukerji, the emphasis on the development of a paradigm of sociology drawn entirely from the Indian philosophical traditions was visualized, but its focus was not on a particularistic Indian sociology. Its aim was to sensitize sociology in general to the perils of gross applications of the methods of positivism and scientism. But, the new debate, initiated by Louis Dumont, suggested that Indian sociology could be confined to the study of ideology of the Indian society. He identified 'hierarchy' or caste as the central ideological principle on which the social structure of the Indian society was anchored. He distinguished this ideology from the western ideology of 'equality' as a measure of contradistinction between the sociology of India and the western sociology. According to him, the Indian sociology is to be founded upon Indology and anthropological observations. The journal *Contributions to Indian Sociology* which was jointly edited by L. Dumont and D. Pocock published the debate between him and Pocock on this premise in the numbers issued in 1957 and 1960. Pocock disagreed with Dumont's proposition as according to him sociology studies not merely structures of society constructed ideologically but also as empirical observable facts. Hence, Pocock felt one could not confine sociology to any particularistic domain. Its findings had inter-societal comparability.

This debate, however, has generated substantial sociological articles and books in which the implications of a sociology for India as a particularistic discipline have been examined. Starting from 1957 the debate has continued in the columns of the *Contributions to Indian Sociology* (new series edited by T.N. Madan et al) well upto the 1980's and continues to simmer. In these debates, the Indian sociologists recognize the need for indigenization of concepts and tools of sociological investigation. The premise of L. Dumont, however, has been overwhelmingly rejected. Even if the centrality of caste system in the social structure of India is accepted, the historical and empirical data on caste in India do not support the hypothesis of its being entirely an ideological system. Caste has many other features rooted in the Indian economy, power structure and instruments of control and exploitation. Indian sociologists tend to accept the need of indigenization of concepts in sociology but at the same time also hold that these may have to be logically integrated with other comparable principles of ranking and social differentiation to offer general explanation. For example, caste could be an indigenous cultural principle of social ranking but its more universal meaning located it in the principle of status determination which may vary from society to society.

Over the years, particularly following the period between 1990 and 2000, the debate on the sociology for India has rather become less resonant. The Indian sociology has gained a very substantial identity of its own which is evident from the size of sociological researches conducted in India. The three consecutive surveys conducted of the researches done in sociology and social anthropology during this period by the ICSSR bear testimony to this fact. In these researches we witness a creative degree of intermix between the uses of the indigenous categories with the application of universal sociological concepts. As the Indian sociologists have expanded the scope of their interests, they have also thrown up methodological and theoretical insights which have been made use of by the sociologists from other societies. Indian sociology is moving fast from the earlier position of self-consciousness to a mature self-confidence, readily interacting and establishing partnership with sociologists at the global level.

The Future Directions

It is hazardous to talk of the future. In the case of the researches in Indian sociology and its future directions of growth, surmises can be reasonably attempted based on two parameters: first, on the basis of the trends in sociological researches conducted so far; and secondly, on the basis of the new challenges that processes of social change and transformation may throw up deserving sociological attention. The trends of researches in sociology so far have indicated that sociology responds closely to examine the new emergent problems arising out of social changes. The researches tend to be both diagnostic or policy-oriented as well as analytical. The future changes in India will result both from the cumulative effects of the previous changes in society and from the new and the predictable as well as unanticipated changes on account of the impact of the globalization and liberalization of economy, and also on account of the revolution in the technology of information and mass media (Singh, 2000). These changes will have deeper impact on culture, style of life, occupational structure, processes of urbanization and the nature of the family and community life. Indian sociological researches will have to focus upon these problems. The analytical and theoretical approaches will have to be creatively adapted to meet with the demands of the researches in the new areas. Already, the involvement of the non-governmental organizations in conducting social researches has highlighted the need for participatory researches. A greater degree of innovativeness and reflexivity would be required in the sociological researches as new issues and problems of social change are encountered. But, the direction of movement in these researches is bound to remain cumulative rather than show unexpected leaps and bounds.

References

Chaturvedi, Jagdish Prasad, *Pravasi Krantikari,* Publications Division, Government of India, New Delhi, 1985.

Indian Council of Social Science Research, Third Survey of Research in Sociology and Social Anthropology, Vols. I & II, New Delhi: Manak Publications, 2000.

Mairet, Philip, *Pioneer of Sociology: The Life and Letters of Patrick Geddes*, London: Lund Humphries, 1957.

Mukerjee, Radha Kamal, *A Philosophy of Social Sciences*, Presidential Address at the Third All India Sociological Conference, 1958.

Mukherjee, Ramkrishna, *Sociology of Indian Sociology*, Bombay: Allied Publications, 1979.

Singh, Yogendra, "Constraints, Contradictions and Interdisciplinary Orientations: The Indian Context", *International Social Science Journal*, 31 (1), 1979.

—, *Image of Man: Ideology and Theory in Indian Sociology*, Delhi: Chanakya Publications, 1983.

—, *Culture Change in India: Identity and Globalization*, Jaipur: Rawat Publications, 2000.

—, *Indian Sociology: Social Conditioning and Emerging Concerns*, New Delhi: Vistaar Publications, 1986.

—, *Modernization of Indian Tradition*, Jaipur: Rawat Publications, 1973.

5

Functional Metaphor in Indian Sociology

In the present state of theory in sociology, most identifications of sociologists with a particular 'theory' indicates not as much their commitment to a process of formal theorizing as to their affirmation of an ideology. Most theoretic attempts towards formalization either end up in application of theory to explain a marginal or insignificant segment of reality or to near abandonment of formal explanations in the face of social realities of macroscopic relevance. This is particularly true for functional theory in sociology, but its parallelism for other 'theories' would not entirely be unfounded. In a formal sense, functional propositions have a teleological character. All institutional interactions and linkages constituting a system must be homoestatiscally integrated. In case of a social system, as examined by philosophers of science, for instance, Ernest Naegel and Karl Hempel, these prerequisites of formalization simply do not exist. The isomorphism between organic system and social system does not exist. In the absence of homology between the two systems functionalist theorizing in sociology takes recourse to metaphors and analogies.

However, these metaphors or analogies in sociology drawn on the model of the organic systems have undergone deeper and variegated logical and intuitive transformations, based on both in-depth observation of comparative social systems and refinement of the logical structure of categories. The richness of observational experiences in cross-cultural settings has in progressive stages contributed to the conceptual refinements in functional sociology. In this process, one witnesses ascendancy of metaphoric reasoning over that of simplistic analogy. The emphasis shifts not only to systems in self-maintenance but also in self-transformation. Merton's portrayal of basic similarity between the functional and dialectical paradigms particularly takes note of this point. Others have been inclined rather to giving up the nomenclature of functional sociology by encompassing it in the very structure of sociological craftsmanship. These tendencies clearly indicate the triumph of 'metaphor' over 'analogy' in the paradigm of functional analysis. Analogous mode of theorizing does not disclaim formal theory. Its commitment to positivism or even scientism persists. Its claim to value neutrality is rather strong and it sharply distinguishes between science and ideology. All attempts towards model-building using organic assumptions about society may belong to this category of theorizing. Its catholicity in respect of system maintenance or consensus as being the primary tendency of societies is uncompromising. The place for conflict in this paradigm only exists as a deviation.

It might appear that during the fifties the functionalist orientation in the Euro-American setting began to undergo a metaphoric transformation. Merton's adumbration of a middle-range theory was its beginning, but the contributions of Talcott Parsons and N.J. Smelser in the *Economy and Society*, and those of Lewis Coser and Ralph Dahrendorf later, tend to manifest its near-maturation. What does this metaphor of functionalism imply? The answer to this question may be briefly summed up as: (1) Assumption of a system in a process of self-maintenance within its internal-external setting through dual mechanisms, (a) that of socialization at the level of personality, and (b) of institutionalization at the level of roles or human activities. (2) Postulate of consensus in the maintenance of the system (derived from the above premises) together with possible *autonomy* of conflict in the system triggering needs for. (3) Reworking of consensus leading to even radical social transformations. Smelser's explanation of the industrial revolution falls within this category of functionalist metaphor. The nature of this conflict might even inhere dialectical reasoning occasionally through the process of polarization on binary lines or as arising out of a symmetry of values or power. Most conflictual situations imply such a symmetry. But, the notion of dialectics as used here departs basically from its formulation in Marxism, where it is endowed with evolutionary historicity. The use of dialectics in functionalist metaphor, especially in the early works of Parsons and the contributions of Coser and Dahrendorf, are of structuralist variety. Parsons, in his thesis on 'evolutionary universals', does depart from this cognitive frame. But he used the term 'evolution' without being fully historical. (4) The functionalist metaphor treats change both as adaptive deviation from the dominant system pattern as well as an occasional system transformation. It thus deals both with changes in the system as well as changes of the social systems. Implicit distinction here is between what is normal and what is historical. In actual practice, however, the studies using functionalist metaphor abound to the near-paucity of social movements or revolutionary transformations. (5) The metaphor of functionalism commits itself strongly to scientific methods and empirical techniques. Indeed, its major contribution to sociology has been not only in the domain of conceptual categories but more prominently in the fabrication of tools of observation, analysis of data and construction of social reality. On this account, however, functionalist sociology has been charged with 'abstracted empiricism', scientism, fallacies of instrumentation and reification. But, most of these refer only to the abuses of certain tools of investigation rather than their logic of discovery.

We have dwelt at some length with this metaphoric shift in functionalism in sociology in order to balance the perspective in our evaluation of the Indian sociology. In most critical commentaries functionalism has been charged with being an ideology of status quoism, bourgeoisie conservatism and mindless positivism. It is also considered to be devoid of a radiological content. In his treatment of Talcott Parsons, Elvin Gouldner makes most of these points with only one exceptional departure in his perception, that is, possibilities of convergence between the Marxist and the western (an euphemism for functional) sociology. Though critical of functionalism of Talcott Parsons, Gouldner does not discard totally the metaphors of this theoretical orientation which he has used effectively in his own studies of complex organization. The idea of theoretical convergence, however, is evocative of the general crisis in sociological theorizing. This refers to a host of cognitive and historical forces generated during the past few decades in the western societies that impel most social scientists to move away from the quest for formal theory. C. Wright Mills' quest for 'sociological imagination' was a product of this crisis and the quest for a new metaphor.

One may ask: why substitute metaphor for theory? There is a basic reason. A theory in its formal sense implies a historicity and near-universal validity. It refers to a level of abstraction where the specificities of historical experiences become blurred if not evanescent. However, at this level of theorizing, the social science products, though high in explanatory power, are low in social relevance. Tautologies replace reasoning. In such a situation, even intuitive reasoning begins to take better of social science theory. The hiatus between the formal and the substantive becomes acute. The metaphoric thinking in sociology is a halfway house between abstracted and empty formalism and dense substantive empiricism in social sciences. I must, however, confess that such metaphoric tension is not only characteristic of functional sociology. One might witness similar tensions in Marxism and phenomenological sociology as well. The search for 'parameters' in place of 'variable' by Peter Worsely, and for middle range theory by Merton only refer to this dilemma of sociological theorizing. An important implication of this, however, is that functionalism as a metaphor offers possibilities of creative variations in different socio-historical contexts. This point assumes significance when we try to analyze the elements of functionalism in Indian sociology.

Indian Sociology

Cognitive structure and methods in Indian sociology have been deeply conditioned by colonial historical experience. One does notice in this context some dissociation between the sociological works of the Indian sociologists and the foreigners, especially the colonial administrators-turned-sociologists or social anthropologists. In the works of C.H. Hutton and W. Wiser, the elements of early functionalist orientation tend to be obvious, but not so is the case of pioneer sociologists, G.S. Ghurye, Radhakamal Mukherjee and D.P.

Mukerji who were all engaged in monumental efforts to understand the Indian reality.

The difference of perspective here is not to much of social anthropology as against sociology. The difference is primarily between the colonial and the nationalistic perspectives. The British administrators and scholars tended to look at the Indian society from the framework of comparative functionalism and comparative history. The objective was not only to understand but also to govern. The mix of politics with social science in the works of these scholars is an affirmation of social conditioning of theory and its metaphoric existence. The recurrent themes in the early sociological and social anthropological writings of western scholars on India tend to revolve around a series of polarities, such as caste-race, primitive-civilized, peasantry-aristocracy, country-city, outcaste-Brahmin, Hindu-Muslim, etc., which posits, on the one hand, questions of cultural lag, or evolutionary back-dating, regression and, on the other, structural dissociation or autonomy for each of the polar categories. Effort seldom was to see the interconnections between these structures in a historical civilizational depth. For instance, the British administrators always portrayed village as an autonomous reality which indeed it was not. Perhaps to see the place of an Indian village in the background of its organic linkages with regions, of the towns, capital city or sacred city would have involved the dynamic unity of the economy, polity and culture of the Indian society which colonialism was systematically attempting to play down.

The shift of emphasis in the treatment of such systems as village, caste, tribe, family, kinship, etc., in heuristic isolation of the one from another by early British and other foreign social anthropologists and sociologists becomes the centre piece of Indian functional sociology which was to be continued by some Indian sociologists even after independence. The mainstream of the early Indian sociologists, however, did not succumb to such temptations. In their writings we find emphasis on history, civilizational unity and continuity, identification of regions and their economic, political and cultural integration, both internal and in the context of the nation as a whole, the study of social structures, such as caste and class, agrarian strata and political economic systems in comparative historical frame of reference, and analysis of the place of the Indian tradition and forces of transformation within it, in the context of western contacts, both colonial and non-colonial. The dominant themes of these studies appear to have their anchorage in these sociologists' quest for national identity, systematic needs of development and change through reform, synthesis and innovation in the culture and social structure. The cultural and political encounter with the west and its sociological implications for our society constituted the central matrix of their consciousness and their intellectual response.

The theoretical choices in most writings of the pioneers of Indian sociology were at best eclectic, emphasis generally being on comparative historical and ideological foci. An interplay of vague theoretical responses ranging from the British evolutionism to German historicism, from American institutionalist and regional sociology to Vedantic dialectics, an Indianized form of Marxism, reflect the intellectual perspective of this age of macroscopic sociology. Though application of functionalism in the works of social anthropologists of this period could be discerned, especially in their studies of caste and tribes, it did not dominate the theoretical orientation of the Indian sociology of the forties and about. The culture of 'research methodology' which began to dominate the sociological thinking and practice in the fifties had not yet emerged in India and most sociological researches were based on individual scholar's own entrepreneurship, innovate the insights and intuitive sensitivities. The emphasis on a methodology, which forms the most significant element in the functionalist metaphor of sociology, was thus non-existent in this period of Indian sociology.

Specific Sociologies and Functionalist Metaphor

The fifties saw in India a shift from the earlier tradition of macroscopic sociology of the pioneers to what may be called, for the lack of a more expressive term, 'specific sociologies' of individual entities and sub-systems. This also coincided with the rise of a culture of research methodology, 'scientific' precision in tools of observation and reproduction of interpretive meanings from facts. It was also a move away from philosophical and historical anchorage of categories of sociology and its broader and bolder intuitive generalizations. Such efforts in sociology, which referred to matrices of civilization, cultural movements and comparative history of institutions, were now treated as of no 'scientific' consequence or even as 'unsociological'. The meaning of sociology in this phase of research does indeed seem to identify sociology with a set of categories in systematic logical interconnection, which had all the frills of a science. Emphasis on structure, role and status, power, institutions and value processes of institutionalization, differentiation and change, in categorical sense, constituted the vocabulary of this new sociology. This tendency was reinforced by rapid influx of American-British textbooks in sociology and contacts between scholars from these countries and our own scholars.

When we closely observe the process of inclusion and exclusion of categories in the sociology of the fifties in India, we witness two major consequences: one, it indeed developed a more tightly structured and logically closed system of concepts. Concepts were such that could be easily operationalized (most of them were already operationalized in the western setting), had close empirical referents, were devoid of obtuse historico-philosophical generalities, and intuitive value judgments. Most importantly, the feedback between categories and empirical verification became more rigorous and the basic element of the sociological craft. Secondly, the problems which now sociologists began to select for study were more specific and defined largely in microscopic setting. The selectivity of problems was determined by this internal shift of orientation in the cognitive and methodological self-image of sociology; but it was also influenced by external factors, such as governmental funding of research in specific developmental areas, setting of styles by foreign sociologists, and the continuity of past traditions in the choice of problems for research.

The most popular areas of research in sociology during the fifties were village community, tribe, caste, family and religion. In addition, many studies of planning and development constituted specialized concerns by a considerable amount of sponsored research. The studies of village community were undertaken with a variety of frames of reference, but three tendencies could be clearly discerned. These are evaluative studies trying to diagnose sociologically the interaction between village social structure and institutions and the targets of planned socio-economic development. Such studies only accidentally tried to offer generalized postulates about the nature of the village community.

These studies were not designed as such for construction of social reality in the context of a 'theory'. Metaphoric associations could, nevertheless, be associated in their findings: that institutions do not inhibit development, that social structure and its hierarchy, especially economic power, does tend to channelize the benefits of development to a narrow caste-class grove, and that factors both within the village as well as without constitute the forces of social change, especially mass communication and politicization. Most studies of community development and panchayati raj in the villages come closer to confirming this. No criticism of the structure of public policy, however, was implied or attempted in these village studies.

In addition to the above, we have two types of preeminently sociological studies of village community in India during the fifties. One, which drew its inspiration from the British social anthropology, its emphasis being on the construction of the structure of village as a social entity, with all ramifications of its internal differentiation and external linkages. Emphasis here was not so much on values, traditions and ideas as on categories of status, role, power and institutions in totality, generating processes of interaction. Bailey's village studies in Orissa come closer to the explication of this orientation, but several studies could be included in this category. The second kind of village studies have their inspiration in the American social anthropology led by Robert Redfield and his associate Milton Singer. In these studies, there was a designed conceptual project that we have analyzed elsewhere as that of civilization and tradition. More than on social structures, focus here was directed on the structure of values, institutions and traditions. The forces of social and economic changes were in these studies seen within the framework of the integrative and conflictual mechanisms of tradition. Hence, the study of festivals, rituals and deities along with the ethnography of the village. The teams led by Singer and Marriott have generated considerable material on village reality in India.

The village studies conducted by prominent Indian sociologists during this time, such as M.N. Srinivas, S.C. Dube, A.R. Desai and others, though bearing some impress of both the above orientations, belong, to my mind, to different approaches. Among the Indian sociologists, Desai clearly followed Marxist orientation in his studies. Dube's Indian village is a sociological construction of a village in all its facets of integration and tensions, primarily undertaken from a role-status differentiation perspective. Dube also attempts to analyze the processes of change in response to both internal and external forces. Srinivas carried the sociological perspective much deeper in his studies and offered as it were a masterly synthesis of both structure and tradition as analytical categories. It is this unique effort in the village sociology of Srinivas that constitutes a distinctive contribution.

The studies of caste were an organic part of the village studies. The processes of caste differentiation, mobility and hierarchy constituted its main foci. Much data was generated on the mobility in the caste system through the processes of sanskritization, westernization and accumulation of resources and power. The phenomenon of dominance and cultural persistence in the operation of caste hierarchy was particularly investigated. In all these studies, not only the element of segregation but also unity of the worldview of pollution and purity was highlighted as the main thread that rendered caste studies symptomatic of the changes in Indian structure and tradition. The principles of community and cooperation, the symbiotic role of the *jajmani* system, and the aspiration to move up in caste hierarchy within the cultural matrix of pollution-purity were aspects which drew the attention of sociologists.

The attributes of functional analysis in Indian sociology are in popular image associated with this phase of village and caste studies. It, however, needs to be closely examined. The factors which impel sociologists to characterize these studies as functional are first, an overt systemic assumption about village and caste within the framework of principles of cooperation and compatibility. In the caste system it was assumed through the universal dominance of the pollution-purity values and in the village context the integrative relationships of caste, *jajmani* and family, kinship and social ecological distinctiveness. Thus, a consensual worldview about the social structure of the village and caste was an implicit element in most of these studies. The entire debate on whether village could be treated as a valid *sociological* reality for investigation or whether the village had a collective consciousness as a unit of social reality related to this theme. The principles of communality in rural social relationships were indeed overportrayed. Oscar Lewis, in his studies of factions in villages, drew a very benign picture of these otherwise contentious and jealous institutions. He went even so far as to suggest usage of this institution for developmental purposes.

The second aspect of these studies relates to their treatment of social change. The notion of change in most of these studies is that of systematic adaptations. The time dimension is simply diachronic. The notion of conflict exists but it is reconcilable within the overarching canopy of the structure and tradition. The historical sensitivity is missing from most paradigms of changes used by this generation of sociologists. On the issues of policy of change and its phenomenology sociologists do not raise any questions; they do not even attempt to judge it or evaluate it. They simply accept the model of change as sponsored by the state as given. The critical element in sociological thinking is thus largely mute. Thirdly, these studies are conducted with much methodological sophistication. Meticulous care is taken about the objectivity of observations, recording of data, and the use of designs of investigation. The 'scientific' sociological craft dominates in these studies, which is also an organic part of the functionalist culture in social science.

Despite all this, the affinity of these studies to functionalism is simply metaphoric. The teleological assumption about the nature of either caste or village as a system is at no stage projected, nor it is substantiated. On the contrary, the systems both of caste and village are exposed to serious doubts qua systems, their linkages outcrossing the confines of a local ecology in case of the village or lineage and kinship in case of caste. The system boundary of both these entities tends to be regional if not pan-Indian in character. At this level of exposure, homoestasis self-corrections are ineffective and nebulous. On the contrary, contradictions are generated by the forces outside the system which not only cannot be accommodated but call for restructuration of roles and values. Bailey's concept of 'bridge action', Srinivas' focus on village disputes and Orenstein's portrayal of inter-village rivalries and tensions, not only draw our attention to the conflicts in the systems of village and caste but also their pervasive dynamic significance. This dynamics is not always intra-systemic as most crucial contradictions emerge from state legislation, constitutional enfranchisement of people and jural reforms in social, economic and political rights. These several forces contributing to sanskritization, to which Srinivas drew attention of sociologists, had them in the making in the process of census operation initiated during the British rule. The literature on the sociology of caste and village of this period does visualize the systems in states of adaptive accommodation, but it also leaves the system boundaries undefined and also the encounter that these systems have with outside systematic forces reflect often that contradiction. Such formulation of the system properties does at no account harmonize fully with a functionalist model. Its similarity with this model is only metaphoric.

The same is the case of the studies of religion. Srinivas' *Religion and Society among the Coorgs of South India* might be cited as the best sociological study of this period. It has obvious links with structural notions, especially in the analysis of rituals. But it also indicates the multiplier ideological inconsistencies in the co-existence of the Sanskritic and non-Sanskritic rituals and beliefs. Srinivas writes:

> Both the Sanskritic and non-Sanskritic modes of propitiation exist cheek by jowl as far as the bulk of Coorgs are concerned. The more enquiring of the men see the two modes of propitiation as mutually inconsistent, but such inconsistency does not seriously trouble anyone. All over India, Sanskritic and non-Sanskritic customs, often involving beliefs, regarded as mutually inconsistent, are found existing together. Usually, the non-Sanskritic custom, either drops out or is transformed to suit the Sanskritic custom, but this process takes a very long time. There is also no doubt, however, that the non-Sanskritic customs of every caste as well as those of sects and peripheral groups are continually being Sanskritized. This has been happening for over 2,000 years all over India (1952: 167).

I have quoted the above passage to illustrate the fact that in Srinivas' study of the structure of rituals the emphasis on the historical process is not subdued. Within the framework of interaction over time the Sanskritic and non-Sanskritic elements in religious beliefs and rituals undergo self-transformation, which is not merely adaptive but total. To understand it, one has to not only go beyond the static or even diachronic time frame, look through the passage of history. Thus, we once again witness but also in whatever functionalist orientation that may exist in the analysis of rituals, the tendency to go beyond it, to search for transformative principles through history. Such a cognitive frame is obviously not of functionalism, even though it is replete with functionalist metaphors. Other studies of religion under the inspiration of the Redfield's model of organization of tradition conducted by several sociologists and anthropologists in India also bear affinity to a similar sense of history. This is clearly highlighted later in the works of L.P. Vidyarthi and Milton Singer, among others.

Structuralist and Typological Constructions

Indian sociology in the sixties and seventies underwent major changes both in theoretical orientations and ideologies. The debate initiated by Dumont and Pocock towards the end of fifties on the one hand, and on the other, the increase of self-consciousness among the Indian sociologists about the nature of their discipline and its objective, led to new theoretic tensions. It also contributed to the widening of the substantive base of sociology as it moved from caste and village studies to that of agrarian structure, peasantry, social movements and social history. The sociological thinking became more analytical from its highly descriptive ethnographic orientation of the past. Even in the village studies, now emphasis shifted from cataloguing of mere facts to discussions of principles and categories. In the use of categories the method of using analytical typologies becomes prominent introducing the shift from the notion of continuation to that of levels in the understanding of the dynamics of social change. There is both a substantive and meta-theoretical shift in the sociology of this period. Substantively, the unit is no longer a territory or a single entity but a system defined conceptually or even axiomatically with the help of a set of categories. This renders these studies simultaneously more theoretical as well as more comparative. The conceptualization of systems or changes therein through categories like 'tribe, caste and nation', 'caste, class and power', 'mind', 'body' and 'wealth' (Pocock, 1974), etc., which are seen to proliferate during this period, though not all equally rigorous in methodology, tend to highlight the change. This was also the period of substantive differentiation of sociological research interests. The questions of 'equality and inequality', 'peasantry' and social movements particularly became new interests of sociologists. The spur to studies of peasantry and agrarian structure came from the field of economics, and the historians' works generated the interest in the studies of social movement.

The exposure of sociology to economics and history, with ensuing new trends in these disciplines, introduced new theoretical and conceptual sensitivities in sociology. Marxological orientation in agrarian studies, quite popular among the dominant group of economists, and the studies of social history, the movement with subtle linkages with the Annales School of French History among the Indian historians, to my mind, also influenced the theoretical preferences of some sociologists studying peasantry and peasant movements. Historical studies in the areas of kinship and family were conducted which used historical material and geneaologies and also family cycle and its self-reproduction from one generation to another. I.P. Desai's study of family cycle in a township effectively countered the theory of continuum in the family change.

During the seventies and eighties, however, the same trend in the selectivity of problems and conceptual orientations persisted. Only we now come across some systematic studies of social structures which have a clearly Marxist orientation in conceptual design. Studies also tend to have more regional and macroscopic dimension in their cognitive organization.

In totality, the contributions of sociologists during the sixties to eighties can be seen as a period of differentiation rather than consolidation of methods or paradigms. In some aspects, especially in dialectical or Marxist orientation, one might see elements of revival of the traditions of the early forties-fifties when Marxism was seriously debated among sociologists at several centres of learning. But 'revival' would not be adequate to describe the new phenomenon, since Marxism now has two additional characteristics: first, emphasis on empirical fieldwork and secondly, interpretive elasticity and cognitive differentiation. Marxism was not used now merely as critical social philosophy or as a tool for analysis of historical data, but as a project for empirical observation of facts and generation of data. Hence, many village studies, studies of agrarian systems, of townships and industrial centres and social movements were conducted using Marxological methods. During this period, one thus finds that along with the tendency of structural and comparative historical studies, which continue to dominate, the Marxological studies, particularly by a number of sociologists of the younger generation, come into being.

The three rather novel conceptual and methodological orientations of this period are: *structuralist, typological* and *dialectical.* The linkages, however, among the three orientations are so close that it would be difficult to identify any particular work of this time with anyone of these specific approaches. The structural as well as structuralist notions in the study of caste, religion, knowledge and culture interpenetrate during this period. Within the overall structuralist framework, one does come across notions of substantive relationships and their implication to the system under study. The studies are not entirely formal. In the typological studies, which use analytic type categories, we find preeminent role of observation, construction and interpretation of concrete institutions and relationships. It is for this reason that allusion to neo-Weberanism in such studies by some sociologists would have to be qualified. In essence, these studies bear closer resemblance to monographic studies of rural and caste structures during the fifties. Their sophistication in terms of analysis and use of categories is, however, so designed that the power of their generalizations tends to be wider and more logically anchored. Otherwise, the notions of system, differentiation of structures, institutions and adaptive changes are as much part of the studies using typologies as were in the former village studies. Amongst the functionalist metaphor these studies do not share the teleological assumptions but the notions of system, structure and change in these studies quite harmonize with the functionalist metaphoric contents. This would be as much true for many studies of agrarian structure, social stratification and cultural institutions as of the studies of social movements.

As we mentioned above, the study of social movements and revolution had come to be recognized as an important new element of the functional metaphor of sociology. It may be interesting to investigate as to how far the contemporary studies of social movements in India depart qualitatively in their paradigmatic content from this model. The sequence of events in the functional analysis of social movement for structural change are: initial dissatisfaction with existing condition, initial resistance and binary differentiation of interest groups, positive-negative emotional tensions and rationalizations of these interests, covert processes of handling these tensions by mobilization of resources and ideas, etc., supportive tolerance of new ideas without commitment to specific responsibilities, positive attempts to select specific new ideas and demands which will become objects of commitment, and finally suitable transformation in the structure to incorporate the new system (see, Parsons and Smelser, 1956: 249–74).This sequence inheres the life cycle of social processes which initiate fundamental changes in the social structure as well as lead to its transformation.

The pertinent question in the sociology of social movements that arises is as to whether all paradigms of movement studies inhere a model of structural transformation or revolution, and whether the outcome of all social movements are structural transformation. Obviously, the answer to both of these questions would be in the negative. It is more as a matter of emphasis and not theoretic conditioning that social movement sociology deals with structural transformations as social change. It would not be without basis to suggest, therefore, that with the coming into fashion of agrarian sociology and social movement, the functional metaphor in sociological practice has not withered away. One could even establish its persistence in many such studies. Both the notions of conflict and contradiction as we mentioned above have been incorporated in the structure of the functionalist metaphor.

The new development in the sociology of the seventies or the eighties is not so much the decline of the functionalist metaphor as such, as the rise of the systematic dialectical-materialist 'theory' for the understanding of social reality. It is still in its nascent form, and does not have, particularly in sociology, much wealth of data to fall back upon in order to test the validity and plasticity of its categories; but it has to its credit some serious efforts in all these directions. Much more basic work in India in the dialectical-materialist analysis is being done by economists and a group of historians rather than sociologists. It would thus be premature to go into the question of theoretical consolidation or synthesis of the alternative metaphors of functional and dialectical materialism in Indian sociology.

However, the nature of internal differentiation within the Marxist paradigm during the past two to three decades, the debates on the notions of 'caste' and 'clan', the nature of the infrastructure versus the superstructure, the role of structural differentiation and integration or even institutionalization in the socialist revolutionary societies (which necessitate recall of functionalist metaphor as such) and their sub-systems, the existence of teleological notion of immanent historical formations within the paradigm of Marxism, etc., tend to suggest both possibilities of convergence and co-existence of the two major metaphors in the contemporary world of sociology. In India, to look for convergence as such would be premature as the bulk of work continues to have anchorage in the functionalist metaphor of sociology. In the absence of concrete and comparative studies of Indian reality by the alternative paradigms most debates tend to be ideological rather than deeply sociological. I should think that if one wished to closely examine the nature of dialectical-materialist orientation in the sociological studies, one would once again encounter the two-fold problem of theory-building in sociology: one of near-impossibility of formalization and secondly, the metaphoric content of the structure of categories and their operationalization for research. This problem is equally shared by most so-called theorists of sociology. The paucity of space does not permit me at this stage to go into the metaphoric aspects of the dialectical-materialist theory. It would, however, be not far-fetched to state that in ways that it has been applied to the study of the Indian reality, its nature too has been more metaphoric than formal.

An important implication of the metaphoric nature of theories in sociology is their deep anchorage in ideology. When formal-logical closure of propositions, concepts and their internal relationships remains inadequate, there is always scope for allusions of values and motives to individual scholars in their work which is largely extraneous to the requirement of theory. It is my impression that such ideological allusions though relevant in the context of evaluation of the relative power and relevance of a theoretic metaphor should be appreciated only at an appropriate level. A simplistic method is that of debunking an individual scholar's work by invoking his social conditioning. It is forgotten that social conditioning ceases to be sociologically relevant if it does not have collective structural character. The conditioning only at the level of personal deprivation or, 'trouble', as C. Wright Mills noted, does not become a matter of sociological inquiry, but an 'issue', a collective deprivation does constitute such a subject matter. How does such a social conditioning influence the choice of paradigms and metaphors, is a relevant proposition. Ideology operates rather normatively also at the unconscious level in the inscription of cultural norms in linguistic structure. This is the form in which a deeper level of ideology exists in social science vocabulary. It is this element particularly which further renders theoretic efforts in sociology largely metaphoric.

References

Parsons, T. and Smelser, N.J., *Economy and Society,* New York: The Free Press, 1965.

Singh, Yogendra, "Ideology, Theory and Method in Indian Sociology" in *A Quarter Century of International Social Science* by Rokkan Stein (ed.), New Delhi: Concept Publishing Company, 1979.

Srinivas, M.N., *Religion and Society among the Coorgs of South India,* London: Asia, 1952.

6

The Relevance of Social Sciences in India

The quest for relevance has been pervasive in the social sciences from their very inception. These sciences originated with the emergence of a kind of societal self-awareness under which indifference by social scientists to social problems could not have been possible. It is not mere chance that long ago August Comte, who gave sociology its name, linked sociologists' roles to that of 'priests' for creating a new social order, and again late in the seventies, Alvin Gouldner is struck by the fact that most American sociologists entering this profession had at some stage thought of taking to priestly calling. This recurrent pull towards acting as saviours of men in society undergoing industrial transformation is one manifestation of the quest for relevance. No doubt, its form and context vary with the nature of each social science, and its historicity.

A significant feature of social sciences is their intrinsic double dialectics: first, epistemological, as a social scientist endeavours to formulate (use) categories to replicate societal realities of which he himself is a part; and secondly, ethical, where a social scientist bears responsibility towards society for the uses of his knowledge which is a social product, a historical product, where the tensions of contemporaneity bear heavily upon him. The meaning of relevance in the social sciences is deeply entangled with and arises out of this double dialectics.

At the first level, relevance is defined cognitively. It refers to formulation of concepts and methods in social sciences which satisfy the principles of *adequacy* and *validity* in the understanding or explanation of social reality. Questions asked here are: To what extent are the social science concepts and methods or their operationalization adequate or valid? Is there a universal social science language equally applicable to societies and cultures historically distinct? Does the advocacy for a universal model in a social science contain ideological packages to perpetuate dependency relationship between the social sciences in the developed 'metropolitan' nations and the developing nations of the 'periphery'? It is obvious how matters apparently conceptual or theoretical in nature tend also to involve ideological and politico-economic issues defining the scope of relevance. Nevertheless, the primacy of the context of relevance at this level is grounded in the nature of *explanation* or *understanding* of the social reality that is offered by social sciences.

At the second level, the notion of relevance is posited in the social responsibility of the social scientist. Caught as he is in the tensions of contemporaneity of which he is a social product, and sharp as is his self-consciousness to transcend the bondages of partisan loyalties, which he attempts to overcome through an epistemological leap towards objectivity in his craft, he seeks a way out of this dilemma in the notion of *policy science*. Most widely acknowledged meaning of relevance in the social sciences is associated with this connotation. Policy science implies an interdisciplinary social approach to resolve social problems. At the level of individual social sciences, however, it involves policy researches. In defining the relevance of social sciences in this context several questions arise: Are the values which define the goals of social engineering or social policy consensual or partisan? What is the nature of the relationship between the social scientists who conduct policy researches and the state apparatuses or the agencies which sponsor such researches? Is this relationship autonomous, advisory or dependent? How consensual is the character of the ruling elites of the state apparatus itself which defines the goals of policy planning?

A distinction should be drawn between the role of the social scientist as policy planner working within the framework of the ideology of the ruling elite, and his role as 'organic intellectual' as postulated by Gramsci where he aims at basic transformation in the entire social system, including the elite structure of the society. Relevance is defined here not as an elite-sponsored programme for social construction which tends merely to replicate the patterns of domination (Bottomore, 1971: 51). It implies attempts to expose the truly 'partisan' character of the projects of social reform or developments (based on class, ethnicity and nationality, etc.) which mark the constraints of the structure of inequalities behind a facade of surface consensuality.

Indeed, several models of relevance can be formulated depending upon the manner in which the ideological bases of social planning are defined. A study of the models of relevance in American sociology postulates five such types. These range from '*no net-effect model*', which postulates societal processes to be so powerful as to be beyond manipulative control to '*direct and positive-effect model*' which assumes a degree of consensuality in social systems and social policies on the basis of which social scientists could attempt the betterment of man's life in society. In between are the positions of the '*special constituency*' models, where the relevance is defined with particular reference to the interests of (a) the '*proletariat*' (as in the Marxist sociology, (b) the '*un-co-opted*' categories as in the writings of C. Wright Mills (1956) and Gary Marx (1972), and (c) the '*government officialdom*' (see Eule, 1978: 78–93). Evidently, neither the constituencies of the interest groups in whose favour relevance may be determined, nor the profession of the social sciences, which is concerned with both theoretical and applied potential of the sciences, offers a consensual perspective on the notion of relevance. The meaning of relevance under these circumstances tends to be structured in ideology.

Mystification and Relevance

This brings us to the process of mystification in both the paradigmatic and ideological foundations of social science which plays a vital role in the understanding of the notion of relevance. This is so whether we locate the meaning of relevance within the theoretical structure of social sciences or whether we posit the same in the 'special constituencies'. Mystification is a process of rationalization of models of society or of ideology which either consciously or unconsciously encapsulate meanings or values to serve partisan interests. It is a historical product of the inherent structure of inequalities in society and the social scientist's place in it which contributes to his alienation from a consensual understanding of social reality.

All paradigms of social sciences, particularly of sociology, offer to construct a model of society. Each of these models abstracts from reality a certain notion of order which posits a quality of relationship among its parts based, depending upon the model, upon either truce or consensus, or conflict or contradiction in society which severally constitute the degree of mystification in the societal model, and define the meaning of relevance. The meaning of relevance is thus pre-structured in the paradigms of social science. Each model of society selectively reveals and hides elements of reality in the manner it constructs the structure of society. It is a logical requirement in the formulation of models of society on the known cannons of science or objectivity. However, in each attempt of this kind, the existential background, of which the social scientists are product, introduces value loads which determine the nature of inclusion and exclusion of parameters in the model (see Saberwal, 1979: 242). Thus, social sciences mystify reality as they attempt to demystify it. The dilemmas of mystification become acute when one counterpoises paradigms like functionalism and dialectics in sociology. The functionalist assumes a consensual nature of society through shared values by mechanisms of socialization, enculturation and institutionalization. The dialectical models (both Marxist and neo-Hegelian) treat these values as manifestations of *estrangement* of meanings and symbols from man's species-self through labour on which he has no command. To functionalists the value system of a society *reveals* the character of the society, its achievements and deficiencies which may help in identifying the character of relevance, whereas to Marxists, these values tend only to *mystify* the true nature of reality which is pregnant with crucial contradictions irreparable through tinkering by policy sciences. The notion of relevance assumes two far different connotations in the two models of society.

The problem of mystification in the models of sociology has been aptly summed up by Alain Touraine in his formulation:

> The sociologist does not study facts but documents. In order not to become the prisoner of a 'reality' that he believes himself to be looking in at from outside when he is in fact part of it, he needs to subject himself to an intellectual access that will lead him to the discovery, behind society's organization and discourse of its social relations, in other words of its conflicts and its domination, as well as what that domination keeps concealed in the shadows (1977:11).

There is a certain model of society in this formulation. For Touraine, society is "not just reproduction and adaptation; it is also creation and self-production". It has a "capacity to act on itself", a *historicity*, which creates its contradictions, e.g., its class relations and historical actions through social movements. This only illustrates how models of society might inhere a normative statement about the nature of society which in turn defines the models of relevance. This is how competing models of relevance of social sciences arise. Since each model is a product of historicity, of which the social scientist himself is a product, the notion of relevance also becomes a problem of sociology of knowledge (see Singh, 1976). For instance, the eurocentricity of most paradigms of social sciences is widely acknowledged (Gellner, 1969).

At the 'special constituency' level of the meaning of relevance, the dilemma of mystification is ideological, and it is much more clearly visible. All social science projects of social engineering do reflect the critical differences between the definition of the 'desirable' by the donor 'elite' and the 'recipient' masses of the society. Mystification of relevance in these contexts of social policy lies not only in the partisan manner in which the objectives of social well-being are formulated, but also in the manner in which the strategy for its realization is outlined as measures of reform. The ruling elite does, under certain constraints, such as popular protest which threatens its position, yield ground by enacting policy measures for distributive justice. The manner, however, in which such legislations are drafted and the mechanisms through which their objectives will be ensured, leave deliberated loopholes to render them ineffective for fuller implementation. Such gaps between profession and policy level execution are concrete illustrations of mystification in models of relevance. The terms like 'development', 'modernization' and 'social justice', which evoke various models of relevance, also inhere acts of mystification.

The Quest for Relevance in Indian Social Sciences

The context of relevance in the Indian social science has been deeply influenced by the historical situation in which it has developed: colonialism and movement for independence are two interlinked historical experiences which define both the theoretical orientations and policy relevance of Indian social science. We attempt to analyze these factors at the levels of (a) theoretical and conceptual models of Indian social science, (b) social science researches and social policy in India, and (c) the emerging models of relevance in the Indian social sciences, with particular reference to sociology. The significance of mystification in the process of formulation of social science paradigms and welfare policies would be examined at all the three levels mentioned above. It may also be useful to raise some questions regarding the sociological character of social science profession in India as it may offer useful insights to related issue of ideology, theory and practice of Indian social science.

The history of social sciences in India is embedded in the colonial and post-colonial contacts with the west, particularly with Britain. From the late 19th century to the first quarter of the 20th century, the tradition of humanistic rationalism of the British universities spurred on a series of attempts towards rationalization of these powerful ideas in terms of the Indian intellectual tradition. More than universities, the social reformers of the 19th century made solid contribution to this process. The question of relevance was one of the most important objectives in these debates. Question was how to imbibe the western philosophical and social scientific constructs into the traditional Indian constructs and in what measure. The Brahmo Samaj in Calcutta, the Prarthana Samaj in Bombay and the Veda Samaj in Madras were reform movements which sponsored vigorous drives for selective assimilation of the ethical and philosophical presuppositions of the western social sciences and humanities into the Indian intellectual stream. This assimilation was itself considered to be a measure of relevance at this time. The project for relevance was westernization.

The kind of response by Indian intellectuals was conditioned by the acceptance of the historical superiority of the western cultural models reinforced by western colonial conquests and their industrial and technological progress, and its rationalistic ideology of that time. At this stage of the evaluation of the east-west relationship, the facts of colonial expropriation and exploitation were secondary. This did, however, surface in Indian social science during the first and the second quarters of the 20th century with rising nationalism, when ideological differentiation among the Marxists, the rational-positivist and nationalist orientations in the social sciences began to sharpen. Attempts to analyze the naught of caste, and the economic institutions, the use of a Marxist framework to analyze the eastern social structure and its intellectual traditions, and the treatment of the phenomena of capitalism and colonialism in India created new cultural self-awareness. This development in India also echoed the contradictions within the European social sciences due to the challenges from Marxism and Freudianism. Historically, the aftermath of the First World War and the emergence of a socialist society in the USSR also spurred this orientation.

The theoretical orientations of early 20th century social sciences were products more of scholar politicians and literateurs than of the university academics whose works continued to mirror the paradigms of the western social sciences. The challenges to this orientation began to emerge from outside the university system in the nationalist movement led by Gandhi. His emphasis on to 'swadeshi' was not only an economic challenge to the British colonialism but also a cultural response to encounter the tide of westernization. Attention may specially be drawn to a chain of educational institutions that were started under this inspiration on indigenous models. No systematic study of the content of curricula or the nature of social science paradigms taught in these institutions has been made from the viewpoint of inherent models of relevance. It would, however, appear that the quest for alternative paradigms of Indian social science did not succeed in this experiment as well.

These developments, nevertheless, had an impact on the university-level teaching and research in social sciences.

Comparative institutional frameworks increased in social science teaching. The awareness of the impact of colonialism on the rise of Indian business classes, the nature of the relationship between Indian and European capitalism and the consequent processes of de-industrialization and de-urbanization in India began to emerge as the foci of teaching and research. Sociology was just beginning to establish itself as a university-level discipline during this period. Its substantive and intellectual concerns were deeply influenced by the national debates on the merits and demerits of western interpretation of the Indian society. The evolutionary social science approaches of the 19th century social anthropologists, and their formulation on the religion, caste and tribes in India, constituted the foci of such debate. The search for relevance in the paradigms of Indian social science at this stage was more meta-theoretical than theoretical. Questions were addressed more to the nature of presuppositions implicit in western theoretical treatment of Indian social realities, rather than to the theoretical models themselves.

The intellectual context of the social sciences underwent a basic change following independence. The reference model now shifted from the U.K. to U.S.A., which had emerged as the most dominant international power. This contact also coincided with the rapid erosion of colonialism in most parts of the world. But, the fear of neo-colonialism and imperialism in the mind of the Third World social scientists remained equally sharp. The socialist revolution in China added a new dimension to this process. Academic colonialism and 'dependency' in the relationship between the social science of the developed capitalist nations and the nations of the Third World now began to be examined.

In the Indian social sciences, particularly sociology, a two-way development took place: first, there was a substantial increase in the policy-oriented social research with the help of tools and methods of American sociology; and secondly, there was unprecedented growth in an empirical study of social structures in the rural, urban and tribal settings using a functional theoretical approach. There was also much research conducted on Indian societal reality directly by American sociologists, political scientists and agricultural economists. The model of society implicit in the paradigms of these sociological studies was consensual and plural. At this stage, the questions were not raised as to how far in the historical and cultural settings of the Indian society these models were relevant for its understanding. The doubts about the American intentions in studying Indian society were expressed by a group of social scientists led by D.N. Majumdar and D.P. Mukerji at the Lucknow University, in the early fifties. They highlighted the neo-colonialist design of American sociologists and social anthropologists in these studies and also challenged the relevance of the paradigms used in these studies as such.

Soon, however, a more systematic effort questioning the relevance of some Euro-American models in sociology for the study of Indian society followed. Towards the end of the fifties D.P. Mukerji wrote extensively on the need to formulate basic concepts in Indian social sciences and sociology commensurate with its distinctive history and tradition. Radhakamal Mukherjee offered a model of studying society in general from a neo-dialectical approach in which one finds a mixture of the notion of Hegelian and Vedantic dialectics. This was followed by a seminar of Indian sociologists in the sixties on the possibility of an Indian model of sociology. This seminar was the Indian sociologists' response to issues raised by Dumont and Pocock in their essays in *Contributions to Indian Sociology*. These debates generated substantial reflective writings in the sixties on the possibility of conceptual and theoretical specificity in Indian sociology, and the relevance of the western sociological paradigms for understanding the Indian sociological reality (see Unnithan, et al, 1967; Singh, 1979). This concern was coupled with the awareness of the politico-economic dimension of the social science relationship between the developed and the developing nations and its distorting effects in its theory and practice (see *Seminar*, No. 112: 1968).

The concern for conceptual specificity and relevance grew into the general ethos of social sciences in India during the seventies. It is reflected in the continued dialogue among social scientists during this period on the role and relevance of social sciences in India and the tensions in their development. The publication in 1976 of *Social Sciences and Social Realities: Role of Social Sciences in Contemporary India* (ed. S.C. Dube), which is a report of the seminar organized by the Indian Institute of Advanced Study, Simla, in collaboration with the ICSSR, explicates this concern. Ramakrishna Mukherjee analyzed the trends in Indian sociology in terms of theory and methodology, reviewing its past, its present and the emerging future orientations in his *Main Trends in Indian*

Sociology (see Mukherjee, 1977) which offers critical insight into successive paradigms of sociology and their ideological interface. In this work, and more systematically in a later work, Mukherjee deals with the question of relevance from a formal methodological perspective (see, Mukherjee, 1979). Using an inductive inferential approach he postulates that the question, "what will it be?", can be answered for each value load of a social science model using 'inductive inferential' methods. He suggests a set of statistical techniques through which social science propositions could be tested and generated irrespective of the value premises involved. Mukherjee deals with the question of specificity of paradigm of sociology only at the level of concept formation and operationalization. Otherwise, his approach is nomological and based on statistical abstractions. He does not deal with the phenomenology of relevance as such.

The seventies mark a distinctive change in the concerns about theory and method in sociology. There is a shift away from the 'abstracted empiricism' of the fifties; there is more intense awareness of the need to explore the nature of structures and their processes using historically founded type-concepts and categories, which may vaguely resemble the Marxian, Weberian or functionalist traditions; the influence of neo-Marxist conceptual schemes is visible in many researches. But, the emerging strong impress is that of concern with history in the understanding of the process as within structure such as social mobility, modes of production and their social structures and social movements. Emphasis is more on the deeper understanding of structures, their symbolic significance and interlinkages using the native categories rather than the conceptual packages from abroad (see Jain, 1977; Singh, 1974; Dhanagare, 1977; Mukherjee, 1977; Saberwal, 1979a, 1979b). The attempt here is not to postulate master theories couched in abstract principles but to offer analytic understanding of concrete social structures and processes at significant points of historical conjuncture.

Simultaneously, further exposure of the limitations of the western models of social science for the developing countries is made through notions of academic colonialism, dependency (in transfer of social science technology) and ideology (see Chossudovsky, 1977; Forrester, 1974; Saberwal, 1979; Momin, 1972; Uberoi, 1968). These arguments assume new significance in the light of the rethinking in the western social sciences on the question of unity of paradigms. Functionalism, structuralism and Marxism are no longer treated as unified paradigms, but as synthetic theoretical schemes. This reinforces the plea for orientating concepts and methods in the social sciences to the specificity of the socio-cultural reality of each society concerned.

This concern is reflected in recent efforts made by Indian economists, sociologists, social workers, political scientists and psychologists through a series of UGC workshops to modernize the syllabi. The question of relevance has been analyzed in most workshop reports both at the paradigmatic and policy levels. The report on economics states: "Standard economics is supposed to explain the *modus operandi* of an idealized capitalist economy. The Indian economy being anything but that, the orthodox paradigms must perforce collapse." It concludes: "Most of the theoretical concepts evolved in the context of the developed industrial societies of the west are mechanically doled out to unsuspecting batches of students in this country. Not unnaturally we find these rarefied tools of analysis to be of little avail in comprehending their own situation" (1977). The reports on sociology and political science have also recognized the need for the indigenization of paradigms and have suggested that such attempts should proceed in phases keeping in view the unevenness in the development of these sciences in the country. Indirectly, these reports reflect the tensions that exist in social science today about the indigenization of their paradigms in order to render them relevant for the understanding of the Indian reality (see Singh, 1979).

The proposition that social science paradigms do not have a universal scientific (explanatory) relevance and should, therefore, increasingly disaggregate their structure in accordance with the historically or culturally specific experiences has, in the seventies, gained firm support in most social sciences at the international level too with the possible exception of economics. Here too it appears that the Indian experience is at variance. The 25th Anniversary Round Table of the International Social Science Association, which was devoted to an assessment of a quarter century of international social science (1952–1977), had several papers that highlighted the inadequacy of universal theoretical models or methods in social sciences and argued for the indigenization of social sciences (see

Lousber, 1977). Reporting on the state of geography during this period Jones writes:

> Models in geography today have all been derived from our own western culture. We are in danger of accepting them as if they were universally applicable. Dealing with every city in the world as if it were Chicago is bad enough. A vast computerized exercise on the social areas on Calcutta does not mean very much to studies of urbanization; it must mean less to 600,000 who sleep in the streets of Calcutta at night. The trend in geography is towards the incorporation of value systems as essential elements in any organized use of space. *Relevance means not only relevance to the existing problems but relevance to the existing cultural system.* We are reminded of Pahl's statement that "geography is the product of a sub-culture" (italics added, see Jones, 1977).

The above establishes how the tensions both within the national and international professions of the social sciences is slowly converging to reinforce the disenchantment with the quest for universal paradigms. The context for such awareness is clearly the demand for relevance from the social sciences as tools for social explanation and understanding, and as aids to the development process in societies. The notion of relevance, however, has varied significance at the two levels despite the apparent convergence of meanings.

Policy Research and Social Science Relevance

The most widely acknowledged level of social science relevance relates to the contributions that researches make in the formulation and implementation of policies of social welfare and development in societies. India has a long history of policy-oriented research. The British colonial administration found it indispensable to understand the nature of the Indian society, its system of stratification and the rituals and customs of the Indian people in order to rule over them. Immense ethnographic researches on tribe, caste, language and culture, rituals and belief systems were conducted by the missionaries and administrators. Their objectives broadly were to aid Christianization and colonization though in varying degrees of enthusiasm. The census operations, land settlement and codifications of penal and civil laws were all policy oriented to perpetuating a social order for colonial expropriation of surpluses. The British rule contributed in an unprecedented measure to the institutional, organizational and administrative innovations, establishing the legitimacy of policy-oriented research. The 19th century utilitarian rationality and colonial urge to exploit resources provided a spur to this process. This phase of policy research offers a pure case of the linkages between the modes of power structure, its interests and policy researches.

Independence led to further rationalization and proliferation of policy research in India. Both in terms of institutional set-up and funding, there was expansion. Universities and colleges, government-funded autonomous research agencies, aided research institutes with governmental and private control and research organizations of the government attached to various ministries offer a variety of institutional apparatuses through which researches were sponsored. During the fifties, most sociological researches were conducted in policy relevant areas in the form of urban surveys, demographic studies, village studies and evaluation of community development schemes and panchayati raj systems, etc. Similar policy-related researches were also conducted in other social sciences, particularly economics and political science. Researches by professionals in the institutes and agencies contributed a large proportion of the total output.

In order to examine the relevance of these researches a few questions arise; these are of the value loads in terms of which relevance of policy research is determined, the relationship between the state, its ideology and its definition of relevance, the extent to which the ideology of the state is consensual or partisan. Added to these questions are the problems of the conceptual and theoretical structures of social sciences, and the extent to which the sciences are autonomous or dependent in the matter of the technology of research and personnel.

Moreover, the policy researches have a heterogeneous character. There are researches which simply generate data on a periodic basis for purposes of social and economic monitoring and planning. The census operations, the national sample surveys and other surveys and descriptive researches conducted by numerous public agencies belong to this category. The question of value load is not directly involved in such researches, except in the definition of concepts, their operationalization and the inclusion or exclusion of items from observation. A second category of policy researches is where the goals of social or economic development are normatively built into the objective of research, the problem is defined as to how to achieve such an objective most efficiently. Researches of this kind are in the very heartland of the dominant ideology defining relevance. The third type of policy research may be of an evaluative nature, a follow-up study of the consequences of measures of social engineering or planning. The urgent problems in such researches are not of ideology or sponsorship but of technology of research, its designing and operationalization. Finally, one may also include in policy researches studies which attempt to examine the value loads of social policy measures and their impact on society; such researches by implication also suggest alternative strategies of planning for development by exposing the contradictions inherent in the social forces which contribute to the various types of policy researches.

On a rough estimate it would appear that policy researches of the above three kinds in India have been in most cases conducted outside the university and college systems, mainly through public or private institutional facilities. There researches of the fourth kind, the 'critical' policy researches have originated more from the university systems. This pattern of orientation in research is logical, because the manner in which research is socially organized to a large extent conditions its orientation, cognitive boundaries and responsibility.

To our mind, the assessment of Myron Weiner in regard to the relatively inadequate role of the universities in policy researches (see Weiner, 1979: 1581) does not take into consideration the differentiated nature of the policy researches as such. His inventory of general attributes of policy researches, however, indirectly supports our thesis. Weiner finds that most policy researches in India are "not social science studies, but are intended to provide a data base for policy". Secondly, "a large number of the research studies conducted in these institutions centre on individual development projects" and thirdly, "none of the studies (cited above) are comparative". These characteristics of policy researches, if true, put them in a very unenviable light. These also seriously damage the many assumptions with which Weiner argues his case for internationalization of policy researches in India.

Considering the types of policy researches in India it is not necessary to expect that all of them should be 'social science'. Similarly, it is also not legitimate to characterize all varieties of basic researches as non-policy oriented researches, since the role of criticism, demystification and alternative modes of social construction of reality is helpful in correcting the premises on which policy researches are based. For instance, the class character of Indian society, especially the existential and structural conditions to which most poorer sections of our society are shackled, offers a more viable explanation of why several developmental measures do not appeal to them, and why to some others they are violently apathetic. A huge bulk of funds and efforts in policy researches in family planning and community development during the fifties and sixties went near-waste in the absence of the appreciation of such basic sociological phenomena.

Policy researches are grounded in the most varied presuppositions about the model of development in a society. At any time, this ideal is represented by its ruling elite. Depending upon the character of this elite, and of the state, the ideal of development may be placed on a continuum of *consensuality* and *partisanship*. The credibility of the policy researches depends upon the extent of consensus that the policy under consideration evokes. Given our socio-political reality, relevance in the short run can be determined only through the degree to which the objectives of developments as set by the ruling elite are promoted by sponsored policy researches. Within the framework of policy researches the scope for formulating them can be only technical, not ideological. An ideological appraisal of policy researches implies structural changes in the character of the ruling elite. It implies alternative models of relevance.

It we take sociology as a case in point, we find various models of relevance in policy researches. The very notion of the relevance of sociology has been rejected by A.K. Saran in his numerous writings. To him, sociology is a symptom of the sickness of modern industrial society, it is a false ideology which modern man restates as a substitute to the disintegrating traditional worldview. Saran has few followers in sociology but many from other disciplines like philosophy and divinity. In the fifties, the dominant model of relevance in sociology was policy research for the government—a tendency which in the sixties and seventies has declined in professional circles of sociologists in the universities. The relevance model now in vogue tends to be more in favour of what Rule calls the constituency of the 'proletariat' or of the 'un-co-opted' strata. Diagnostic and analytic sociological studies now use either class or interest groups as the framework for understanding the contradictions in the Indian social structure. Emphasis on the study of social movements, agrarian structures, social inequality and power structure is the new direction of research implying alternative models of relevance.

An interesting feature of the emergence or co-existence of these models of relevance is that they have remained independent of the influence of the funding agencies like the UGC or government ministries. The ICSSR sponsored a number of national level research projects in the priority areas of national concern. These have been mainly in the nature of fact-finding studies rather than structural or comparative in perspective. These also reflected the interests of the concerned ministries of the government of the time. It would be doubtful if these researches have generated any significant sociological ideas or propositions which could form the basis for significant debate in sociology. It is noteworthy that sociological contributions which have evoked relatively more interest in the profession have come from individual research scholars working as one-man team with limited funds at their disposal rather than from expensive sponsored projects.

The points raised in this paper may be summed up as follows: The notion of relevance in social sciences is a product of double dialectics: (i) social sciences as epistemological systems, and (ii) as ideologies. Relevance at the epistemological levels directs our efforts towards examination of the validity of concepts and methods in terms of their universality, historicity and cultural specificity. Increasingly, social sciences are tending to articulate that most concepts and theories of social sciences are historically and culturally grounded. Hence, one measure of relevance for Indian social science should be to search for autonomy and indigenization of paradigms and methods of social enquiry.

The second level of relevance, ideological, is associated with policy researches. Policies of social welfare and social development are based on normative projects of the ruling elite. These projects have hidden in their normative structure a model of society which is seldom made fully explicit to the people at large. This is true for all ideological systems. This is implicit in the existential teleology of functionalism as well as the historical teleology of Marxism. Its realization is a painful experience for those social scientists who are neither mystagogues or ideologues. To determine social scientist's responsibility in terms of relevance at this level is difficult indeed. He is apt to play the role of supporter of a ruling elite merely as a technician to oil the wheel of the state apparatus. Short of this, he may play the role of a critic of the dominant ideology by demystifying it, by objective and critical analysis of the structure of social reality and its processes.

The quest for relevance in the Indian social sciences has been mounting at both levels mentioned above, i.e., epistemological and ideological. Within the domain of each social science, the awareness for autonomy and indigenization of concepts, paradigms and methods has increased. The social sciences have not arrived at any definitive solution of this problem on their agenda except through increasing use of the native categories and comparative Indian data for the understanding of the historicity of social processes. The attempt is bound to gain momentum with time.

The nature of policy researches in India is not uniform. These range from mere data-generating activities to preparation of cultural and social profiles of tribes and communities. The challenges that social sciences face in the context of the issue of relevance, therefore, do not equally apply to all types of policy researches. In most policy researches in India, the relevance signifies the attempt to use most objective and valid methods and concepts, commensurate with the specificity of the concerned social phenomena. The model of society implicit in any notion of social development does not operate here as a significant frame of reference. The problem of relevance in such researches is technical and operational. The challenges of indigenization of social science research at this level are in terms of devising appropriate categories and methods. The policy researches, where the objective is formulated in terms of a specific developmental target, are also those where a normative model is *ipso facto* implicit. To maintain relevance in researches of this kind, the quest for historical and cultural specificity of social realities should be combined with rationalization of the technology of research. Sociologist's role as social critic may not always be relevant in researches of this type. However, social sciences as social criticism, or as instruments of demystification also belong to the domain of relevance in a more fundamental sense. But their relevance at this level is caught up in the whirlpool of power structure to which the social scientist is not always a 'marginal'. He is a social and, a historical product, and his existentiality enters into the notion of relevance he postulates as a critic of society. Logically, social science as social criticism inheres a transcendence from such historicity defining the limits of relevance. But, the limits of this transcendence are also set by the historical nature of the social forces, of which the social scientist is a product. All social sciences have a truly historical character.

References

Bottomore, T.B., *Sociology as Social Criticism*, New Delhi: S. Chand and Company Ltd., 1979.

Chossudovsky, M., "Dependence and Transfer of Intellectual Technology: The Case of Social Sciences", *Economic and Political Weekly*, Vol. XII, No. 36, 1977.

Dhanagare, D.N., "Agrarian Conflict, Religion and Politics: The Moplah Rebellion in Malabar in the Nineteenth and Early Twentieth Centuries", *Past and Present: A Journal of Historical Studies,* No. 74, February 1977.

Dube, S.C. (ed.), *Social Sciences and Social Realities: Role of Social Sciences in Contemporary India*, Simla: Indian Institute of Advanced Study, 1976.

Eule, J.B., "Models of Relevance: The Social Effects", *American Journal of Sociology*, Vol. 84, No. 1, 1978.

Forrester, D.B., "Western Academic Sophistry and the Third World", *Economic and Political Weekly*, Vol. IX, No. 40, 1974.

Gellner, E., *Thought and Change*, Chicago: The University of Chicago Press, 1965.

Jain, R.K., "Class and Classification Among the Peasantry of Central India: Relations of Production in Village Parsania, Madhya Pradesh", *Sociological Bulletin,* Vol. 25, No. 1, 1977.

Jones, E., "A Quarter Century of International Social Sciences Developments—1932–1977: Geography" 25th Anniversary Round Table: A Quarter Century of International Social Science 1952–77: International Social Science Council, October 24–26, Paris (mimeographed), 1977.

Loubser, J.J., "The Need for the Indigenisation of the Social Sciences", 25th Anniversary Round Table: A Quarter Century of International Social Science—1952–1977: International Social Science Council, October 24–26, Paris (mimeographed), 1977.

Marx, Gary, *Muckraking Sociology Research as Special Criticism*, New Brunswick: N.J., Transaction, 1972.

Mills, C. Wright, *The Power Elite*, New York: Oxford University Press, 1956.

Momin, A.R., "The Facade of Objectivity: An Inquiry into the Epistemology of Value-Free Sociology", *Economic and Political Weekly*, Vol. VII, No. 44, 1972.

Mukherjee, Partha Nath, "Social Movement and Social Change: Towards a Conceptual Classification and Theoretical Framework", *Sociological Bulletin*, Vol. 26, No. 1., 1977.

Mukherjee, R.K., *What Will It Be*? New Delhi: The Macmillan Company of India, Ltd., 1979.

Saberwal, S., "Inequality in Colonial India", *Contributions to Indian Sociology*, Vol. 13, No. 2., 1979a.

—, "Sociologists and Inequality in India: The Historical Context", *Economic and Political Weekly*, Vol. XIV, Nos. 7 and 8, 1979b.

Singh, Rajendra, "Agrarian Social Structure and Present Unrest: A Study of Land Grab Movement in District Basti – East U.P.", *Sociological Bulletin*, Vol. 23, No. 1, 1974.

—, "Constraints, Contradictions and Interdisciplinary Orientations: The Indian Context", *International Social Science Journal*, Vol. XXXI, No.1, 1979.

Touraine, Alain, *The Self Productions of Society*, Chicago: The University of Chicago Press, 1977.

Uberoi, J.P.S., "Science and Swaraj", *Contributions to Indian Sociology*, (New Series), Vol. 2.

Unnithan, T.K.N., et al., *Sociology for India*, New Delhi: Prentice-Hall of India, 1967.

Weiner, M., "Social Science Research and Public Policy in India", *Economic and Political Weekly*, Vol. XIV, No. 38, 1979.

7

Challenges of Globalization, Identity and Economic Development: An Indian Perspective

The process of globalization has generated universal discontent and disenchantment. Those who applaud its arrival are fewer. Disenchantment prevails not only in the developing but also in the developed world. It needs to be analyzed as to what lies at the root of such discontentment. Also, globalization almost everywhere has given rise to a newer and sharper self-consciousness of identity. Such consciousness tends to be pervasive; it is not confined to the cultural minorities, local cultures, ethnic groups, tribes or weaker sections. The surge of identity consciousness and anxiety about preservation of cultural identity extends also in the relationships between nations. The nation or the set of nations which plays the dominant role in controlling the financial resources or the institutional instruments of globalization is perceived to have an unchallenged monopoly on the extension of its 'symbolic power' through marketing of its cultural products, practices, styles and symbolic forms. Amongst nations or communities which feel culturally subordinated, the sense of resentment generates forces leading to cultural nationalism or even fundamentalism. Can we treat these twin processes as contemporary pathology of globalization? The issue needs to be examined in all its dimensions. Moreover, we notice that despite massive literature being generated on the treatment of the specific dimensions of globalization such as its social, structural, economic, cultural and political correlates and consequences, a very substantial degree of ambiguity persists about its historicity, ideology and epistemological or conceptual status as a factor in the integrated social and economic development of the contemporary societies. This problem is global.

Globalization is a composite process. It results from the convergence of a series of developments in society which are qualitatively new. These include: contemporary revolution in science and technology of communication, high velocity movements of finance, capital and market, increased social mobility, migration of personnel and the emergence of a global diaspora. Its associated contributory processes are: intensification of cultural interaction among diverse groups through media exposure, increased incidence of leisure-time activities, growth in tourism, infrastructures of entertainment and marketing of cultural products, personnel and styles. These developments have an evolutionary character, as they are generally irreversible despite societies going through the cycles of growth and depression in economy, polity and social system. This attribute of globalization has social structural and political consequences which are often overlooked as most treatment of this process has focused upon a segmental rather than a holistic analysis of its nature and consequences. In a segmental approach, analysts have studied 'financial or capital globalization', 'telecommunication or media globalization' and 'cultural globalization' as separate developments, and then tried to view the impact of the one, for instance, 'financial or capital' globalization upon other segments such as the 'media', 'communication' or 'culture'. This approach has two weaknesses: first, it fails to help us in comprehending the role of the residual social structural realities and their emergent properties and the way they interact with any one of these three aspects of globalization, be it capital, communication or culture. Consequently, such treatment is unable to explain why some societies, communities or groups resist globalization and reject its institutions and ideology, whereas others accept it and celebrate its arrival. It is necessary to take note of this reality since it determines the historicity of globalization in specific societies, cultures and nationalities and takes into consideration the 'initial' historical and social-cultural realities of each society as it encounters the pressure for globalization. Secondly, the segmental approach does not give enough weight to a holistic treatment of the process of globalization. Particularly, it misses the point that globalization plays a vital contributory role in the evolution of a 'new' society, variously described as an 'information society' or a 'post-modern society'. The emergence of such a society inheres a basic structural transformation of economy, polity and culture, and the potential to go beyond the systemic features of a capitalist or a post-capitalist social order. Its unfolding may eventually contribute to the birth of a new social order.

This new social order, variously described as the "information society or the post-modern society" is yet to come into being; it does not exist as yet in a systemic form in any part of the globe. We see today only a selected set of institutional, structural and cultural attributes of such a society, which is probably in the process of being born. For instance, we witness substantial growth of homogenized occupational workforce of skilled manpower, such as in the professions, technology and services; there is growing global mobility and interdependency among societies in need of such skilled workforce. It contributes to the emergence of social and cultural diaspora with huge influence upon the economy and culture both of the nation of its origin as well as that of its settlement.

The increased social mobility and cross-cultural interactions release the forces of change in each society. In the developed world, it has released intense feeling of cultural identity leading to the growth in the ideology of the 'right' on the one hand and on the dissatisfaction with the existing form of political participation in democracy on the other. Focus now is on the movement from 'representative' democracy to 'participatory' democracy; from state sponsorship of social and economic agenda of societies to its formulation and management by the civil society and voluntary associations. The new slogan is to 're-invent democracy'. The revolutionary changes brought about in the communication technology, such as telephony, internet and new mass media, make it possible to envisage the possibilities of political, social and cultural interaction within and between societies and interest groups which are truly participatory and which bring about self-governing civil society into existence.

In this process, we witness radical changes at the economic level. The basic organs of economy, such as capital, market, modes of production and trade, are getting increasingly entwined into a web of global interdependence. This interdependence is not merely geographical or of capital and market, but it increasingly draws its synergy from new technological advances in the fields of communication through satellites, internet, television, telephony, etc. These technologies are helping not only the educated and the professional sections but also the fishermen, farmers, horticulturists, floriculturists and people engaged in many other occupations. These extend the scope of their operations such as technology uses, marketing and capitalization. Similarly, branding of commodities is increasingly transforming production processes in an idiom which is cultural, communicative. It universalizes that which was once considered to be local.

To deal with its implications for a specific national society, institutional innovations within and at the international level are required. The contemporary institutions such as the World Bank, International Monetary Fund (IMF), World Trade Organization (WTO), etc., are some of the responses, but these do not yet inspire the level of consensus and confidence that could make the acceptance of the goals of globalization smooth. This fact, combined with the reality of the existing social inequalities among societies and its varying levels of intensity within each individual society, do not inspire confidence about the final outcome of globalization. Many questions are posed and many challenges are faced by societies yet in the process of new transformation. The recent experiences of near-economic breakdown in Indonesia, Malaysia and Thailand, once lauded as 'little tigers' due to the flight of capital, has left memories in the developing world which evokes disenchantment rather than reassurance from the processes of globalization.

Ideology and Globalization

These operational contradictions of globalization have generated several ideological nuances in its contemporary conceptual and substantive evaluation. A range of ideologies, such as neo-Marxism-Leninism, post-modernism, critical theories of development, particularly those related to the impact of globalization on ecology, human rights of the weaker sections such as women, minorities, working classes and other marginalized groups, have generated a strident debate on the social, cultural and economic consequences of globalization. The fact that globalization has not yet resolved some of the basic contradictions in the realms of culture, economy and human relationships and in some cases it is supposed to have contributed to internal social conflicts goes only to lend credence to such ideologies. According to the contemporary Marxist-Leninist critique, globalization is only other manifestation of cosmopolitan capitalism with its classic imperialistic orientation remaining intact. Instead of contributing to trans-nationalism, it exposes societies and nations to endemic 'disasters' such as the recent food crisis in Africa and the onset of fundamentalism and communalism, both at the global and national levels. The acute social distresses, cultural conflicts and alienation (see, Patnaik, 1996) of the weaker and marginalized communities contribute to this process. No doubt, globalization with its emphasis on the supremacy of the market, quest for optimization of profits by the multinational corporations, continual unemployment due to the fluctuations in economy and capitalism-friendly labour laws and control over the management or governance of globalization by the Bretton Wood inspired institutions of the rich capitalist nations who set the agenda, policies and practices of globalization lends credence to this critique. In fact, the Human Development Report (2002) echoes this despair and calls for reforms within the international institutions of development such as the WTO, World Bank, IMF, etc., by making them more accountable and representative.

It is said that, "nearly half the voting power in the World Bank and International Monetary Fund rests in the hands of seven countries. And though all countries have a seat and a vote in the WTO, in practice, decisions are taken in small group meetings and heavily influenced by Canada, the European Union, Japan and U.S. In 2000, 15 African countries did not have a single trade representative stationed at the WTO" (*The Hindu*, July 25, 2002). This political domination contributes to the acute differences in the perception as to the extent that globalization decrease or increase the levels of economic and social inequalities within a society.

The Marxist-Leninist critique of globalization is anchored into a theoretical paradigm which recognizes the role of the historical forces, systems of political economy and social structure. Yet another ideology, the post-modernist criticism of globalization, is essentially cultural. It derives sustenance from an epistemology which rejects the idea of a system or structure, and posits human social and cultural realities in a perpetual state of symbolic transience or flux, continually in the process of making and unmaking. "It challenges the postulate of rationality (the foundation of market economy) on which most social science categories such as, 'structure', 'system' and 'change' are anchored; it also attempts to invalidate the notions of the 'actor' or the 'subject' from the social science discourse or their moorings in the structure of social values. The French sociologist, J. Baudrillard articulates this view when he says that in matters of social discourse, "the things have never functioned socially, but symbolically, magically, irrationally". Social systems, according to the post-modern reckoning, are illusionary facades characterized by "micro-orders of domination" (Singh, 1998: 1). Thus, in the logic of its analysis, history has no role or significance. It treats the conjuncture of events and processes largely in terms of space as 'co-happenings' and not in order of temporal succession. The diversity of existence of identities is recognized but the causality of the same is rejected.

We also witness yet another ideology about globalization which emanates from the assorted movement of the NGOs. These NGOs represent a variety of 'interest groups' and many institutionalized forms of activism. The issues of their concern are as diverse as human rights, ecology and sustainable development, rights of the minorities, women, tribes, working classes, etc., which seem to converge upon their opposition to globalization for reasons some of which have a common basis, and others which are contradictory. Their ideology in some parts may seem eclectic with the underpinnings of Marxism, post-modernism, ecological and developmental humanism and focus on human rights etc., which are articulated in a generalized form.

In my view, globalization is a unique process. It is a product of such developments in the field of science and technology which are entirely new to human history. And, these offer new opportunities to humankind as also pose many challenges. It is a fact, however, that several of its features taken individually did indeed exist in the past, such as international trade by sea and land routes, capitalism and imperialism, market and capital mobility and transfer of workforce from one country to another. But, devoid as these processes in the past were of the advantages of the modern technologies, their total impact upon society and its direction of change was qualitatively different. Therefore, the nature of challenges was also different. Hence, to understand its fuller implications, a new ideological paradigm is necessary. It must be of an interdisciplinary nature, because globalization is a multidimensional and multidirectional process. Its implications have to be understood and analyzed from a holistic perspective. The particularistic perspective, either on the basis of political economy as we find in Marxist-Leninist critique or that of culture, symbols or images as we find in the discourse on post-modernism, remain inadequate. While highlighting some of the aspects of globalization, each one of them leaves a much larger segment of globalization, its nature and consequences etc., unaccounted for. Sociology, to my mind, could be one such discipline which has a broad enough integrative theoretical perspective to offer a paradigm for the analysis of globalization. It focuses upon the study of the 'specific' or local in the perspective of the 'total' and the historical. Its methodology and epistemology offer both variety and flexibility of an approach to deal with social realities that may be 'normal' or 'enigmatic' or paradoxical. Globalization is a good candidate to merit its attention.

Challenges of Globalization

Any revolutionary transformation in society brings in its wake both challenges and opportunities. This is true also for globalization. Not that these challenges are confined only to a developing society like India. The developed world is also not immune from them, as it too faces the challenges of globalization; only its character is different. In the developing societies, the tensions and anxieties on account of globalization are primarily economic which spill over to the anxieties about culture and identity. In the developed world, culture seems to top over all other anxieties on account of globalization. In Europe, we witness this in the crescendo of debate on multiculturalism and in the revival of the ideology of the 'right and the racial-cultural exclusiveness'. In India, however, the cultural and ethnic aspects of the challenges of globalization do exist, but these are in most cases derivatives of the anticipated unpredictable consequences to the economy, polity and social structure.

In terms of social structure, India remains essentially a rural-agrarian society. Only about 30 percent of our population is urban and the pace of urbanization remains slow. The addition to our urban population comes mainly from the rural poor, who migrate in search of employment. They remain marginalized in the urban economy and hold the lowest position in the urban social structure. Thus, a major challenge that globalization is likely to pose to our social structure is related to the nature of inequalities in the society. We witness these inequalities at several levels, such as between the village and town, between the middle classes and the working classes, between males and females, between marginalized ethnicities and the dominant castes or communities and between the mobile metropolitan diaspora and the illiterate masses in the villages, urban slums and at the periphery of the tribal lands. How is globalization going to affect these sections of our society? Its pace at present is no doubt measured and slow due to choice of policies and also because of the limitations that our social structure itself imposes upon the pace of globalization, but the challenges are likely to grow and pose serious problems in the future.

The impact of globalization on the structural changes in the society comes generally through the changes in the economic policies. India, since independence, has been following a policy of import-substitution and inward-looking market economy. This policy handicapped the economy in global competitiveness, in the manufacturing sector and in exportable commodity production. But its focus upon higher education in science and technology and agricultural infrastructures did compensate the loss. It is evident in 'green revolution' in agriculture, in our growing strength in the sectors of information technology, the professions, the rising middle classes and in the space research which has added edge to our growth in telephony, television and mass communication. Also, the investment in the capital-intensive sectors, such as steel, petrochemicals, power, etc., have generated an economic and technological potential strong enough to cope up with the exposure to the contemporary challenges of globalization. The existing economic, social and cultural resilience of our society is to a large measure influenced by the rising middle class. It is estimated that by 2020 the half of the Indian population would comprise the middle classes even at the contemporary rate of the economic growth! Despite this, the challenges of globalization felt by India in early 1990's made it inevitable to change these policies. Of course, the difference (see, Herzog, 1999; Malhautra, 2001; Panchamukhi in Chadha, 2001) of opinion on matters related to economic liberalization continues to persist.

The Indian economic policies on globalization have rightly tended to be cautious. This does not rule out the need for faster movement in several areas. To some extent, our political-structural reality, our democratic path of development imposes restraints to our speed. This is inevitable, as the structural reality of our democracy is still deeply embedded in our social and economic inequalities. Besides, democracy is not merely an instrument of social and political development. It constitutes a fundamental ideal or normative principle of human development. It is an irony that globalization of economy does not by itself translate into the growth of a democratic society. The Human Development Report (2002) recognizes this fact and laments about it.

In our appraisal of the inward-looking economic policies of the past or in our overenthusiasm for the quick embrace of full economic globalization, we should not neglect our developmental goal of growing as a strong democracy and civil society. This goal, when posited against many policy objectives of economic globalization, calls for caution and graduated response. Our membership of the WTO and IMF etc. has devolved upon us the responsibilities for moving towards an open market economy. It exposes our farmers, consumer good industries, small-scale sector industries and those employed in the unorganized sectors to unequal competition from strong economies, which may increase unemployment or lead to many forms of economic and social displacement.

To take these factors into account and yet to encounter the challenges of globalization, an integrated policy is required. Increased export earnings and foreign trade on the one hand, and the need for massive foreign capital investment on the other depend upon how fast we move in this direction both at the federal and the state levels. In foreign trade and export earnings, we have a temporary advantage of low wages and human resources, but economies of scale and technological modernization of the production process are required. Reforms in management, governance, labour legislation and fiscal and monetary policies are required. Capital investment on a massive scale is needed to develop the infrastructures in the sectors of power, roadways, railways, airports and ports etc. India has lagged behind in foreign capital investment, apart from other reasons also because of our weak infrastructure. Its inadequacy hampers the growth of our trade and modernization of agriculture. No doubt, globalization does create a "mismatch between growth of trade, growth of output and growth of employment" (Panchamukhi in Chadha, 2001: 11), but its negative consequences can certainly be avoided if our infrastructure is modern and our policies with regard to various sectors of economy are adequately synchronized. We may need to reinforce our legal expertise, laws about the intellectual property rights, banking and insurance policies and measures to protect our economy from unfair trade policies from abroad.

Modernization of agriculture is an urgent requirement as 70 percent of our population depends upon it. About 90 percent of employment in our country is offered by the unorganized sector, of which agriculture is a primary component. Studies reveal that during 1990–98 nearly 7 million Indian workers, of which about 4 million in the rural and 3 million in the urban sectors, lost their jobs. Also, the quality of workforce in the rural areas is poor; during 1993–94 NSS round, 44 percent of rural males and 80 percent of rural females were found to be illiterate (see, Chadha, 2001). Hence, the urgent need for the improvement of the rural human resource base of our country. This would reduce the crisis of inequalities in the social and political structure and also strengthen the pace of our economic modernization. The farming sector in our economy has chronically suffered from underdevelopment due to lack of investment and adverse terms of trade and tariff policies. Despite this, globalization has so far not caused any massive dislocation, may be only because of its slow pace in our country or because of our policies. But, eventually, agriculture would have to become commercial and oriented to value added production. This is slowly taking place as some studies reveal (see, Panini, 1999), but its scale is still miniscule due to lack of investment and poverty of infrastructure and human resources.

These challenges of economic globalization have indeed created a social structural crisis of change in our society. The social inequalities have increased in relative terms. But to call it structural dualism may be an oversimplification. The studies on the consumption data indicate that the rural areas constitute about 80–90 percent of the market for the factory-made consumer goods. There exists a strategic linkage between the rural economy and the industrial sector producing consumer goods. A middle class has emerged in the villages and it continues to grow in size.

In bringing about these changes the expansion of the mass media has played an important role. The incidence of telephony, access to radio and television and in some areas even the uses of the internet are linking the rural social structure and economy with the outside world as never before. It reinforces inter-regional and inter-state linkages, alters the character of the social mobility of skilled and unskilled labour and in some measures it also creates inter-regional or inter-state inequalities. These changes have the potential in the long run to influence the nature of social inequalities in our society and also the pattern of political and cultural interactions among groups and regions within and across the states.

Challenge of Identity

These developments do impinge upon the issues of identity. The social and economic developments augment the societal self-awareness within every society. The larger question of identity is related to the growth of social, economic, political and cultural self-awareness among groups and communities. Identity has its subjective root in the person, but it manifests itself objectively as a social product through the mobilization of collective self-consciousness. This consciousness is forged by a chemistry of several factors, such as history, mythology and instrumental rationality. The sense of identity is created by one's realization of the presence of the 'other'. For this, a historical context is necessary. The past and present experiences of social and cultural interaction with other cultures give shape to people's consciousness of their own identity. What form the identity consciousness will take, whether it would promote adaptive, assimilative, alienative or hostile attitude towards the other culture depends upon a variety of factors. Among them are included the presence or absence of a tradition of pluralism, the nature of the civilization and its past historical experiences of cultural contacts with the outside world. For instance, exposure to colonial control and its impact upon local culture and economy play a material role in the perception of cultural globalization in India.

Most discussions on the impact of globalization on the cultural and social identity of people relate to questions such as: Will globalization eventually bring about a cultural homogenization among societies which today enjoy cultural diversity? Which culture would dominate in this process? What would be the fate of local cultures? Will they face a total loss of identity? What about the cultural minority groups, religious groups and ethnicities? Will they face extinction through homogenization? Finally, is globalization of culture a new incarnation of westernization—a mark of cultural imperialism? I will like to briefly address some of these issues in the context of our own society.

India has been exposed to cultural contacts with other civilization since millennia. It has been continually making adaptive changes in its cultural styles, traits and forms as it encountered other cultures. It has a history of accommodating identities. The cultural impact of globalization on the identity of this civilization or its impact upon the identities of local cultures, therefore, is bound to be mediated by this resilience. There are several reasons for this observation. In the first instance, the initial historical conditions of the Indian social structure have been unique. It is characterized by immense plurality of communities, languages, cultural diacritical symbols and ethnic styles. A variety of cultural traits and cultural styles have over centuries given identity to communities but not in total isolation. Cultural interaction among regions and communities has persisted in a mode of co-sharing and mutual accommodation. This commonality has existed beyond the religious and ethnic divides. A recent study by the Anthropological Survey of India illustrates this fact. It observes that the sharing of cultural traits among communities in India, in all about 4,635 in number, shows "high correlation of traits among states within macro-regions such as those in the south, north-western India, central and western India and so on. There is very high correlation of traits between the Scheduled Castes and the Scheduled Tribes, between Scheduled

Tribes and Hindus, between Hindus and Sikhs, between Hindus and Muslims (which is very high indeed) and between Hindus and Jains. The high correlation between Hindus and Buddhists may also be explained in the same way. This fact that these communities interact across space or states is important" (Singh, 1992: 99). Thus, we notice that despite the plurality of identities, a macro-linkage of cultural bonds has existed in India throughout history. It continues to subsist even today, and constitutes the cultural unity of India despite plurality of local identities.

The cultural impact of globalization gets enmeshed within this process of internal dynamics and resilience of the local cultures. The perception that globalization threatens local culture is being increasingly invalidated. It is observed that in the process of globalization local cultures are reinforced and also globalized. Ronald Robertson has called this process *glocalization*. It indicates how local cultures get increasingly enmeshed with the global culture through selective adaptation of symbolic forms and styles in their products through micro-marketing. Based on the Japanese experience, this process affirms how local cultures begin to occupy a global space by constructing differentiation of consumers. Its examples are witnesses in the field of tourism and the popularity of ethnic supermarkets (see, Robertson, 1994). In India, we witness how our local cultural traditions are also making adaptive responses in the forms and styles of cultural products in tune with the inter-regional and global requirements. For instance, regional languages are being creolized across regions or even in global terms. The incidence of bilingualism has increased in our country from about 13.4 percent in 1971 to 64.2 percent in 1991. The culinary styles, the pattern of dress, local ethnic cultural objects, rituals, religious icons and local customs, etc., are now increasingly becoming pan-Indian and even global due to the increasing size of the Indian diaspora. The process of micro-marketing is penetrating deep into this sphere. The momentum for this is, of course, provided by the emergent forces of economic development. It has triggered a new wave of internal and external migration, and establishes a linkage between culture and market. It also extends the space for cultural interaction as never before. No doubt, it generates a threat perception about cultural identity, but correspondingly it also reinforces the identity consciousness. This ambivalence notwithstanding, the Indian response towards the 'other' cultures has throughout remained selective and adaptive. Globalization is, therefore, leading increasingly towards hybridization or fusion of cultural styles and forms rather than their total displacement. This only shows the strength of cultural resilience of the Indian society.

Economic Development and Clash of Identities

This resilience, however, is not without tensions, both social structural and cultural. It is a global phenomenon. India, since independence, has been making conscious efforts through its democratic institutions, policies of welfare and devolution of power to the regional, ethnic and cultural minorities to establish a synergy between local identities and national development. The linguistic reorganization of states, the policies of protective discrimination, the continual effort to bring about better and more effective federal structure of governance by improving the centre-state relationship, the policy of offering protection to the ethnic-regional and cultural entities etc., have been continually implemented and updated to accommodate cultural, social and political identities. We have largely succeeded, but not in all cases, and not without conflict and violence. Globalization, to the extent that it generates new inequalities or sharpens the consciousness of inequalities, does contain within it the seeds of social and cultural conflicts in society. It makes the intensity of symbolic transmission across lands more effective and easier, and it also sharpens in people's mind the sense of social, economic and cultural deprivations. It has a regional, national and global dimension. The premise that globalization generates conflict in societies which sometimes have disastrous consequences is based upon the possibility of extreme mismatch between globalization and removal of poverty or deprivation of classes, communities and ethnicities. It is true that organized violence such as terrorism and insurgency erupts in societies where people feel that they are being subordinated culturally, politically or economically, where dominant powers are perceived to be totally unresponsive to democratic protest, and where basic human rights are denied. Does globalization increase poverty in a society or reduce it? Does it enhance the ability of some nations to structurally dominate the weaker ones? Ideological debate on these issues goes on but the result remains inconclusive. The evidence available so far suggests that globalization reduces the absolute level of poverty but does enhance the incidence of relative inequalities among people.

If we observe the pattern of social mobility and incidence of poverty since independence in our country, we find that measures of social welfare, education and economic development have contributed to the reduction of poverty, but the relative social inequalities have increased. In absolute terms, the standard of consumption has qualitatively improved in villages and towns; the reservation policy together with focus upon education has created a 'limited' middle class among the weaker sections, minorities and ethnic groups; the quality and extent of participation in politics and power sharing by the backward classes, tribes and scheduled castes etc. has radically changed. A substantial degree of empowerment of these groups has taken place in the political realm, but in the economic and educational fields the gap between them and the dominant classes or castes persists. In my view, globalization does pose challenges on several fronts, foremost of which may be economic. For reasons of history, pluralistic social structure and culture and the democratic path of development that we have adopted, we enjoy tremendous resilience to meet with the challenges of globalization. Notwithstanding this, a cautious fine-tuning and synergy in our economic policies is required. To my mind, the most strategic aspects of such a policy relate to the development of our human resource base, agriculture and infrastructure. Economic development in a balanced manner holds the key to our ability to meet with the challenges of globalization and accommodate the upsurge of identities.

References

Chadha, G.R., "India and WTO: Some Suggestions for Internal Corrections and External Initiatives" in Chadha, G.R. (ed.), *WTO and the Indian Economy*, New Delhi: Deep & Deep Publications Pvt. Limited, 2001.

Herzog, S., "Globalization and Poverty Alleviation in India", *Liberal Times*, March 1999.

Malhautra, M. (ed.), *New Century: Whose Century*? New Delhi: UBSPD, 2001.

Panchamukhi, V.R., "World Trade Organization and India: Challenges and Perspectives", in Chadha, op. cit.

Panini, M.N., "Trends in Cultural Globalization: From Agriculture to Agribusiness in Karnataka", *Economic and Political Weekly*, July 31, 1999.

Patnaik, Prabhat, "The Antinomies of Transnationalism", *Social Scientist*, Vol. 24, September-October 1996.

Robertson, R., "Globalization or Glocalization?", *Journal of International Communication*, Vol. 1 No. I, 1994.

Singh, K.S., *People of India: An Introduction*, Calcutta: Anthropological Survey of India, 1992.

Singh, Yogendra, *Culture Change in India: Identity and Globalization*, Jaipur: Rawat Publications, 2000.

The Hindu, July, 25, 2002.

Bibliography

Adorno, T.W., *Negative Dialectics*, London: Routledge and Kegan Paul, 1973.

—, *The Authoritarian Personality*, New York: Harper, 1950.

Aggarwal, Pratap C., *Caste, Religion and Power: An Indian Case Study*, New Delhi: Shri Ram Centre for Industrial Relations, 1971.

Aurora, G.S., *Tribe, Caste, Class Encounters: Some Aspects of Folk-Urban Relations in Alirajper Tehsil*, Hyderabad: Administrative Staff College of India, 1972.

Bailey, F.G., "Closed Social Stratification in India", *European Journal of Sociology*, Vol. IV, No. I, 1963.

—, "For a Sociology of India", *Contributions to Indian Sociology*, No. III, 1959.

—, *Politics and Social Change: Orissa in 1959*, Berkeley: University of California Press, 1963.

—, *Tribe, Caste and Nation: A Study of Political Activity and Political Changes in Highland Orissa*, Manchester: Manchester University Press, 1960.

Barnes, *Social Thought from Lore to Science*, New York: Dover Publications, Inc., 1961.

Baudrillard, Jean, *Simulacres et Simulation*, Paris: Galilee, 1981.

Bauman, Zygmunt, "Sociological Response to Postmodernity", *Thesis Eleven*, 1989.

Becker, E., *The Lost Science of Man*, New York: George Braziller, 1971.

Bell, D., *The Coming of Post Industrial Society*, London: Heinneman Educational Books Ltd., 1974.

Berger, P.L. and Luckmann, *The Social Construction of Reality*, U.S.A.: Doubleday and Co., 1966.

Berger, P.L. et al., *The Homeless Mind*, Pelican Books, 1974.

Berger, P.L., *The Sacred Canopy*, New York: Doubleday and Company, 1969.

Berna, J.J., 1960, *Industrial Entrepreneurship in Madras State*, New York, 1960.

Berreman, Gerald D., "Social Categories and Social Interaction in Urban India", *American Anthropologist*, 74, 1972.

Beteille, Andre, "Ideas and Interests: Some Conceptual Problems in the Study of Social Stratification in Rural India", *International Social Science Journal*, Vol. 21, No. 2, 1969.

—, "The Future of the Backward Classes: The Competing Demands of Status and Power", *Perspectives: A Supplement to the Indian Journal of Public Administration*, Vol. 12, 1965.

—, "The Politics of 'Non-antagonistics' Strata", *Contributions to Indian Sociology* (New Series), Vol. 3, 1969.

— (ed.), *Social Inequality*, Harmondsworth: Penguin Books Limited, 1969.

—, *Caste, Class and Power*, Berkeley: University of California Press, 1965.

—, *Castes: Old and New: Essays in Social Stratification*, Delhi: Asia Publishing House, 1969.

—, *Harmonic and Disharmonic Social Systems*, Sydney: Sydney University Press, 1971.

—, *Inequality and Social Change*, Delhi: Oxford University Press, 1975.

—, and Madan, T.N. (eds.), *Encounter and Experience: The Personal Dimension of Social Anthropological Fieldwork*, Delhi: Vikas Publishing House, 1975.

Bettelheim, B. and Janowitz, M., *Dynamics of Prejudice: A Psychological and Sociological Study of Veterans,* New York, 1950.

Bettelheim, C., *India Independent*, London: MacGibbon and Kee, 1968.

Bhaduri, A., "A Study in Agricultural Backwardness under Semi-Feudalism", *Economic Journal*, March 1973.

Bhalla, Sheila, "New Relations of Production in Haryana Agriculture", *Economic and Political Weekly*, Vol. XI, No. 13, March 27, 1976.

Bhambhri, C.P., "Political Science" in S.C. Dube (ed.), *Social Sciences and Social Relations: Role of the Social Sciences in Contemporary India*, Simla: Indian Institute of Advanced Study, 1976.

Bhatt, Anil, Caste, *Class and Politics: An Empirical Profile of Social Stratification in Modern India*, New Delhi: Manohar Book Service, 1975.

Bose, N.K., "Inequality and Social Changes", *Searchlight*, 68, 1968.

Bottomore, T.B., "Sociology in India", *British Journal of Sociology*, 13(2), 1962.

—, *Sociology as Social Criticism*, New Delhi: S. Chand and Company Ltd., 1979.

Bourdieu, Pierre and L.J.D. Wacquant, *An Invitation to Reflexive Sociology*, Chicago: University of Chicago Press, 1992.

Brass, P., *Factional Politics in an Indian State: The Congress Party in Uttar Pradesh*, Berkeley: University of California Press, 1965.

Brass, Paul R., *Language, Religion and Politics in North India*, New Delhi: Vikas Publishing House, 1975.

Broomfield, J.H., *Elite Conflict in a Plural Society: Twentieth Century Bengal*, Bombay: Oxford University Press, 1968.

Burns, Tom, *Industrial Man*, London: Cox and Wyman Ltd., 1969.

Chadha, G.R., "India and WTO: Some Suggestions for Internal Corrections and External Initiatives" in Chadha, G.R. (ed.), *WTO and the Indian Economy*, New Delhi: Deep & Deep Publications Pvt. Limited, 2001.

Chanana, Dev Raj, "Sanskritization, Westernization and India's North-West", *Economic Weekly*, 13 (9), 1961.

Chattopadhyaya, Paresh, "On the Question of the Mode of Production in Indian Agriculture: A Preliminary Note", *Economic and Political Weekly*, Vol. VII, No. 13, March 25, 1972.

Chaturvedi, Jagdish Prasad, *Pravasi Krantikari,* Publications Division, Government of India, New Delhi, 1985.

Chauhan, B.R., "Rural Studies", in *A Survey of Research in Sociology and Social Anthropology*, ICSSR, Vol. I, Bombay: Popular Prakashan, 1974.

Chossudovsky, M., "Dependence and Transfer of Intellectual Technology: The Case of Social Sciences", *Economic and Political Weekly*, Vol. XII, No. 36, 1977.

Cicourel, A., *Cognitive Sociology*, London: Cox and Wyman Ltd. 1973.

Cohn, Bernard S., "The Changing Status of Depressed Caste", in M. Marriott (ed.), *Village India*, Chicago: University of Chicago Press, 1955.

—, *India: The Social Anthropology of a Civilization*, New Jersey: Prentice Hall, 1971.

Damle, Y.B., "Reference Group Theory and Mobility in the Caste System", James Silverberg (ed.), *Social Mobility in the Caste System in India*, Hague: Mouton and Co., 1968.

Dasgupta, Biplab, *The Naxalite Movement*, Bombay: Asia Publishing House, 1974.

Davis, K., "The Myth of Functional Analysis as a Special Method in Sociology and Anthropology", *American Sociological Review,* 1951.

De Souza, Alfred, "Dialogue between Religions in India", *Social Action*, XXII, 2, 1972.

Derrida, Jacques, *The Margins of Philosophy*, Sussex: Harvester Press, 1982.

—, *Writing and Difference*, Chicago: Chicago University Press, 1978.

Desai, A.R. (ed.), *Rural Sociology in India*, Bombay, Popular Prakashan, 1959.

—, *Social Background of Indian Nationalism*, Bombay: Popular Prakashan, 1966.

—, *State and Society in India*, Bombay: Popular Prakashan, 1975.

—, and Pillai, S. Devadas, *A Profile of an Indian Slum*, Bombay: Popular Prakashan, 1972.

Desai, I.P., *Some Aspects of Family in Mahuva*, Bombay: Asia Publishing House, 1964.

Dhanagare, D.N., "Agrarian Conflict, Religion and Politics: The Moplah Rebellion in Malabar in the Nineteenth and Early Twentieth Centuries", *Past and Present: A Journal of Historical Studies,* 74, February 1977.

—, "Social Origins of the Peasant Insurrection in Telengana (1946–51), *Contributions to Indian Sociology* (New Series), 6.

—, "The Politics of Survival: Peasant Organization and the Left Unity in India 1925–46", *Sociological Bulletin*, 24 (1), March, 1975.

D'Souza, Alfred (ed.), *Women in Contemporary India*, New Delhi: Manohar Books Service, 1975.

D'Souza, Victor S., "Caste Structure, in India in the Light of Set Theories", *Current Anthropology*, 1972.

—, "Scheduled Castes and Urbanization in Punjab: An Exploration", *Sociological Bulletin*, 24 (1), 1975.

—, "Urban Studies", in *A Survey of Research in Sociology and Social Anthropology*, ICSSR, Vol. I, Bombay: Popular Prakashan, 1974.

— and Sethi, Raj Mohini, "Social Class and Occupational Prestige in India: A Case Study", *Sociological Bulletin*, XXI, 1972.

Dube, Leela, *Sociology of Kinship: An Analytical Survey of Literature*, New Delhi: ICSSR, 1974.

Dube, S.C. (ed.), *Social Sciences and Social Realities: Role of the Social Sciences in Contemporary India*, Simla: Indian Institute of Advanced Study, 1976.

—, "The Study of Complex Cultures", in T.K.N. Unnithan et al. (eds.), *Towards a Sociology of Culture in India*, New Delhi: Prentice Hall of India, 1965.

Dumont, Louis, "A Fundamental Problem in Sociology of Caste", *Contributions to Indian Sociology*, No. 9, 1966.

—, *Homo Hierarchicus*, Delhi: Vikas Publishing House, 1970.

—, *Religion, Politics and History in India* (Collected Papers in Indian Sociology), Paris: Ecole Pratique des Hautes Etudes, 1970.

— and Pocock, D.F., "For a Sociology in India: Rejoinder to Dr. Bailey", *Contributions to Indian Sociology*, 4, 1968.

Durkheim, E., 'Le Dualisme de la nature humaine et ses conditions sociales', *Socientia*, XV 1914.

—, *The Division of Labour in Society*, New York: Macmillan Company, 1933.

—, *The Elementary Forms of Religious Life*, New York: Macmillan Company 1915.

—, *The Rules of Sociological Method*, New York: The Free Press of Glencoe, 1950.

—, *Suicide*, New York: The Free Press of Glencoe, 1951.

Eule, J.B., "Models of Relevance: The Social Effects", *American Journal of Sociology*, Vol. 84, No. 1, 1978.

Fischer, E., *Marx in his Own Words*, Pelican Books, 1973.

Forrester, D.B., "Western Academic Sophistry and the Third World", *Economic and Political Weekly*, Vol. IX, No. 40, 1974.

Fox, Robin, *Kin, Clan, Raja and Rule: Hinterland Relations in Pre-Industrial India*, Bombay: Asia Publishing House, 1971.

Frank, A.G., "The Wealth and Poverty of Nations", *Economic and Political Weekly*, 1970.

Fromm, E., *Escape From Freedom*, London, 1942.

—, *Man for Himself*, New York: Holt Rinehart and Winston, 1964.

—, *The Crisis of Psychoanalysis*, Pelican Books, 1973.

—, *The Sane Society*, New York: Holt Rinehart and Winston, 1955.

Galbraith, J.K., *The New Industrial State*, U.S.A., 1967.

Gellner, E., *Thought and Change*, Chicago: The University of Chicago Press, 1965.

Giddens, Anthony, *Consequences of Modernity*, Cambridge: Polity, 1990.

—, *Modernity and Self-Identity: Self and Society in a Late Modern Age*, Cambridge: Polity, 1992.

Goffman, E., *Asylums*, New York: Doubleday and Co. Inc., 1961.

—, *Presentation of Self in Everyday Life*, London: Penguin, 1971.

Gough, Kathleen, *Class Developments in South India*, Montreal: McGill University Press, 1975.

Gould, H., "Time Dimension and Structural Change in an Indian Kinship System: A Problem of Conceptual Refinement", in Milton Singer and B. Cohn (eds.), *Structure and Change in Indian Society*, Aldine: Aldine Publishing Company, 1968.

Gouldner, A., *Coming Crisis in Western Sociology*, New York: The Free Press, 1970.

Gupta, Dipankar, "The Political Economy of Fascism", *Economic and Political Weekly*, XII, No. 25, June 25, 1977.

Gupta, Krishna Prakash, "Sociology of Indian Tradition and Tradition of Indian Sociology", *Sociological Bulletin*, 23 (1), 1974.

Habermas, Jurgen, *The Theory of Communicative Action*, Vol. 2, Cambridge: Polity Press, 1987.

Harper, E.B., "A Hindu Village Pantheon", *South Western Journal of Anthropology*, 1959.

Hazlehurst, L.W., *Entrepreneurship and Merchant Caste in a Punjab, City*, Duke University, 1966.

Henderson, L.J., *Pareto's General Sociology*, Cambridge: Harvard University Press, 1937.

Herzog, S., "Globalization and Poverty Alleviation in India", *Liberal Times*, March 1999.

Homans, G.C., *Social Behavior: Its Elementary Forms*, New York: Harcourt, Brace and World, 1961.

—, "Bringing Men Back In", *American Sociology Review*, December 1964.

Horkheimer, Max and Adorno, T.W., *Aspects of Sociology*, London: Heinemann Educational Books Ltd., 1973.

Indian Council of Social Science Research, Third Survey of Research in Sociology and Social Anthropology, Vols. I & II, New Delhi: Manak Publications, 2000.

Jain, R.K., "Class and Classification Among the Peasantry of Central India: Relations of Production in Village Parsania, Madhya Pradesh", *Sociological Bulletin*, Vol. 25, No. 1, 1977.

Jameson, Fredric, "Postmodernism and Consumer Society", in (ed.), *Postmodernism and its Discontents: Theories and Practices*, by E.A. Kaplan, New York: Verso, 1988.

Jones, E., "A Quarter Century of International Social Sciences Developments—1932–1977: Geography" 25th Anniversary Round Table: A Quarter Century of International Social Science 1952–77: International Social Science Council, October 24–26, Paris (mimeographed), 1977.

Jones, Rodney W., *Urban Politics in India*, New Delhi: Vikas Publishing House, 1975.

Joshi, P.C. and Damodaran, K., *Marx Comes to India*, New Delhi: Manohar Book Service, 1975.

—, *Land Reform and Agrarian Change in India and Pakistan* (Report), 1971.

—, *Land Reforms in India*, ICSSR Trend Report, 1974.

Kothari Rajni (ed.), *Caste in Indian Politics*, Delhi: Orient Longman, 1970.

—, *Politics in India*, New Delhi: Orient Longman, 1970.

Ladejinsky, Wolf, "How Green is the Indian Green Revolution" *Economic and Political Weekly*, Vol. VIII, No. 52, December 29, 1973.

Leach, E.R., et al. (eds.), *Politics in South Asia*, Cambridge: Cambridge University Press, 1970.

Loubser, J.J., "The Need for the Indigenisation of the Social Sciences", 25th Anniversary Round Table: A Quarter Century of International Social Science—1952–1977: International Social Science Council, October 24–26, Paris (mimeographed), 1977.

Lowenthal, L. and Gutman, R., *Prophets of Deceit*, New York, 1949.

Lynch, Owen M., *The Politics of Untouchability* (Ph. D. dissertation), Department of Anthropology, New York: Columbia University Press, 1966.

MacIver, R.M., *The Ramparts we Guard*, New York: The Macmillan Company, 1950

Madan, T.N., "For a Sociology of India: Some Classification", *Contributions to Indian Sociology*, 1965.

Mairet, Philip, *Pioneer of Sociology: The Life and Letters of Patrick Geddes*, London: Lund Humphries: 1957.

Majumdar, D.N., *Caste and Communication in an Indian Village*, Bombay: Asia Publishing House, 1958.

—, M.C. Pradhan, C. Sen and S. Misra, "Inter-Caste Relations in Godhankallan, A Village near Lucknow", *The Eastern Anthropologist*, 8, pp. 191–214, 1955.

Malhautra, M. (ed.), *New Century: Whose Century*? New Delhi: UBSPD, 2001.

Mannheim, Karl, *Man and Society*, London: Routledge and Kegan Paul Ltd., 1940.

Marcuse, H., *Eros and Civilization*, London: The Beacon Press, 1955.

—, *Reason and Revolution*, Boston, 1960.

—, *One-Dimensional Man*, London: Sphere Books Ltd., 1964.

Marriott, McKim, *Caste Ranking and Community Structures in Five Regions of India and Pakistan* (Ph.D. dissertation), Chicago: University of Chicago Press, 1955.

Marx, Karl and Engels, F., *The German Ideology*, Moscow: Progress Publishers, 1968.

Marx, Gary, *Muckraking Sociology Research as Special Criticism*, New Brunswick: N. J., Transaction, 1972.

Marx, Karl, *Economic and Philosophical Manuscripts of 1844*, Moscow: Progress Publishers, 1974.

Mead, G., *Mind, Self and Society*, University of Chicago Press, 1934.

—, *Philosophy of the Present*, The Open Court Publishing Co., 1932.

Mencher, Joan P., "Conflicts and Contradictions in the 'Green Revolution': The Case of Tamil Nadu", *Economic and Political Weekly*, Annual Number, Vol. IX, Nos. 6, 7 & 8, 1974.

Merton, R.K., *Social Theory and Social Structure*, The Free Press of Glencoe, 1968.

Mills, C. Wright, *Images of Man*, New York: George Braziller Inc., 1960.

—, *The Power Elite*, New York: Oxford University Press, 1956.

Momin, A.R., "The Facade of Objectivity: An Inquiry into the Epistemology of Value-Free Sociology", *Economic and Political Weekly*, Vol. VII, No. 44, 1972.

Moore, W.E., *Man, Time and Society*, New York: John Wiley and Sons, Inc., 1963.

Mukerjee, Radhakamal, *A Philosophy of Social Sciences*, Presidential Address at the Third All India Sociological Conference, 1958.

Mukerjee, Radha Kamal, in Barnes and Becker (eds.), *Social Thought from Lore to Science*, Vol. III, New York: Dover Publication, 1966.

—, *Social Indicators*, Delhi: Macmillan, 1976.

—, *The Rise and Fall of East India Company*, Berlin, 1958.

—, *The Sociologist and Social Change in India Today,* Delhi: Prentice Hall of India, 1965.

Mukherjee, Parth Nath, "Social Movement and Social Change: Towards a Conceptual Classification and Theoretical Framework", *Sociological Bulletin*, Vol. 26, No. 1, 1977.

Mukherjee, R.K., *What Will It Be*? New Delhi: The Macmillan Company of India, Ltd., 1979.

Mukherjee, Rama Krishna, *Sociology of Indian Sociology*, Bombay: Allied Publications: 1979.

Mukerji, D.P., *Diversities*, Delhi: Peoples Publishing House. 1958.

Mumford, L., *Conditions of Man*, London: Martin Secker and Warburg, 1944.

Nicholas, R., "Economy of Family Types in Two West Bengal Villages", *Economic and Political Weekly*, 1961.

—, "Structure of Politics in Village of Southern Asia", in Milton Singer and B.S. Cohn (eds.), *Structure and Change in Indian Society*, Chicago: Aldine Publishing Co. 1968.

O'Neill, John, *Sociology as a Skin Trade*, New York: Harper and Row Publishers, 1972.

Oommen, T.K., "Sociological Issues in the Analysis of Social Movements in Independent India", *Sociological Bulletin*, 1977.

—, "The Concept of Dominant Caste: Some Queries", *Contribution to Indian Sociology*, New Series, No. IV, 1970.

—, *Charisma Stability and Change*, New Delhi: Thomson Press, 1972.

Panchamukhi, V.R., "World Trade Organization and India: Challenges and Perspectives", in Chadha, G.R., op. cit.

Panini, M.N., "Trends in Cultural Globalization: From Agriculture to Agribusiness in Karnataka", *Economic and Political Weekly*, July 31, 1999.

Parsons, T., *The Social System*, New Delhi: Amerind Publishing Co. Pvt. Ltd., 1972.

—, *Toward a General Theory of Action*, New York: Harper and Row, 1962.

— and Smelser, N.J., *Economy and Society,* New York: The Free Press, 1965.

Patnaik, Prabhat, "The Antinomies of Transnationalism", *Social Scientist*, Vol. 24, Nos. 9–10, September-October 1996.

—, "Imperialism and the Growth of Indian Capitalism", in Robin Blackburn (ed.), *Explosion in a Subcontinent: India, Pakistan Bangladesh and Ceylon*, Penguin Books, 1975.

Patnaik, Utsa, "Economics of Farm Size and Farm Scale", *Economic and Political Weekly*, Special Number, Vol. VII, Nos. 31, 32, 33, 1972.

Pocock, David F., "Inclusion and Exclusion: A Process in Caste System in Gujarat", *South Western Journal of Anthropology*, 13 (1), 1957.

—, *Mind Body and Wealth: A Study of Relief and Practice in an Indian Village*, London, Blackwell, 1974.

Raghavan, V., "Methods of Popular Religious Instructions in South India", in Milton Singer (ed.), *Traditional India Structure and Change*, Philadelphia, 1952.

Rastogi, P.N., *Cybernetic Analysis of Complex III: Defined Problems in Organization* (mimeographed), Kanpur: Indian Institute of Technology, 1976.

—, *The Nature and Dynamics of Factional Conflict,* Meerut: The Macmillan Co. of India Ltd., 1975.

Reisman, D. et al., *The Lonely Crowd*, New York: Yale University Press, 1950.

Robertson, R., "Globalization or Glocalization?", *Journal of International Communication*, Vol. 1, No. I, 1994.

Rosenthal, D.B., *The United Elites: Politics and Government in Two Indian Cities*, Chicago University Press, 1970.

Rudolph, L. and S. Rudolph, "Surveys in India: Field Experience in Madras State", *Public Opinion Quarterly*, 22 (3), 1958.

Saberwal, S., "Inequality in Colonial India", *Contributions to Indian Sociology*, Vol. 13, No. 2, 1979a.

—, "Sociologists and Inequality in India: The Historical Context", *Economic and Political Weekly*, Vol. XIV, Nos. 7 and 8, 1979b.

Saberwal, Satish (ed.), *Towards a Cultural Policy*, New Delhi: Vikas Publishing House, 1974.

Saran, A.K., "For a Sociology of India", *Eastern Anthropologist* 15 (1), 1962.

—, "Sociology of India", in Roucek (ed.), *Contemporary Sociology*, New York, 1957.

—, "Sociology of Knowledge and Traditional Thought", *Sociological Bulletin*, 14 (1), 1965.

—, "The Concept of Social Science", in K.D. Sharma (ed.), *Basic Issues in Social Sciences*, Bombay: Academic Journals of India, 1968.

—, "The Faith of a Modern Intellectual", in T.K.N. Unnithan, I. Deva and Y. Singh (eds.), *Towards a Sociology of Culture in India*, New Delhi: Prentice Hall, 1965.

—, "The Natural Sciences and the Study of Man: The Problem of their Synthesis in Contemporary Culture", *Eastern Anthropologist* 14 (2), 1961.

—, "Theoretical Anthropology and the Cult of Man", *Ethics*, LXVI, 1956.

Sau, Ranjit, "On the Essence and Manifestation of Capitalism in Indian Agriculture", *Economy and Political Weekly*, Vol. VIII, No. 13, March 31, 1973.

—, "Political Economy of Indian Agriculture: What is it All About?" *Economic and Political Weekly*, Vol. VIII, No. 20 May 19, 1973.

Schutz, A., *On Phenomenology and Social Relations*, London: The University of Chicago Press, 1970.

Seth, Ashwani and Tankha, Ajay, "Agrarian Transition and the Differentiation of the Peasantry A Study of a West U.P. Village, *Economic and Political Weekly*, Vol. VIII, 14, 1972.

Shah, A.M., "Basic Terms and Concepts in the Study of Family in India", *Economic and Social History Review*, Vol. I, 1964.

—, "Historical Sociology (A Trend Report), in *A Study of Research in Sociology and Social Anthropology*, Vol. I (ICSSR), Bombay: Popular Prakashan, 1974.

—, *The Household Dimension of the Family in India*, New Delhi: Orient Longman, 1973.

—, Shroff, R.G. and Shah, A.R., "Early Nineteenth Century Village Records in Gujarat", in Tapan Roychaudhari (eds.), *Contributions to Indian Economic History*, 1963.

Shah, Ghanshyam, "Traditional Society and Political Mobilization: The Experience of Bardoli Satyagraha (1920–28), *Contributions to Indian Sociology* (NS) 8, 1974.

Shils, E., "Charisma, Order and Status", *American Sociology Review*, 1965.

Silverberg, James (ed.), *Social Mobility in the Caste System in India*. The Hague: Mouton Publishers, 1968.

—, "The Great Tradition in a Metropolitan Centre: Madras", in Milton Singer (ed.), *Traditional India: Structure and Change*, Philadelphia: The American Folklore, 1959.

Singer, Milton (ed.), *Traditional India: Structure and Change*, Chicago: Aldine Publishing Company, 1968.

—, *When a Great Tradition Modernizes*, New York: Praeger Publishers, 1972.

Singh, K.S., *People of India: An Introduction*, Calcutta: Anthropological Survey of India, 1992.

Singh, Rajendra, "Agrarian Social Structure and Peasant Unrest, A Study of Land Grab Movement in District Basti – East U.P.", *Sociological Bulletin*, 1977.

—, "Politicization, Protest and Peasant Movement in Uttar Pradesh: A Study in the Politics of Land Control in District Basti", in M.S.A. Rao (ed.), *Social Movements in India*, 1977.

—, "Agrarian Social Structure and Present Unrest: A Study of Land Grab Movement in District Basti-East U.P.", Sociological Bulletin, Vol. 23, No. 1., 1974.

—, "Constraints, Contradictions and Interdisciplinary Orientations: The Indian Context", *International Social Science Journal*, Vol. XXXI, No.1, 1979.

Singh, Yogendra and Oommen, T.K., *The Craft of the Social Sciences in India,* Centre for the Study of Social Systems, Jawaharlal Nehru University, New Delhi.

—, "Constraints, Contradictions and Interdisciplinary Orientations: The Indian Context", *International Social Science Journal*, 31 (1), 1979.

—, *Image of Man: Ideology and Theory in Indian Sociology*, Delhi: Chanakya Publications, 1983.

—, "Chanukhera: Cultural Change in Eastern Uttar Pradesh" in K. Ishwaran (ed.), *Change and Continuity in India's Villages*, New York: Columbia University Press, 1970.

—, "Ideology, Theory and Method in Indian Sociology" in *A Quarter Century of International Social Science*, by Rokkan Stein (ed.), New Delhi: Concept Publishing Company, 1979.

—, "Role of Social Sciences in India: A Sociology of Knowledge, in S.C. Dube (ed.), *Social Sciences and Social Realities: Role of the Social Science in Contemporary India*, Simla: Indian Institute of Advanced Study, 1976.

—, "Social Anthropology of the Study of Rural and Urban Societies", *Economic Weekly*, reprinted in M.N. Srinivas, 1962, 1959.

—, "Sociology for India: The Emerging Perspective in T.K.N. Unnithan et al. (eds.), Delhi: Prentice Hall of India, 1967.

—, "The Case of the Potter and the Priest", *Man in India*, 39 (3), 1959.

—, "The Desired Role of Political Leadership in Economic Reforms", in *Indian Economy and the Institutional Set-Up*, in J.L. Bajaj (ed.), Delhi: Policy Group, 1999.

—, "The Dominant Caste in Rampura", *American Anthropologist* (February).

—, "The Scope and Method of Sociology in India", in T.K.N. Unnithan and others (eds.), *Sociology for India*, Delhi: Prentice-Hall of India, 1967.

—, *Culture Change in India: Identity and Globalization*, Jaipur: Rawat Publications, 2000.

—, *Indian Sociology: Social Conditioning and Emerging Concerns*, New Delhi: Vistaar Publications, 1986.

—, *Modernization of Indian Tradition*, Jaipur: Rawat Publications, 1973.

—, *Religion and Society among the Coorgs of South India*, Bombay: Oxford University Press, 1952.

—, *Social Change in Modern India*, Berkeley: California University Press, 1966.

—, *Social Stratification and Change in India*, New Delhi: Manohar, 1978.

Spencer, H., *Principle of Sociology*, New York: D. Appleton and Company, 1898.

Srinivas, M.N., "Mobility in the Caste System", in Milton Singer and B.S. Cohn (eds.), *Structure and Change in Indian Society*, Chicago: Aldine Publishing Company, 1968.

—, "Social Environment and Managements, Responsibilities", *Economic and Political Weekly*, 10, 11, 1975.

—, "Village Studies, Participant Observation and Social Science Research in India", *Economic and Political Weekly*, Special Number, 1975.

—, *Religion and Society among the Coorgs of South India*, London: Asia, 1952.

Staal, J.F., "Sanskrit and Sanskritization", *Journal of Asian Studies*, 22, 1963.

Stark, W., *Social Theory and Christian Thought*, London: Routledge and Kegan Paul Ltd., 1958.

Taylor, Charles, *Sources of the Self: The Making of the Modern Identity*, Cambridge: Harvard University Press, 1989.

—, *The Ethics of Authenticity*, Cambridge: Harvard University Press, 1992.

Thapar, Romesh, *Tribe, Caste and Religion in India*, New Delhi: The Macmillan Company of India Ltd., 1977.

Thapar, Romila, *Past and Prejudice*, Delhi: National Book Trust of India, 1975.

Thorner, D., "The Peasantry Confronted with Industrial Capitalism", 1777–1970, 1973.

—, "Marx on India and Asiatic Mode of Production", *Contributions to Indian Sociology*, 1966.

Tiryakian, Edward A., *Sociologism and Existentialism*, New York: Prentice-Hall Inc., 1962.

Touraine, Alain, *Critique of Modernity*, Oxford: Blackwell, 1995.

—, *The Self Productions of Society*, Chicago: The University of Chicago Press, 1977.

Uberoi, J.P.S., "Science and Swaraj", *Contributions to Indian Sociology*, (New Series), Vol. 2, 1968.

Unnithan, T.K.N., et al., *Sociology for India*, New Delhi: Prentice-Hall of India, 1967.

Verba, S., Ahmed, B., and Bhatt, A., *Caste, Race and Politics: A Comparative Study of India and the United States*, Berkeley Hills: Sage Publications, 1971.

Vidyarthi, L.P., *Conflict, Tension and Cultural Trends in India*, Calcutta: Punthi Pustak, 1969.

—, *The Sacred Complex in Hindu Gaya*, Bombay: Asia Publishing House, 1961.

Wagner, H.P., "The Scope of Phenomenological Sociology" in *Phenomenological Sociology* by George Psathan (ed.), New York: John Wiley and Sons, 1973.

Weber, Max, *Essays in Sociology*, London: Routledge and Kegan Paul Ltd., 1952.

—, *Sociology of Religion*, London: Methuen, 1966.

—, *The Protestant Ethic and the Spirit of Capitalism*, London: Unwin University Books, 1965.

Weiner, M., "Social Science Research and Public Policy in India", *Economic and Political Weekly*, Vol. XIV, No. 38, 1979.

Weiner, Myron and Kothari, Rajni, *Indian Voting Behaviour*, Calcutta: Mukhopadhayaya, 1965.

Whyte, William H., *The Organization Man*, New York: Simon and Schuster Inc., 1956.

Winch, P., *The Idea of a Social Science*, London: 1968.

Zeitlin, I.M., *Rethinking Sociology*, New York: Appleton-Century Crofts, 1973.

Index